Shopping while drunk

Shopping
while drunk

confessions from
modern life

o   o   o

AMANDA ASTILL · TOM BROMLEY
MICHAEL MORAN · SIMON TREWIN

JOHN MURRAY

First published in Great Britain in 2007 by John Murray (Publishers)
An Hachette Livre UK company

1

A CIP catalogue record for this title is available from the British Library

ISBN 978-0-7195-2176-8

Typeset in 11/12.5 Galliard by Servis Filmsetting Ltd, Manchester

Printed and bound by Clays Ltd, St Ives plc

John Murray policy is to use papers that are natural, renewable and recyclable
products and made from wood grown in sustainable forests. The logging and
manufacturing processes are expected to conform to the environmental
regulations of the country of origin.

John Murray (Publishers)
338 Euston Road
London NW1 3BH

www.johnmurray.co.uk

Introduction

Shopping. Who doesn't like wasting a few hours and several pounds buying stuff you don't want, clothes you don't need and gadgets you really can't afford? Drinking. What better way is there to spend a sunny afternoon than gently nursing a pint of warm ale and a pack of pork scratchings down your local, if you have one? So far, so socially acceptable. But bring these two fine traditions together, and suddenly you have invented a pastime that is best not mentioned in polite company: shopping while drunk – an activity that results in giggling at shop assistants, falling over in changing rooms and flexing your flexible friend into positions it didn't know it could go. But where, you might ask, does a book come into all this? Did I buy it when I was drunk? Well yes, but not exactly.

This book is about stuff. Lots of stuff. Not just tipsy shopping, but other stuff too. The kind of stuff that everybody likes, but sort of wishes they didn't. What we aim to do is point out that *everybody* likes that stuff that you wish you didn't, so you might as well enjoy it. It's essentially a self-help book. If you've ever pushed an empty Yorkshire pudding mix packet into the lower strata of the bin when you've had people round for Sunday lunch, or been so racked with guilt over chucking a sickie from work that you've ended up with a psychosomatic slight sniffle, then this book is for you. Or, as is normally the case with this sort of book, it's for someone you like a bit but not enough to get a proper present for.

By the way, while we applaud the merits of shopping while drunk, we draw the line at shipping while drunk. That's just dangerous.

Abu Hamza

The most perfect pantomime villain ever seen outside the Alhambra Theatre, Oldham: Dame Abu Hamza (not to be confused with those other denizens of the tabloid press, Abi Titmuss, Abbey Clancy or Richard Hamster) rocks the hook and eyepatch look like no one since Calico Jack took the King's Pardon. He's younger than you think, although much less handsome than he looks, and has been a civil engineer and nightclub bouncer as well as a tabloid pin-up. While real villains operated in secret, subtly weaving evil plans watched only by researchers from Spooks, Uncle Abu opted for the loud-mouthed Jihadi Pirate approach. Coming inevitably to the attention of some sleepy local constable, he was banged up for behaviour liable to cause excessive sales of the *Daily Express* and is only allowed out on special occasions, when newspaper sales are flagging and we need a quick story about him having a gold-plated hook paid for by the taxpayer or something. And how does that hook stay on anyway? The power of prayer?

AC/DC

'Giving the Dog a Bone'. 'Beating Around the Bush'. 'Let Me Put My Love Into You'. 'Finger of Fun'. 'Go Down'. 'Put the Finger on You'. 'Inject the Venom'. 'Love at First

Feel'. 'Squealer'. 'Hard as a Rock'. 'Cover You in Oil'. The fascinating thing about the DC is that only one of those titles is made up. A sort of Finbarr Saunders meets hard blues boogie, AC/DC have spent thirty years peddling their teenage boy version of life to the world, symbolized by guitarist Angus Young dressing up as a schoolboy. Puerile but great: who else can you smirk at and play air guitar along to at the same time?

Accessorize

Take a look at any high street in the UK and most of the shops are pretty much self-explanatory: Sock Shop sells socks, Tie Rack sells ties, Costa Coffee sells . . . erm sandwiches. But, when you think about it, what does Accessorize actually sell? What are all those people looking for in those poorly-lit and cramped surroundings? They can't *all* be someone's Secret Santa. Not in *August*. No. What we witness when we are tempted into that mahogany grotto is the hysteria of the jumble sale stripped of its concomitant odour of damp dog. It's irresistible. We have no idea what most of these products are actually for. Most of us may have, at some time or another, been playfully tied to a bed with one of those vaguely ethnic scarves, but no one's ever worn one outdoors and certainly nobody has ever worn those strangely uncomfortable slippers that seem to be on sale year after year in defiance of market trends. But there's always a chance that there will be some earrings that don't make us look like a school fete fortune teller, or a hat that really would do for our sister's wedding after all – and as long as that remote chance exists, we will carry on rooting through the bins of the precinct's best-marketed pound shop in search of those unlikely bargains.

Accommodation Allocated on Arrival

How long will it take travel agents (on-line or off) to realize that 'Accommodation Allocated On Arrival' is only a selling point for a twisted cheapskate minority of the population whose way of evaluating a potential holiday destination is based solely on price, whether the locals speak English and the chances of scoring? Shameful that people can behave like this – we take months choosing our Tuscan villas and can't understand who would get a kick out of a Magical Mystery Tour-style holiday where a cheerful Holiday Rep bungs you on coaches destined for concrete flats that no one in their right mind would book out of choice. That said, it does sound like a bit of a laugh and you might even end up on telly – on *Holidays From Hell* – so it can't be all bad.

Adding Cheese

One of our favourite interviews of recent years was when Liverpool captain Steven Gerrard was asked what his favourite sort of cheese was. After a moment's deliberation, his answer could not have been more definitive – melted cheese, he replied. Now, while it might be easy to mock a footballer's culinary tastes, it has to be said that Stevie G has a point: how many recipes are there that cannot be improved by a helping of cheese? Shepherd's Pie? Macaroni Cheese? Nachos? We say, bring on the melted stuff. Cheesy chips? It's a main and a pudding all in one. Additional pizza toppings? It can't be only us who ask for extra cheese. In a word, grate. See also **Cheese on Toast**.

Adopting Little Brown Babies (to Enhance Your Celebrity)

Give a man a fish and he'll eat today – but organize a photo shoot to show the world that you're giving him a fish and you just can't buy that kind of publicity. Indeed, you may not need to: very few of those picturesque little ethnic orphanages actually receive the promised fish (or cheques) once the cameras stop rolling and *OK!*'s run the story. If you do end up actually taking a little foreign chap home to one of your various enormous houses, don't worry about feeding him or anything. That's what your Polish nanny's for.

Agent Provocateur

No wonder they stock spanking paddles – when a pair of knickers cost £125, it makes sense that you'll need a little something for guilt-ridden self-flagellation later.

Airfix Models

When we were writing this, Humbrol had just acquired the assets of Airfix after months of uncertainty. Hundreds of thousands of British men breathed a collective sigh of relief as a vital part of their heritage was preserved for at least one more generation of mildly obsessive young boys. All right, you probably haven't made one of those things for years, but we bet you still slow down a little bit if you pass a shop window full of Spitfires and Focke-Wulfs, and you can still remember the taste of the glue, can't you?

Airline Seats (Reclining)

In this glorious age of budget air travel, holidaymakers are packed as tightly as flowers in a Victorian maiden's diary. Only not half as fragrant. No wonder then that, in a vain bid to offset the onset of deep vein thrombosis, most of us are fumbling for the little switch that makes the seat recline before the end of the announcement about 'what to do in the event of a landing on water'. Of course, if you do put your seat back, you'll empty the contents of that wobbly tray on the back of your seat into the lap of the person sitting behind you. Because the little trays of airline food are always volcanically hot, depositing the alleged chicken chasseur on your flying companion may be looked upon askance. You don't really have any choice, though, because the fat bloke in front of you will be doing exactly the same thing. Still, it's the only way to travel; as you lean back in comfort, travelling at 500 m.p.h., with a cool gin and tonic soaking into your pants.

Alpha Women

A new breed of scary women for the noughties. She's more than just a cigar-chewing match for a city-slicker and, unlike trophy wives, just as likely to want him for his boner as his bonus. But just in case men find her a bit too scary, she'll have an oddly reassuring, maternal name – like Horlicks, or Ovaltine – something that suggests a hot milky drink, someone who can pay the mortgage and put you to bed. Unlike the ball-breaking Superwoman who came before her, Alpha Woman hasn't filed her ovaries under F for fat chance. No, even Alpha Woman's reproductive system is a paragon of hyper-efficiency. She's a queen of multi-tasking, and manages to pop a baby out during break time at the annual board meeting. As many cultures have realized, eventually the world will taken over by a super-race of über-matriachs. They're already here. They work for Goldman Sachs. And they can do anything you can do – just a million times better.

Alternative Fireplace DVD

Think of the quintessential romantic setting – sitting in front of a roaring open fire with huge crackling logs and tender licking flames caressing the brick surround and occasionally spitting a spirited spark upwards. Perfect for romance and for relaxation. Now try to transplant that scene into a one-bedroom conversion on the edge of the South Circular, or into a Barratt home near the Hangar Lane gyratory system, and it becomes problematic – maybe you are in a smokeless fuel zone, maybe carrying huge logs up a narrow winding staircase is too much for your back or maybe, most likely, you don't have a fireplace. That was the position we found ourselves in until we discovered the ridiculously addictive Alternative Fireplace DVD, which enables you to have a cosy evening in front of the television selecting one of seven different-styled crackling log fireplaces to watch. Choose a different one every day of the week, if you must, but save up the retro student digs two-bar (count 'em) gas fire for when your parents come over. With the whole package lavishly filmed in widescreen with Dolby 5.1 Surround Sound, this is a must-have for any bone idle lazy sinner.

Amateur Footage on the News

Rubbish production values, wild focus-pulling, snow-storm grainy and with sound that is reminiscent of two tin cans and a ball of twine, the joy of watching this amateur footage on the news is that there is a real sense that, even in this multi-channel environment where civil liberties are infringed by CCTV cameras everywhere, there are still some newsworthy events where no one has got the evidence except for a man or woman in the street who happens to be in the right place at the right time. We love the slight embarrassment of the newsreader when he announces, 'Paris Hilton's naked ascent of Nelson's Column was captured by a passerby', and we love the fact that, no matter how shocking it is, whether footage of the Paris Concorde catching fire or the Zappruder footage of JFK's assassination, we can't stop ourselves thinking a) wish that had been mine and b) wonder how much cash they got. Action!

American Idol

The British invented the show. The Americans do it fifteen times better. Maybe it's because they've got a wider pool of potential people that they end up with a list of finalists who can actually sing? Maybe it's because we're British that Paula Abdul's judging – 'judging' that consists of telling the contestants how wonderful they are – is so hilariously nauseating? And maybe it's because they're American that Simon Cowell's tell-them-like-it-is comments are met with gasps of sheer disbelief from the crowd? Give it that glossy sheen you get when American programmes are 'translated' for British TV screens, and you've got one gorgeous 'naughty but nice' slice of entertainment. Does anyone know what happened to Fantasia, by the way?

Ankle Bracelets

As folklore would have it, wearing an ankle bracelet used to be a sign you were a lady of the night. Now it means you've been to Thailand and lost more than a money belt at a full moon party. In a way, ankle attire is an early warning system announcing what class of traveller you are. An elaborate adornment harking from a Karnatakan gypsy means you've, like, been to India, man. A thread of red string means you're too cool for jewellery but don't want people to think something dreadful like you're down with the tourists. And a turquoise thread with some shell thingy hanging off it means, sadly, you're on a package holiday and you think a spiritual epiphany will get you hammered at the beach bar later on. Interestingly, it is virtually illegal to wear shell ankle bracelets unless you're in possession of world-class ankles and a very thick calf.

Anne of Green Gables
Written by Lucy Maud Montgomery, *Anne of Green Gables* is one of those children's classics that has captivated female hearts ever since it was first published in 1908. Anne is an orphan who ends up (how did you guess?) at Green Gables. She's bright and has got red hair for which she is mercilessly (rightfully?) teased by, among others, Gilbert Blythe, who she originally hates, but then changes her mind . . . If you're over, well, twelve, you should know better than to hire the TV mini-series and spend the whole day watching it with equally should-know-better friends. Doesn't stop it being indulgent fun, though.

Anne Summers (Nurse's Uniform)
Kate Moss might float around in Agent Provocateur underwear, but the real thrills are to be had strapping yourself into some Anne Summers finery – like the PVC nurse's uniform. It says 'I'm cheap, so you can get me dirty,' (the outfit, that is), and will instantly turn your bedroom into a modern day *Carry On* set. Of course, the overall effect will be more Nurse Gladys Emmanuel than Emmanuelle. But at £24.99 with a free stethoscope thrown in, what can you expect?

Announcers Saying 'We Interrupt this Programme'
This happens less than it used to – probably because we live in a 24/7 news-orama world of live feeds, scrolling subtitles

and text message alerts, so when it does happen you know that this is a WHERE WERE YOU WHEN YOU HEARD THE NEWS MOMENT. No matter how tragic the event and how devastating the consequences or even simply how big the 'name' involved is, we all love the drama, the repetition of sparse facts until more information becomes available, and the shots of a shifty-looking reporter speculating wildly into a camera next to hundreds of others doing the same. We love drama – all in the name of media analysis and our constant quest for a greater understanding of global issues, of course.

Annual Bonus

The word 'bonus' is actually a misrepresentation of what happens in your pay packet every year. A bonus suggests a pleasant surprise, something over and above what you expected, something that could buy a small farm in France outright. Obviously, if you work in the City, you can buy a quaint holiday home with your loot, but seeing as you were expecting enough to buy a small Lear jet, it still registers as a bitter disappointment. Not an 'oh you shouldn't have' type bonus. But what can us mere mortals expect as a gracious acknowledgment of all our painful toil over the past twelve months? Two hundred quid. Max. Still, mustn't be negative, you think, we can have that mini-break to Bridlington now. Until the tax man mauls it. And you're left with a pitiful £79. Which mysteriously correlates with the bank charge you just got hit with for going 1p over your overdraft limit for one day.

Anti-Wrinkle Creams

Anyone who has even the most superficial understanding of quantum chronodynamics realizes that time and gravity are essentially intertwined and ineluctable. That's annoying, because it predicts that we will keep getting older and bits of us will get increasingly saggy. Not even Cher can turn back time, and she's probably got better access to beauty products and particle accelerators than the rest of us.

Consequently, all we're left with is little pots of cream that promise to miraculously defy the ageing process. Of course it's impossible: if you eat really healthily all the time and don't drink a box of wine every evening, you might live to quite an advanced age. We're not trying to be old, though, quite the opposite. What we're looking for is action liposomes that are scientifically proven to make us look 63 per cent less hag-like. What we're looking for is snake oil advertised by serious-looking men in white coats. The more expensive an anti-ageing product is, the more likely we are to believe its frankly impossible claims. Ideally, some endangered species needs to have secreted something into it for maximum value. If you can't get unicorn milk night cream, though, the next best bet is some sort of wonder molecule with a magical name like Totalmugathon, or Bollockonium. It may not change a thing, but rubbing sixty quid's worth of moisturiser into our cheeks feels like success to us.

Apple Product Announcements
You've already got a computer. And a mobile phone. And, for that matter, some little fag-packet sized affair that plays all the music you've downloaded illegally from the Internet and has funny little earphones that smell of earwax. And yet there you are, sitting in front of that perfectly good computer that you've already got, watching a man in a black polo-neck telling a room full of whooping fanboys about a new computer/mobile phone/earwax thingy that will transform your life in some magical and strangely ill-defined way. It's almost impossible to resist Steve Jobs' reality distortion field: the only way to preserve the integrity of your bank balance is to not leave the house for twenty-four hours after the end of an Apple keynote speech. Otherwise, next year you'll be watching one of those captivating speeches on a very shiny computer indeed. And nobody wants that.

Aquadrops
These weird sweets come in a flip-top plastic box reminiscent of dental floss and also come with a weird claim – that

not only can they give you lasting refreshment but also instant hydration. They look like New Age pebbles, are sugar free, and are so addictive that it is truly impossible not to finish an entire packet within minutes of popping the first one. Oh yes – and they come in two flavours – Apple and Citrus. Yum.

Arctic Monkeys

Oh, how the mighty fall. Once upon a time they were an insider tip, traded in whispers on community sites like MySpace. Then they gang-banged the charts so viciously that even Gordon Brown claimed to be a fan. Which must have felt as wrong as your parents claiming you had a 'cute ass'. Still, at least now we can all use the cheesy chat up line 'Bet You Look Good On My Bedroom Floor' rather than 'Get Your Coat You've Pulled'. And that's where *real* creative immortality lies.

Aromatherapy

If we could shoot up aromatherapy oils, we would. But until things get that desperate (i.e. Christmas), we'll chase the Lavender dragon with our £2.99 Ikea oil burner. See **Scented Candles**.

Artful Combing

There comes a moment in every man's life when – unless he's some sort of ladyboy – he begins to lose some of his hair. Those first couple of years (when there's still enough to play with, but not quite enough to offer full coverage unaided) are to be savoured: once you give in to the inevitable and buy a pair of clippers, you'll never get to play with hair gel again.

Arthouse Cinema

Men like films where plenty of stuff happens. Ideally films where plenty of stuff blows up. That's no great surprise. It's not just men: *everyone* likes films with homicidal androids from the future and no one really likes films where Bill Murray just sits around waiting for his foundation to dry. Still, it's one of the few enigmas that women as a sex have managed to preserve despite men having cracked the menstrual code, the shoe cipher and pretty much every other secret except the washing machine instructions, and it's perhaps the best test yet devised of just how desperate to please he really is. After all, if he'll do that, he'll do *anything*.

Asking Leading Questions

Boxing Day. A house somewhere in the Home Counties. Everyone a bit tiddly. Great time to start lobbing hand-grenade statements guaranteed to get a huge amount of tension going into the middle of the table. Here are our favourites: 1. (to a bitter spinster sister in her forties) – 'Wouldn't it be lovely if you could get a boyfriend next year?'; 2. (to closet-queen uncle) – 'I expect you'll be watching that Judy Garland film later'; and 3. (to overweight sister-in-law) – 'Don't you think Kirstey Alley looks so much better now she has slimmed down so much?'

Asking the Waiter Questions

Men see a menu as a list of dishes that a restaurant knows HOW to cook pretty well, CAN cook pretty well and WILL cook and deliver to your table within fifteen minutes. How unadventurous – we women prefer to see a menu as a list of ingredients we know they have in the kitchen and we take it from there. Not content with ordering the Chicken from the Chicken Sandwich and adding it to the Spinach from the Spinach Tart and then Olives from the Tapenade, all 'on the side' from the main event of the mixed salad, it is also CRUCIAL to cross-question the waiter AT LENGTH about the origins of each ingredient, the fat content, whether it comes in a sauce (and, if so, whether the ingredients are all organic) and what the second cousin of the Pastry Chef's greengrocer's hygenist ordered last time they were in. Once this is all settled and we have established the sodium content of the water and whether you can have the ice in a separate glass, there is just time to call the waiter back and change your mind all over again. It is all part of the ritual and we ain't changing for nobody. Actually – hold on a sec – is the paper this is printed on from renewable rainforests? And is the pulp bleached . . . ? Maybe we could have a different typeface? (ad lib to fade)

Australian Princess

Any programme that is shown exclusively on ITV2 is a show you know you shouldn't be watching. Any programme that is shown exclusively on ITV2 *and* is hosted by Paul Burrell is a show that not only you shouldn't be watching but you should also allow a couple of month's cooling off before you consider leaving the house. *Australian Princess* finds Paul Burrell taking a host of flying doctors, beach bums and other Australian stereotypes and attempting to turn them into 'Princess' material. Watch as women with names such as Kylie Booby are escorted through a selection of upper class classes such as drinking Pimm's, watching Polo, copulating with their cousins and beating up paparazzi photographers outside Boujis at three in the morning . . . Sorry, we're getting confused between the reality show and the reality now.

Baby-Talking to Men

People wonder why there's a direct correlation between commitment and crap sex. Couples rub their chins in despair trying to work out why their once hot sex lives have dwindled to every other Saturday with the lights off and a flannel nightie on. Is it because of those moobs he grew by mistake last summer after one too many beers? Is it because your cellulite is mimicking a contagious disease and spreading uncontrollably all over your body? No, it isn't. Such is the human drive for duvet action it can survive even the most appalling physical decline. It's the fact that you say 'I wuff you soooo much' in a tone that Paris Hilton wouldn't even use to baby talk her dog. It's because you call him 'little bear'. When you first met he was that 'totally hot guy' – now he's 'snookums'. No one wants to give someone whose vocabulary has descended to kindergarten level a good seeing to. Frankly, it's just wrong.

Back, Crack and Sack Waxing

The thought of someone pouring hot wax over your back and into your important little places, allowing it to set and then RIPPING YOUR HAIRS OUT VERY FAST WITH NO MERCY AT ALL WHILE YOU STIFLE HUGE SCREAMS sounds either like a medieval torture or something that is a little bit . . . well 'gay', and you would never tell your friends or colleagues about it, but the end product (before the itching starts) is rather smooth and lovely. Allegedly.

Backhanded Compliments

Women weren't designed to nurture and nest. They were designed to decimate other women's egos with a few carefully chosen words. Like 'wow, that really suits someone your size'. Or 'he's gorgeous, and he's not choosy now he wants to settle down'. It's passive aggressive taken to the extreme. As you're mentally drop-kicking the backhanded compliment giver and tearing her manicured nails off one by one, you have to smile and say THANK YOU. That's right, you actually have to graciously accept such an insult and proffer gratitude. It's OK, though, because the next time you meet you'll always get the chance to slip in a little dig of your own. 'I LOVE that dress, it was so on-trend last year . . .'

Backstage Riders

In the classic documentary, the (if you will) rockumentary *This Is Spinal Tap*, one famous scene shows band guitarist Nigel Tufnell freaking out at the backstage catering – to summarize: small bread, large filling. If only we were famous, we too could revel in the delights of the contract rider, making ridiculous demands on some stressed out promoter (three bottles of champagne, two packets of Monster Munch and a Filipino ladyboy, since you ask). But until we hit the big time, we'll have to make do with applauding the stars for what they can get away with. M&Ms with all the brown ones taken out? Hilarious, Van Halen. No stairs? We'll just rearrange the building infrastructure for you, Mariah. Organic soup? Oh, do try harder, Coldplay.

Banana Caramel Frappuccino Blended Coffee

Try going into a Starbucks and asking for a coffee. Just 'a coffee'. Nothing else. Watch the bewildered panic that starts to flicker across the barista's face. Now imagine turning the clocks back maybe only a decade and walking into the refreshment bar of a British Rail station and asking for a Banana Caramel Frappuccino Blended Coffee. How evil does this drink sound? Firstly, there is the terrible punning 'frappuccino' element, then we have the notion of 'blended' (which usually means lots of brown beans mixed up to pretend to be something it isn't), then, of course, the main offender is the 'banana' (a fruit that doesn't belong in a mug under any circumstances), and that is without throwing in the frippery of the 'caramel', which is, last time we checked, a sweet and not a beverage. So why, oh why, does it taste so good?

Bananarama

In today's world of pile 'em high, sell 'em cheap quick turnover flat-pack pop acts, it's hard to believe that Bananarama ever happened. Appearing first as a troupe of über-hip Wurzel Gummidges in the pages of the irreproachably cool *Face* magazine, they morphed themselves gradually into a teutonically efficient pop behemoth under the guidance of every musician's favourite production team, Stock, Aitken and Waterman. Everybody had their favourite Banana. Teenage girls tended to go for future Shakespeare's Sister Siobhan because her quirky individuality made them feel unique and empowered. Teenage boys tended to plump for Keren because she looked as if she might know how to do all the *sex stuff.*

Band on the Run

Yes, yes, yes . . . It's all so cool, isn't it, the ironic music choice. Top it off with a 1980s hair metal T-shirt and a Stan Laurel haircut and you're in with the In Crowd. Until the next wave of silliness comes along. *Band on the Run*, though, that's forever. The way that the songs interweave and cross-reference one another certainly improves on Paul's previous stab at the idea on *Abbey Road* and arguably kicks lumps out of the George Martin *Love* masheroo too. Plus, as if that were not enough, 'Jet': back of the net.

Bandslash

You've got to love teenage girls. Those scary, hormonally challenged, psychotic purveyors of unrequited love. Back in the 1980s it was all about putting up a poster of Wham and daydreaming of a white wedding with George Michael (bless those poor, deluded souls who wasted so many hours on that one). By the nineties you were allowed, with parental supervision (e.g. a horny housewife masquerading as your concerned mother), to go and see Take That in concert. Then came the noughties. With eight-year-olds throwing their diamanté thongs at Busted and MySpacing McFly for a threesome. Where could you go from there, without involving the strong arm of the law, and possibly the NSPCC? The answer is bandslash, where overexcited tweenies blog about made-up gay sexual experiences between their favourite musical dishes de jours. That's right, imagine Johnny Borrell slowly fingering Liam Gallagher's pantie line as they explode in an orgasm of mutual desire. Oh dear.

Bandwagon Jumping

Every week it seems like another million CDs, DVDs and books are dumped on the market by companies apparently oblivious to the enormous time constraints placed on ordinary people like you and us by the proliferation of magazines, TV channels, video games and nosepicking opportunities that vie for our attention. Just working out which of these choices would be worth investigating further would entail spending our entire lives in front of a computer listening to free samples of this, watching trailers of that and reading online extracts of the other. No one's got time for that. Not even that tubby film review guy off the Internet. That's why bandwagons are so handy. Someone else, and indeed a large number of someone elses, picks the bones out of the bewildering kedgeree of modern culture and hands us an Arctic Monkeys CD and a copy of *The Da Vinci Code*, leaving us with a bit of spare time to watch *Big Brother*. Which, candidly, is all we wanted.

Banksy

Do you remember when you used to graffiti a huge speed-nob on your desk when the teacher wasn't looking? Do you remember when you used to change signs, hilariously, from TO LET to TOILET and NO SMOKING to the gut-achingly funny SMOKING (geddit?)? Imagine if you were still doing this now and pretending it was 'art' and being treated as a god by the Primrose Hill/Kate Moss set? You'd be a total tosser and be pissing yourself with laughter. That said, who hasn't looked at his outrageous stunts (such as the seven-foot-high graffiti in the Penguin Pool at London Zoo which said 'WE ARE BORED OF FISH' or the various artworks smuggled into the Tate Modern or the British Museum) without secretly admiring them and wishing, just a little bit, that they hadn't given up Art so they could do Double Maths?

Banoffee Pie

Your eyes mentally surf the menu, slack-jawed at the array of sugar-fuelled fodder dancing before your eyes. Slowly you mouth every syllable of every description to yourself, luxuriating in the possibility that you could actually be eating such a naughty treat in the imminent future. Then your inner diet police kick in. 'I'll have the sorbet,' you tell the waiter firmly. Except you don't. As if a disgustingly obsese poltergeist has inhabited your body, the words 'banoffee pie' slip out, punctuated with splashes of drool hanging from your mouth. Why?? Why THAT one? The slag of all sweets. The one that looks like a dustbin outside KFC vomited up a mush of biscuit and cream? Never mind, you think, I'll just *have* to eat it. You'll need a shower afterwards, and possibly a heart bypass. But hell, it was worth it.

Bar Snacks

Beer is good. The pub is good. There's just one problem: drinking beer in the pub makes you hungry. If only it were possible to solve this unfortunate conundrum without having to leave the pub, stop drinking and wind up the fascinating conversation you're having about thingy from work. Well, hunger no more, thanks to the bright spark who invented the bar snack. The crisp and the peanut are the staple, of course, with Walker's, those cardboard McCoy's or KP being the standard fare. Posh pubs might offer you those small bags of Kettle Chips or those microscopic cans of Pringles – all a bit pricey, if you ask us; a pound for a packet of crisps? And don't even get us started on those five quid 'dips to share'. Hummus? We're down the pub, not in bloody Crete. Buy a packet of crisps and appreciate the simple beauty of traditional bar snack etiquette. Split open the bag, laying the crisps out on its shiny foil for all to enjoy. Once complete, pass the bag to your friend who does the origami thing where he folds it into a tiny triangle. Drop it in the empty pint glass, and buy another bag. By this stage in the evening, it's the nearest you're going to get to supper.

Be Here Now

Popular opinion can swing like a pendulum of epic proportions, and at no time was this more true than with Oasis' third album, *Be Here Now*. When it came out, the critics hailed it as the greatest thing since sliced bread (that's bread as in foodstuff, rather than someone taking a knife to the seventies group). When the nation played it, however, everyone quickly realized it was a bit of a dog's dinner. And yet, and yet . . . we're with Liam on this one – it's not all bad. It's funny calling one of the fastest-selling records of all time a lost album, but that's exactly what this has become. We say, give it another listen – it's nothing like as bad as you remember.

Beating Your Child (at Tennis)

Nothing beats a nice bit of father-child Sunday morning bonding on the tennis court. After a friendly knock-up, the key thing as an adult is to hang back and give away a few easy points to lull your child into a false sense of security, which reinforces their feeling that you are old, rubbish and were born into this world at the age of thirty wearing chinos and a button-down shirt. If you are feeling very generous, drop the racket a couple of times, fall over backwards in pursuit of an easy shot and maybe even get tangled up in the net as you do a sideways roll into it. And then proceed to ruthlessly serve ace after ace, win every volley and then quibble in a very McEnroe-esque way if, heaven forbid, your child protests at any point. Scream 'You cannot be serious' until they cry and then, when you have triumphed at championship point, cheer, leap in the air and maybe even do a lap of honour before cuffing the back of your weeping child's head and say, 'For God's sake grow-up – it is only a game.'

Beauty and the Geek

The fact that Ashton Kutcher, he of beautiful chiselled jaw and buff body, is the executive producer on this American TV import says it all really. The premise is: a bunch of really ugly nerds try and woo a bunch of really thick beauty queens – and get derided and annihilated in the process. Beside the message that it's fine to be thick, but beyond forgiveness to be fugly, it's like being in the gladiatorial pit of male and female relations circa secondary school. Something that, really, we never grow out of. Which suggests that, despite doing the delectable Demi Moore on a nightly basis, Ashton was probably the school geek. Or worse – a fat child. In the end, the comedy becomes painfully like social realism as the bespectacled, genetically-challenged goofers wear their pain and rejection on their tasteless shirt sleeves like a suicide note in motion. The only light relief (and most likely, hand relief) is the swimwear catwalk show. The geeks' reactions to watching the show? Like. Kids. At. Christmas. It's enough to bring a tear to your eye.

Beaver Shaver
The majority of women don't like the au naturel look these days, so no wonder the must-have self-purchase of the moment is something that will have to be delivered in brown packaging from those nice people at www.beavershaver.com. Yes, you read that web address right, but do read it again – we will wait for you . . . OK? Good. If you are keen on a bit of pubic topiary, you know how important precision is, but it is a hard choice between the Seiko S-Yard Model PS-335 Shavy Femini T Handle Trimmer, which has, and we quote, 'an ergonomic design allowing for incredible precision, making it an ideal tool for detail work like fashioning a design with your pubic hair', or maybe you might be tempted by the 'gold standard of pubic shavers' – the Seiko S-Yard Model ES-412 Cleancut Shaver, which handily comes with a free Duracell battery and a little half ounce bottle of high-grade shaver lubricating oil for preventative maintenance and a three ounce bottle of medical-grade, cornstarch-based body powder for use as a dry lubricant. Difficult choice, eh?! And once you have the equipment, do you plump for a Brazilian, a Hollywood, a Lynam, a Widdecombe or a Curly-Wurly?

Bedroom Posedown
Just out of the shower. Quick check in the old mirror. Yep. Still got it. Maybe suck in the gut a bit. Yeah. She's lucky to have you. Twist your arm around a bit as you flex and bingo! Muscles! If you worked out you'd look like bloody Superman. No chance of that, though. Still. The gym's loss is the pub's gain.

Being a Homezilla
Worse than a bride-to-be is the home-owner-to-be. As soon as the offer is accepted, a kind of creeping insanity sets in. The kind that threatens to bore anyone within a

fifty mile radius. For men this manifests in an unnatural interest in the workings of a tracker mortgage and an obsession with the finer points of conveyancing. For women it develops into a nasty dependency on the Laura Ashley home furnishings catalogue and the ability to recite the exact price of every B&Q bathroom suite. Not to mention house prices. Speculation of how much it's appreciated are endless, as are plans for the extension. It's no wonder estate agents are so twisted. Spending every day listening to the tedious yackings of homezillas would poison anyone in the end.

Being a Snob
There is a trick to being a snob – firstly, you must recognize snobbery in other people and despise it, and then do it yourself without thinking about it. Therefore you can happily watch re-runs of *Keeping Up Appearances* and laugh like a drain as Hyacinth Bucket puts newspaper down for the tradesmen to walk on while thanking God you are nothing like her, and then watch *The Royle Family* immediately afterwards and wonder how people can spend their lives on a sofa watching the telly all the time. Shouldn't they be reading a good book instead? Hmm.

Being a Strict Parent
Telling your children off for doing things you secretly do yourself when they are not looking is a tricky skill to get right but, if you can keep a straight face, it is a good wheeze. When you have just come back to the table from having picked your nose, not washed your hands after going to the loo, gulped some orange juice from the carton and picked some crust off the crumble on the work surface, to then sit down and be very Victorian about cutlery protocol is a challenge, but huge fun. Look at me when I'm talking to you and STOP drumming on the table. Honestly – you would not do this in front of your grandparents so don't do it in front of me! Although, obviously, God knows what your grandparents got up to in the sixties – it was probably

all hash brownies and looking up their genitals with hand mirrors, but that's not important right now.

Being a WAGabee

It's beyond tragic, but some part of the female DNA is wired to wear fake tan and shop itself into a coma. Oh go on then, throw a liaison with a footballer in there too. Even though you know you should be studying particle physics, subscribing to *The Economist* and citing Barack Obama as the man who makes you go weak at the knees, it all goes wrong when Mastercard write to let you know they've increased your credit limit. The beast within rises and can only be sated by a consumerist frenzy in Louis Vuitton. Followed by a good half hour in a tanning salon. The only cure for this terrible affliction is to carry a picture of Danielle Lloyd in your purse. It's a sobering thought looking into her vacant lot.

Being Asked to Move Down the Train (Watching Passengers Ignoring)

We have all been the victim of these terrible examples of humanity – they bundle onto the train and then stand in a totally selfish position halfway down the compartment, stopping more people from getting on the train. People mutter and people try staring and then someone (usually an agressive sounding accountant with an umbrella) shouts out 'You – yes, YOU, sir, with the black beret, can you PLEASE move down the train?' One of three things now happens – either the man in the black beret just pretends he can't speak English, or he shuffles about one-and-a-half little footsteps down the carriage, thus allowing about one new person on the train, or he turns round and tries to outstare the accountant. Sometimes even words are exchanged and sometimes, even more excitingly, other people join in and start shouting. In any event, it is a great spectator sport as long as you are comfortably sitting down feigning sleep across a double seat somewhere warm.

Being Duped by Newspaper Headlines

We've all done it – wandered by the billboard, seen TV STAR DEAD, and rushed to buy a copy. Who is it, we wonder, as we fumble for change – Paxo? Clarkson? McDonut? Every time we turn a page with still no news we slightly downgrade our expectations (Cheggers? Dirty Den? Anthea Turner?) until, by the time we have reached page nine and given up all hope of finding out, we see a tiny paragraph right at the bottom telling us that tributes are pouring in for a Mr Ron Ecklethwaite who played love-able Cockney rogue Fred Dawson from 1957–1961 in the much-missed ATV soap opera *Victoria Garage*. Thanks, Mr Headline Writer, we enjoyed the ride.

Being Late

The funny thing about late people is that we are always about ten minutes behind everyone else. If only they'd set their watch ten minutes fast, punctual people sometimes say, they'd be on time like the rest of us. Well, no, we wouldn't. Firstly, we'd just factor in the ten minutes (believe us, we've tried it). And secondly, we quite like being late. We think it makes us look a bit cool, like we're really important or something. We never have to hang around, wondering if we've been stood up. And we never have to be the one to fight for a table, because someone's already done it for us. Put it this way – we get all this, and what do early birds get for their efforts? Worms.

Being Nicer to Temps than You Are to Your Secretary

In a counter-intuitive way, we all behave better in front of people we are never going to see again than in front of our usual colleagues/life partners/family, so getting a temp for a day is an opportunity to spend the whole day playing 'let's pretend' and being the perfect boss. Learn your temp's name, brief her clearly and concisely about what is expected of her, take all calls, answer all your post immac-ulately and on time, ask her politely to do some filing and recommend an inexpensive but rather good sandwich bar for lunch, then give her some interesting and useful tasks to carry out before allowing her to leave ten minutes early, signing her time sheet for an extra half hour and then giving her an excellent reference. Then spend the next day shouting at your normal and long-serving assistant, expecting her to read your mind, saying you are in a meeting every time anyone calls, getting angry at the slightest lapse in efficiency, throwing hissy fits when she asks you to make decisions and then getting her to work late while you swan off early for a 'doctor's appointment'.

Being 'On a Break'
If it is good enough for Rachel and Ross, then it is good enough for us humble mortals. The great thing about being on a break is that anything counts, really, but you know you have the option of a boyfriend to go back to if things don't work out. It is like pressing pause on a favourite DVD, popping along to the local multiplex, watching every film currently on release and then deciding whether you want to go home and press play again. Of course, life is never that simple and one party enjoys the freedom of the break more than the other, and then you end up having a jealousy-fuelled fight and it all goes tits up. But it is fun while it lasts.

Being the Office Fire Marshal
It's great – you get to be officially bossy, hold a clipboard, have an armband and even, in some offices, wear a hat. The only downside is that if there actually ever was a fire, you probably have to be the last person to leave the building so you might get burned alive, although, compared with the hat, that is a small consideration.

Being Welcomed by Name at a Restaurant
In this alienated society we live in, where urban life is an anonymous experience, where eyes rarely meet, where strangers pass in the night and no one knows your name,

there is something pathetically wonderful about going into a favourite restaurant and being met by a smiling maitre d' saying, 'Good Evening, Mr Shopping While Drunk, your usual table is ready, sir, and how is Mrs Shopping While Drunk and your two lovely children – Shopping and Drunk?' Lovely.

Betting Shops

There is a quick way of saving time in a betting shop, and that is to go straight to the counter and hand over your money immediately. But where's the fun in that? Not when you can get stared at by all the tramps watching the dog racing. Not when you can play that most excellent of games, find the little blue pen that actually works. Not when you can humiliate yourself totally by asking, 'So, just remind me, what does "each-way" mean again?'

Big Boy Condoms

In the old days, buying condoms at the local chemist involved either first filling a shopping basket with a lot of items that you really didn't need or wearing dark glasses and trying not to make eye contact. Either way, you were made to feel either like a slag or a lady of the night. Now, thankfully, the process has migrated on to the world wide web, where no one need be embarrassed by anything ever. We particularly like our friends at www.bigboycondoms.co.uk, who offer ample opportunities to titillate or even humiliate your current paramour. For those boyfriends with a warped sense of humour, why not gift them an Erco Novelty hand-painted condom which comes (no joke intended) in a handsome presentation box and a choice of styles between 'Baby's Dummy' and 'Fireman' (with a glistening helmet, of course) or, for the musical among us, there is a range which play tunes when squeezed. We would like to think that the choice of songs includes 'She'll be Coming Round The Mountain When She Comes' or 'A Whole Lotta Shaking Goin' On', but we can't confirm that at this stage. You could also buy a packet of 'Safex Max Extra Large' for the man who needs his condom a little longer with extra width. When they don't fit (which they won't!), look surprised and then say, 'Well, they fitted my last boyfriend no problem.' Hmm.

Big Brother Contestants (of Limited Intelligence)

Let's face it, we're all a bit dim. Educational standards have slipped dramatically in the last twenty or thirty years and no amount of giving A-levels away in cornflake packets is going to disguise it. Luckily, that's not the Government's only idea. They have also rather cunningly loosened the constraints on our once high-quality television broadcasters until the weekday evening schedules are effectively a protracted mong parade. Dozens of optimistic morons appear on our televisions every week equipped with little more than a winning smile and a catchphrase. Always the same one, in fact: 'I'm just going to be myself'. As if they were going to be anyone else? (In fact, it would be entirely refreshing if one contestant assured us that they were going to 'just be Rasputin'.) They know nothing, they can do nothing and their language skills are, at best, marginal. Indeed, they conclude every sentence with the word 'so . . .' Rarely a half hour goes by without one of these fame-hungry dimwits assuring us that 'what we see is what we get' or that that they love somebody 'to bits'. Given that their every utterance is composed of the same half-dozen meaningless clichés, we can pop out to the kitchen for frequent tea and biscuit refills safe in the knowledge that nothing will be said that we won't have heard before, and will soon be hearing again. The brilliance of the scheme, of course, is that, for the price of a few thousand text messages, we are reassured that, as dense as we are, there are people out there who know a good deal less, so . . .

Big Brother's Little Brother's First Cousin's Aunt

Big Brother, being as it is concerned principally with interpersonal relationships, is women's television. During the course of an entire BB series nothing blows up and few, if any, people have complicated and noisy sex. Hardly worth a fine gentleman like yourself bothering to get out of bed at eight o'clock in the evening to watch it then, one might think. But imagine for a moment if all the best and funniest bits were collected together and shown to a hand-picked audience of especially witty homosexual gentlemen and presided over by an annoyingly funny tyke who dresses like a Dickensian street urchin who's just joined The Alarm. Say what you like about our gay cousins but, because they aren't distracted by parenthood and trying to work out what women think, they've got a lot more time to think up brilliantly sarcastic comments about popular culture. And Russell Brand may have been technically irksome, but he still managed to get us hooked. It's a shame he left – that *Blankety Blank* microphone is worth the price of admission alone. Dermot O'Leary's alright too, in a 'Wogan – The Next Generation' sort of way.

Big Lunch, a

The problem with going out on the lash after work is that although you'll be consuming thousands of these mysteriously 'empty' calories, you won't have time to go home for your tea. Consequently, the only rational choice is to line your stomach with something comforting and tasty the preceding lunchtime. Pasta's the intelligent choice. A nice big burger is the most pleasing one. A pub lunch is the only option for the truly dedicated drinker. Don't worry if you don't fancy what's on the pub menu, though. Just treat yourself to a couple of liveners. You're having a fry-up tomorrow morning anyway.

Bingo Wings

The problems start when you stop waving, but your upper arm doesn't, when it continues flapping giddily in the wind like a mottled pork chop on the run. Suddenly middle age beckons with a wobble. And a cap-sleeve T-shirt becomes the serial killer of sex appeal. No more flighty, floaty, strapless sundresses for you. No, instead it's the matronly charms of the cardie. Worn at all times. Virtually bandaging the bingo wing in place, lest it should run amok when you least expect. At this point, strict bingo wing etiquette becomes essential. Never pose for a picture with your arm pressed across your body. The offending wingage will spread like a spilt lard-slick, creating an optical illusion that you're 5 per cent woman and 95 per cent gargantuan, all-conquering arm. And never stand with your arms raised at shoulder height, making the wings hang down like heavy velour drapes. You body should never bring to mind the soft furnishing department at BHS.

Biting Your Toenails

We used to think that the desire to do this went away as one got older, but actually the primal urge to chew your stinky feet stays the same. Alas, your body gets less flexible and less able to agree to your every command, thus the risk gets higher – do you really want to chew your nails to such an extent that you are prepared to risk something going snap, and being stuck in a position that the editors of the original edition of the *Kama Sutra* omitted because it looked too silly and a bit rude? Of course you do! Apparently someone has invented nail clippers, but that's not important right now.

Black Opaque Tights

Forget surgery, thick black tights are the style equivalent to liposuction, honing heavy calves and thick cankles into something acceptable to display amongst polite society. Years ago opaques were the domain of heavy-set nurses and OAPs who needed something to keep their incontinence pants in place. Then fashion, not usually one to come to the rescue of the diet-challenged, swept in and deemed them a style must. Women everywhere sighed into their sofas and got another slice of fudge cake in. Straight to the hips? Yes, but hips swaddled in flattering, lycra-enhanced, support-pant reinforced black tights. The fear for women now is that the fashion police will cast tights into the sartorial wilderness. A bitter blast of how devastating this would be sweeps in every spring, when fake-tan is the only thing between your newly-bare legs and an arrest for indecent exposure.

Blackpool

The town that taste (and the casino committee) forgot. If you were, say, a hapless American tourist who'd wandered far from the Piccadilly Line and found yourself in the wilderness of the north west, the first thing that would surprise you would be the sea. There isn't any. Instead there's an oil slick on the distant horizon. To find out if this menacing waterline is indeed an ocean would mean embarking on a long and dangerous journey across the bottle and sewage strewn beach to find out. Even Christopher Columbus wouldn't have risked it. Luckily, no such tourists exist. Instead, the town is populated by visiting fat slags and ASBO yobs who've hired a National Express coach to celebrate their respective hen and stag parties. Candy floss and a ride on the rollercoaster, followed by a Bacardi Breezer booze up and a blow-job for the bouncer. Perfect. What better way to celebrate your forthcoming nuptials? Quaintly, you might still find someone's nan wandering round, stuck in 1952, wearing a Kiss-Me-Quick hat and asking for a ride back to neighbouring Lytham St Anne's – the toff to Blackpool's chav.

Bloating (Blaming Everything on It)

The phrase dripping from the lips of every woman these days is 'I'm just a bit bloated'. Bloating is *very* different from being, well, a bloater. A fat stomach suggests gluttony and a surgical operation, or worse, a diet to remove it, whilst bloating is more like a medical ailment, a temporary affliction that is in no way your fault, and will be entirely cured by the weekend. Just in time to fit into that dress that, at the moment, won't zip up. NO. NOT because you're too fat for it, you're merely *bloated*. The funny thing is, this bloating business mostly strikes you down when you've been scoffing your body weight in chocolate. Weird that, isn't it? If someone (say your boyfriend) even *dares* to suggest there could be a link, implying it's down to you being a lard-arse, you bring out the big guns. Your food allergies. Then take him down in a barrage of IBS anecdotes. Within minutes he'll be agreeing that, yes, you are a 'bloated' size zero, forced to wear size 12 for medical reasons . . .

Body Type (Lying About on Internet Sites)

Can you imagine a more loaded question for women? *What's your body type?* Well, how long have you got? Women could literally spend a good two years answering this question, and there still wouldn't be a grain of truth in the reply. So it's beyond horror when this little question pops up when you are creating a dating or networking profile. Unfortunately, answers don't include 'thin when I breathe in' or 'in serious need of lipo'. The dilemma comes when deciding if you should put down small or medium. Small would be stretching the truth, as it implies someone with Nicole Ritchie-esque petiteness. But medium has that undertone of Jessie Wallace – solidly built, and *seriously* scary in a fight. Plus, knowing the Internet, everyone upgrades themselves one notch. So answering 'medium' is the equivalent of saying 'I'm a total fatso'. Of course the answer is to go for small. And just wear a flattering outfit and keep your fingers crossed if you meet up with someone . . .

Bog Books

As fewer and fewer houses are equipped with a library or a study for quiet contemplation, so the discerning gentleman turns to his water closet as the last bastion of scholastic tranquillity. Similarly in the workplace, where mounting intolerance of the half-hourly fag break drives the work-shy dandy ever more frequently to the disabled loos, those most fragrant and spacious of the provided facilities. You might well be reading this book on the loo now. It's a bit odd, in that case, us being in here talking to you like this, but it's important stuff so we'll press on.

Look down at your thighs. Are there two red elbow-prints on them? Perhaps revealing a little of the texture of your jacket? If not, read on. A good read ends only when you can't feel your legs. Large format books are inadvisable in most circumstances, as you will end up having to place them on a floor of uncertain cleanliness at the end of the session in order to attend to certain unpleasant necessities. What you're looking for is a trim volume which will nestle snugly in the pocket of a sports jacket, while offering enough content to see you safely through a truly marathon sit-down.

Boob Jobs

British women, by some cruel sleight of God's hand, are often pear-shaped, and are more likely to need a D-cup for their thighs than their breasts. Step in your friendly, chiselled-jawed surgeon, ready to correct with a scalpel the aesthetic apocalypse created by a century of bad genes. The logical thing would be to just amputate the saddlebags and implant them on the chest. But then you only have to imagine Pamela Anderson with a cellulite-ridden cleavage to see the error of that theory. So, until the experts can invent Krispy Kremes that go straight to your boobs, not your bum, the only solution comes in a saline-filled airbag inserted through your nipples. If that seems too radical, let's just hope someone invents an inflatable bra.

Book Groups

It's like school, but with a bottle of wine. And no teachers. No one cares if you've done your homework or not, and there's only one book to remember. No matter what your mum tells you, *these* are the happiest days of your life. In theory, book groups are there for like-minded people to discuss and debate the literary merits of a recent novel they have all read. In practice, the books get tossed aside in the first five minutes and the rest of the time is spent gossiping, bitching and eyeing up members of the opposite sex. Even the attempts at serious discussion are loaded with pregnant meaning: when someone asks you if you thought the sex scenes were smouldering, you know you're in with a chance; if they take them apart for being funny and look at you, maybe you're not.

Book Signings
It was a recent picture of Princess Diana's 'rock', Paul Burrell, that made us remember what fun book signings can be. There he was sitting forlornly with the paparazzi outnumbering the punters queuing up to buy his latest cash-in . . . sorry, 'celebratory' book, and he was quoted as saying, 'I am sure my book will be flying off the shelves nearer Christmas.' Hmm. Book signings by 'proper authors' are traditionally events mounted to suit the vanity of the person concerned and rarely actually sell many books, and, as such, they are a great opportunity to turn up and watch the discomfort of the author concerned; whereas book signings by 'celebrities' can be hilarious media circuses, where the 'author' can barely sign their name let alone profess to have read their own book. To test this theory, grab a copy as soon as you get into the store, then queue up patiently and ask the celebrity concerned a few random questions about the autobiography. 'Move along, sir, please – thank you.'

Borat (Fancying)
In these complicated dating times, the thought of a be-tached berk chasing you with a 'sack' to 'marriage' you suddenly doesn't seem that bad. Obviously the Soviet-manufactured underpants would have to go . . .

Bought It in the States. Coupla Bucks
Is there anything more annoying than the person who gets back from a holiday in the US with a seemingly limitless supply of pairs of new jeans, trainers and incredibly well-fitting T-shirts, all of which, as a result of the dollar's precarious position in the currency markets, seem to have

cost 'a coupla bucks'. Equally, is there anything better than *being* that person? The defence rests.

Bourbon Biscuit Sucking

This is messy but pure heaven – bite both ends off a Bourbon biscuit and suck coffee or tea through it. Then stuff the biscuit in your mouth before it melts in your hand. Yum, yum, yum.

Boyfriend's Baseball Cap

Wearing one of his T-shirts means you weren't expecting to stay for breakfast. Borrowing his sweater means you're really an item, see below. Slipping on his pyjama top means you're trapped in 1963. You can just about excuse any of these on the grounds of general sluttiness, climate change or rips in space-time. There's no way you can get away with wearing his baseball cap though. The fact that you've got a boyfriend with a baseball cap, in the first place means (unless you're dating an actual baseball player) that you're going to be enjoying rather too many romantic tête-à-têtes in your local Harvester than you might like. God forbid that he ever drives a car wearing the thing: you might as well pawn all your jewellery now in that case. You might think that a ponytail held in place by a baseball cap gives you the air of an exceptionally sporty WAG. Frankly, exceptionally sporty SLAG is probably more accurate. A baseball cap is, according to Debrett's, one step *below* a lovebite in polite society. It might do for walking the family staff around the council estate, but pray that no one you know sees you wearing it. A baseball cap says more about you than a sovereign ring ever can.

Boyfriend's Jumpers

What is it about your boyfriend's clothes? We think it's because, unless you're going out with Tom Cruise, chances are that they're likely to be bigger, baggier and pretty comfy. And while, normally, big and baggy might result in a look of disapproval from your bloke, the fact that it's *his* jumper means that he gets a kick out of it too, so everyone's happy. Skilled practitioners will, at this point, take the jumper borrowing to the next stage, by easing the transition from shared ownership to making the jumper yours. Very skilled practitioners will take jumper borrowing to the max by going clothes shopping with their boyfriend, and helping them pick out a jumper that they want to wear. Just resist the temptation to say 'But *this* one will go so well with my jeans . . .'

Brangelina See TomKat.

Bread-Free Sandwich

Only Pret à Manger could dream this one up. It's not a sandwich, whatever the clever marketing men say, it's salad. If you want a salad, have one. If you want a sandwich, tuck in. Just don't call a pile of lettuce and tuna a sandwich without bread. What next? Alcohol-free wine? Oh, actually . . .

Brides of Botox

There are probably some women who would walk, barefoot, to Chernobyl and bathe in chemical waste if it made them look younger. Luckily, they don't have to. They just have to get a cab down to Harley Street. Such is their thirst to imbibe potential anti-ageing agents, they probably stop off at a petrol station on the way for a cheeky go on the petrol pumps. Celebrities are the calling card for the frozen-faced results of the procedure. From looking at a sliding scale of their expressionless foreheads, it seems that Botox is a bit like booze. A couple of shots and you look more or less normal – just a 'little refreshed'. But a full-on binge session unleashes your inner beast, making you look like evolution's justification for extinction. Ironically, in a world headed for eco-apocalypse, when the melted ice-caps end up in a celebrity spa heated whirlpool, the Brides of Botox will be the only part of planet earth still frozen.

Brighton on a Bank Holiday

Ah yes, you may say – city of (principally) homosexual gentlemen and antique shops. We know all about Brighton. It's like an episode of *Sex and the City* with David Dickinson standing in for Manolo Blahnik. You haven't really experienced the place, though, until you've felt a strong gale whipping the near-constant rain into a force ten facial spritz that makes a can of Evian seem like a mere child's plaything. These peculiar climatic conditions only prevail on Easter and August Bank Holidays, so book early for guaranteed disappointment. Paradoxically, the only antidote to this excessively bracing situation is a stiff Sea Breeze in one of the numerous cocktail establishments that jostle for position between the antique shops. With one of these at your elbow and a small barricade of carrier bags from selected boutiques around your ankles, you really are experiencing the very best of this popular seaside resort.

Broken Digestives

It is always a shame to find the bottom two biscuits in a packet of digestives are broken, but sometimes, just sometimes, we break them deliberately and then hide them in a big bowl of either Greek yoghurt (with honey – obviously) or, even better, in a bowl of vanilla ice cream. The combination of smooth cold gooey stuff and crunchy biscuity stuff is irresistible. Oh dear, we have broken another one.

Burning the Dinner

Today's busy professionals don't always have the time to cook a proper meal after a busy day of gossiping, smoking, looking out of the window and pratting around on the Internet. Not when *EastEnders* is on, anyway. That's why it's increasingly common for that final dramatic drum flourish to coincide with a sympathetic screech from the smoke alarm as the remains of your carefully-planned repast ignites. Still, as long as there are chip shops, we have access to a quick replacement supper that covers all the major food groups (mushy peas *are* a vegetable!) and leaves us with sufficient time to prepare for the following day's work, watch *Newsnight* or (and this would be our choice) flick through *heat* while sipping an acceptable mid-priced Pinot Grigio straight from the box.

Bushisms
He didn't say half of those things you read on the Internet. Candidly, he doesn't know that many words. Still, we're right behind him. Even if he does always mix up 'Iran' and 'Iraq' in speeches, he's less frightening than Hillary and Barack put together. Hell, Satan's less frightening than the idea of those two together!

Butter
Banish all thoughts of Marlon Brando and *Last Tango in Paris* – this dirty little secret is much simpler and doesn't mess the sheets up at all. Butter is usually eaten as an accompaniment to the traditional sandwich fillings, such as Marmite, cheese and tomato, and honey, but we like to eat it on its own – preferably off a knife. There is nothing like a bit of pure butter – you KNOW it is going to make you fat, but it tastes far too good to hide in sandwiches. Recent research shows that, in recent years, Americans have been eating about five pounds of butter per person per annum, so we are not alone here. Margarine? What do you think we are? Chavs?

Buying 'It' Bags
Oh God, it's happened: you've turned into a Grazombie – you are now prepared to spend your entire salary on a handbag because a glossy magazine told you to. Just because Kate Moss has one doesn't make it big or clever. But, somehow, the '*Itness*' of the bag is infectious. You're not just buying a Chloe Paddington, you're virtually booking the Lear jet and landing right bang on Rodeo Drive. But who cares about that? Having the designer label du jour on your arm is all that counts. Until you have to sell your kidney on the black market to pay for it. Which, with

brilliant synchronicity, puts you in the same position as the poor worker who made it. Except they sold their kidney for the frivolous stuff, you know, like paying rent . . .

Buying a Box of Chocolates (For Yourself)

You know that guy, the suave, slightly stalkerish Milk Tray man? Not only does he a) not exist, but b) if he did, he wouldn't do home deliveries. Which is a shame. Because this means ladies have to shame-facedly shuffle to the supermarkets themselves to pick up an *entire* box of lardy treats. Blame the PMT monster, but sometimes even a family-sized Dairy Milk won't hit the spot. But an entire box of Celebrations will. Of course, even though you could realistically be buying them for your sick aunt, it's as if everyone knows what you're up to. You can almost hear the disapproving tuts as you and your muffin top loiter nervously at the checkout. The law is, once you've got your stash back home, you must eat the evidence all in one go. Except the coffee creams. No woman is *that* desperate.

Buying New Tools (When You Know You Have What You Need Somewhere in the Cellar But You Can't Be Arsed to Look For It)

If you are an infrequent DIY-er then you never quite know where any of your tools are kept – at the end of each job you scoop them all up and vaguely tidy them away into the cellar or the cupboard under the stairs or the attic or on top of the wardrobe or . . . and this is where the trouble lies. Next time you need them you have a cursory look, can't find them, so, frankly, it is easier to wander off to Homebase and start all over again. Once you have got the paint and nails and screws you need (all of which you probably have at home somewhere), it is so tempting just to sling in a new hammer, set of screwdrivers, paintbrushes (which will never be washed, just binned) and assorted gubbins into a plastic basket and start your job with shiny new tools. A bad workman may blame his tools, but a guilty workman can never find them again.

Buying the Outfit in the Window

Buying the outfit in the window says that you're just too busy and important to waste time browsing the racks. Or it means the window dresser has better taste than you. Which may be true. Or it means that you can't be bothered to think for yourself and would prefer to outsource that job to someone who didn't do all that well at fashion college. Still, beats shopping.

Call Centre Rage

In a way, even getting through to the call centre to be mentally tortured is a triumph. Because that means that you've got through the horror of the automated phone system. 'Can you input the second, seventh and tenth number of your security code, multiply it by four, divide it by 2456 and explain Einstein's Theory of Relativity in morse code', the monotone voice asks you. 'NO I BLOODY CAN'T', you scream at the phone. But, of course, there's no one there. That's the first stage in breaking you down. By the time you get through to Sheila in Leicester (who, incidentally, was trained by the CIA at Guantanamo Bay), it's all over for you. 'I'll need to know your mother's inside leg measurement to access your accounts', she vacantly explains. Anything you ask her to do will, inexplicably, be impossible. Get a balance on your account? No way. Jesus, anyone would think it was *your* money. The more misinformation you're given in the android, emotionless tone of someone who's simultaneously reading *Closer*, the more your rage will froth up. Usually, it's only after being passed to the Belfast branch via India and Angola that your patience really snaps. You would slam the phone down. But, by that time, they've already cut you off by mistake.

Cancelling Dental Appointments

Dentists. Bastards. Sorry if you're a dentist and have just read that, but let's be honest, you don't make it easy for us to like you, do you? All that drilling, the swilling, the paying, not to mention the appalling selection of magazines in the waiting room. The only thing worse than a dental appointment is the anticipation of going. But there is another way – ring up and cancel. Your teeth might twinge a little, but, believe us, you'll feel great for it.

Cancelling Lunch

We've all done it – looked at the office diary for the week (or even day) ahead and thought 'sod it – I really can't be arsed to have lunch with X'. Finding some excuse in this modern day and age to cancel is never tricky ('sorry, but we have had an urgent internal meeting brought forward' will do the trick) and hey presto you have a free period in your busy schedule. The real trick (and what makes it a hell of a lot more guilty) is to make use of the time to do something you really want to do, like gadget shopping or browsing DVDs at HMV, rather than then arranging yet another lunch. Word of warning: if you ignore this advice and do arrange a lunch – DON'T ARRANGE IT IN THE SAME RESTAURANT YOU WERE GOING TO GO TO. Chances are you will be rumbled as you sit down at the next table to your recently cancelled guest. . . .

Carrier Bag Fraud

There's a part of you that never evolves from refusing to carry your school gym kit in a Tesco carrier bag. 'Mum – it's soooo uncool,' you scream petulantly. And that's aged thirty, when you're forced to hit the streets with a Primark bag. Instead, the three times you ever shopped somewhere posh are preserved in the cupboard under your sink in the form of an upmarket carrier bag. Of course it's cheating. But life feels so much better when you're carrying your Somerfield shopping home in a Marc Jacobs bag.

Carveries

If you can set aside the sense that you are stepping back into the 1970s for your dining experience and simultaneously morphing into Alan Partridge (and those are big IFs), then popping along to your local carvery is well worth the trip. Stiffle your giggles at the huge swirly carpets, mahogany-effect furniture, ridiculously oversized laminated menus and comical cruet sets and just feast your eyes instead on the huge slabs of rare roast beef, chicken, pork, crackling, yorkshire puddings, brussels sprouts, huge mutant carrots, too green peas and enormous vats of gravy. Go on – eat as much as you like – it's only £7.95 and, frankly, at those prices it's probably cheaper than doing it yourself. Just keep your fingers crossed that you don't see anyone you know. Double points if experienced alone.

Cashmere

Once a luxury yarn exclusive to Ladies Who Lunch but now, like just about everything else, mass produced in China, probably under terrible conditions, so that our aunts can have a nice Christmas present that doesn't cost as much as they think it did. Or, of course, so that we can stroke our own lovely jumpers at times of stress. Almost certainly the softest and loveliest jumper stuff available, and definitely the most comforting. Oh, those poor Chinese goats, though. Do you think they suffer?

Cassettes

No one's bought a cassette in ages. Really they haven't. Certainly not a pre-recorded one with an album on it. Nevertheless, if you open the right drawer or shoebox in anybody's house, you can find millions of the bastards. All labelled in an adolescent approximation of the research subject's handwriting. Nearly all with 'Top 40 17th Feb 1987' written on them. Kept under ideal conditions, magnetic tape has a life expectancy of around twenty years. The compilations you made for that girl you liked the look of in the fifth form (but never got around to giving her) have been played at a couple of smoky parties before being shoved in a dusty cardboard box and dropped by enthusiastic amateur removals men every couple of years. If you played them they'd disintegrate, writing off your cassette deck in the process. It doesn't matter, though. You don't really need a cassette deck. No one's bought a cassette in ages.

Casualty

Early Saturday night telly is perfectly acceptable. You're getting ready to go out – there's a nice bit of *X Factor* while you do your face/eat your tea. But let's face it – if you're still in when *Casualty* begins, it's a Billy No Mates night for you. Fortunately, the show's scriptwriters are there to cheer you up by handing out brutal and violent accidents to random characters who are out having more fun than you. A man enjoying a drink in the pub; a young couple in a car; if they're not dressed up as a doctor or a nurse and they're on in the first five minutes, you know they're going to get it. The only suspense is what misfortune is going to befall them: is it going to be a fallen tree smashing through the pub window? Someone mis-throwing a dart and hitting an alternative target? Or will he just choke to death on a peanut? Whichever it is, as you watch the victim writhe towards an early grave, however miserable you were feeling before, suddenly the world seems a better place. Which is public service broadcasting at its very best.

CDs with Sexy Covers

As the digital download slowly supplants actual records you can hold, it's difficult to say what will happen to the mystical art of the mildly fruity album cover. Would Roxy Music have sold any records at all without their winning succession of softcore sleeves? Would any of us know anything about Jazz, or indeed Heavy Metal, without the talents of those callypigous young women who adorned the covers of many key recordings. For that matter, would we have *any* Ohio Players records? Perhaps there will be a concomitant growth in pictures of half-dressed young women on the Internet? Who can say? A helpful hint, if sexy album covers are your kind of thing and you're looking for real sauce, Jorge Santana is your man.

Celebrities (Too Fat)

Let's get this straight. According to *heat* magazine, anyone in the public eye over a size 12 is a porker. 'Celebs say stuff the diet!' the coverline screams, with a picture of Charlotte Church eating a ham and cheese sandwich. Er, no. She's probably just having her lunch. 'Ew! Liz Hurley's cellulite shocker' another one gloats with a gratuitous beach bum shot, the horror-struck tone of the caption suggesting that this disgusting development is like having bird flu on your arse. Quite rightly so, as most of the female population will catch it. Then you get poor Fern Britton, pictured in a bikini with the headline 'She loves her curves!' Brilliant, let's hope she does. Though doesn't this suggest that it's gross to be a size 12/14, but that being a size 20 is merely voluptuous? Anyway, let's not waste too much pity on our portly celebs. At least they're bound to make a fortune taking part in a *Closer* diet.

Celebrities (Too Thin)

One minute you're tipping the scale at 'TOO F%^&*£G FAT', the next minute you've lost a pound and weigh a minuscule 'SHOCKING EATING DISORDER'. For celebs, it really is feast or famine when it comes to their weight. Has Nicole got thinner this week? Did Britney eat that gherkin on her burger? Is Lindsay eating her greens? What are you – her bloody mother? This ghoulish obsession with skinny celebs must end now. Until *Now*'s next bikini body special, that is.

Celebrity Autobiographies, Failing to Sell

We all love a good trashy celebrity biography, whether it's Jordan or Geri Halliwell, Robbie Williams or Jade Goody. But what we like even more is when the so-called star signs the squillion dollar deal to spend four weeks talking into a ghostwriter's tape recorder only to discover that, when the book comes out, *very few people want to buy it. Fools Rush In* by Anthea Turner? I guess the nation ain't fools, Anth. *Living the Dream* by Chantelle? If the dream is having your signing session at Brent Cross truncated because hardly anyone has turned up.

Celebrity Golf

We like golf. We like celebrities. But what if we could get celebrities to play golf, *and we were allowed to watch them?* Monsieur Scheduler, with your pro-am programme, you are really spoiling us. Does life get any better than watching Jodie Kidd, Chris Evans and Damien Lewis cross clubs and make a few cheap cracks about 'balls', 'holes', 'lips' and, er, 'balls'? It's a win-win situation all round: real golfers love it for the glamour that rubs off from the stars; the celebrities love it because they feel they are like proper sportsmen. Well, as far as twatting around in a Pringle sweater makes you a proper sportsman. And, somehow, the fact that James Nesbitt is playing means your girlfriend will not only let you watch golf on the telly, she'll sit there and watch it with you. See? Everyone's happy. Well, everyone apart from Brucie and Tarby, who never seem to get an invite any more.

Celebrity Sex Tapes

You can find films of people having sex on the Internet. We know. We found some by accident when we were looking for something about kittens. Some of the people having the sex have clearly done it before and are really rather good at it. A great many of them are genuinely attractive young men and women. So why, then, would you choose to watch some really poorly-lit video of a couple of bumping uglies from a fixed camera angle and dodgy focus? Because that suspiciously hairy buttcrack that's filling the whole frame for five minutes apparently belongs to one of S Club 7. Or somebody off *Emmerdale*. Or that rough bird that got evicted in the first week of *Big Brother* a few years back. And we just can't get enough of celebrities. It's obvious why we keep watching the videos, the only mystery is why these people are dim enough to keep making them. If we'll stoop to pinching the little lady's copy of *heat* to read on the lav then there's absolutely no doubt that we'll be downloading something called Mother_ Teresa.avi, purely for research purposes.

Chakra Crystal Bracelets

Even your accessories have to work hard to secure a better future for you now. A trinket for a tenner from Topshop will no longer do. Why mindlessly fritter money on an imitation gold bracelet like the one that Sienna Miller wore last week when you can wrap chakra crystals round your wrist? Obviously, you're still not quite sure what a chakra is (although you established it definitely wasn't a nickname for Chaka Khan, who, incidentally, you love). But you've been promised they can cure everything from a blocked heart to a blocked toilet. Really, chakra crystals are the cut diamonds of the New Age world. And, yes, simply wearing one will make you more compassionate. So buy loads more – after all, they're like a cashpoint for karma.

Changing Rooms (the Gym)

There are two breed of women who go to the gym: the hard-bodied fitness freak and the blubber-bodied Weight Watcher. One flaunts the spoils of her toils in hot pants and a crop Adidas top, whilst the other waddles around in the gym kit equivalent of a burka. But it's in the changing rooms that the gloves really come off in this war of flesh. Miss Hard Body strips naked (sporting an extreme bikini wax, naturally) and positions herself in the centre of the changing room, in front of the mirror, then proceeds to slather body lotion over every last toned inch of herself, with such over-vigorous application you can't help but think 'get a room'. Meanwhile, Miss Non-Supermodel is skulking in the corner, trying to strip, have a shower and get dressed again, all within the confines of an extra-large towel.

Changing Song Titles in a Puerile and Stupid Way

Songwriters look away – you won't like this one. It is very silly but hugely pleasurable – all you do is simply add the words 'in your big pants' to the chosen song title. Thus, Sting's huge international hit becomes much more fun when called 'Every Breath You Take in Your Big Pants', The Rolling Stones' charming ditty takes on a new resonance when it becomes 'Start Me Up in Your Big Pants', but Wham's 1982 classic sounds worryingly like an advertisement for incontinence pants when it becomes 'Wake Me Up Before You Go Go in Your Big Pants'. Hee Hee!

Charity Shop Clothes

Worse than someone saying 'Yah, it's from Marc Jacobs' is someone showing off that they picked up a designer bargain in a charity shop for a tenner. Was that the mystical charity shop somewhere over the bloody rainbow? Because, quite frankly, any jaunt to an ordinary person's local charity shop is usually rewarded with a vintage C&A tank-top fragranced with the scent of OAP bedpans. Or a Stephen King book for a quid. The truth is, unless you happen to live in Hampstead, Chelsea or Notting Hill, with folks like Madonna donating their cast-offs, the humble charity shop is the sartorial equivalent of rummaging through the bins.

Charity Shops (Looking to See How Much Your Donations Are Being Sold For in)

Owing to a disappointing quirk of physics, wardrobes (unlike arses) are of finite size. Therefore, when we tire of last season's collections (we never grow out of anything, never!) and seek new sartorial challenges upon the racks of top couturiers like Jigsaw and Mango, we must perforce dispense with last year's garments. It would be too much of an admission of defeat to hand them down to poorer (thinner) relatives, so, being as green as green can be, we of course bundle them into (recycled) bin bags and ditch them in the nearest charity shop. But what happens to them after that? To wander back a few days later and look for your old clothes to see how much they were worth (plus to root through the pockets for forgotten earring backs, non-prescription drugs, diaphragms etc.) is one of those joys that make the satisfaction of having given succour to the needy just that little bit sweeter. It's just like being the late Princess Diana. (Except you're alive.)

Chavumentaries

Ever felt a bit, well . . . slatternly? Ever thought that your house is frankly something of a tip and that your kids – should you have any – are more or less completely covered in snot and biro? Have you ever looked at your reflection in a finger-marked mirror and thought 'Jesus, what a slut'. And not in a good way? You need to get yourself sat in front of a chavumentary: these marvellous television programmes, generally set on crumbling sink estates, are essentially re-enactments of the last series of *Shameless* with non-actors taking the principal parts. Whereas *Shameless* and its cousins, Mike Leigh films, consist essentially of middle-class media professionals poking fun at the dim unwashed, using 'real people' lends a certain verisimilitude to the overall sense of futility and hopelessness and is also altogether cheaper. So they can make more of them, so you can sneer at losers all day long, which makes you feel a bit better about yourself. In fact, you feel like a bloody Duchess. A Duchess in a stained dressing gown, but a Duchess nonetheless.

Checking the History Bar of a Friend's Internet Explorer

You can tell a lot about people from what they surf when they think people aren't looking. Next time your flatmate is out, boot up their computer and check out the drop-down History panel of the Browser and you can instantly see into their personality – betcha bottom dollar two times out of three there will be something 'Adult' or 'Specialist' which will give you an insight into their tiny little twisted minds. Find the most extreme image you can and right click it so that it sets as the Desktop Background. Nice little suprise for them next time. . . .

Cheese on Toast
There are some recipes that require a fair degree of culinary skill in order to pull off. And there are others whose sheer simplicity allows their joy to spread to all ends of the cooking ability spectrum. Beans on toast is all very well, but it does involve opening a can, working a hob and stirring, which can seem like too much effort by half. So instead step forward cheese on toast, one of the finest fusions of modern foodstuffs since Mr Fish met Mr Chips. Where can you go wrong? All you've got to do is make some toast, grate some cheese and stick it under the grill for two minutes. Delish. Hang on, what's that burning smell. . .

Cherie Blair
Those consistently awful clothes, her Michael Jackson haircut, that letterbox smile that looks like she could swallow a VHS tape – where did it all go right for Cherie Blair? We think the turning point was probably the reports that surfaced of her once having modelled for a nude portrait. Once you realize that those shapeless tunics are removable, it puts a whole new spin on things.

Chicken Fillets
There's really no point having massive bosoms if the rest of you is so fat that they don't stand out. If you *do* decide to shell out a year's wine budget on a pair of Jade Goody signature edition spacehoppers then they'll smack you in the face every time you run for a bus and, before you know where you are, you'll look like the fat Anna Nicole Smith instead of the *Playboy* centrefold billionaire-marrying one. And nobody wants that. Praise be, then, for the humble

Chicken Fillet. They can mind their own business in the bottom of your bag all day, enabling you to get a decent day's work done without the work experience lad steaming up his glasses, but when it's time to go out in the evening you can pop 'em in your bra, and you're a SuperVixen. Plus they're about a million per cent cheaper than surgery, leaving loads of money left for more lovely wine.

Chip and PIN

Years ago, the only time you needed an evil genius computer wizard to access money was if you were planning to rob a bank. Now even buying your shopping at Sainsbury's requires you to crack the code to your own bank account. Chip and PIN seemed like such an innocent phrase. A bit like a comedy cartoon duo, really. In a way it seemed quite fun – like playing at grown-ups – the way you had to type in a code just to authorize payment for that bag of crisps. But put into the mix five credit cards, two debit cards and a brain mangled by the latest copy of *heat* magazine, and you're in a code red situation. Nope, that's not it, you mutter manically as you punch your grandmother's cat's birthdate in – just on the off chance. Of course, it turns out that your code is 1234, which actually makes you more of an idiot than the checkout girl thought possible.

Chocolate Nutella

Who came up with the concept of spreading not jam or marmalade or honey on their toast, but chocolate? Oh, the Germans. Still, full marks for the no-messing, slap-on-the-calories approach. We like to think we've given the experience a peculiarly British twist by inventing the no-carbs version, i.e. forgetting about the bread and just eating it straight out of the jar. Lick it off a knife for double dirty pleasure.

Chopsticks

We're not Elton John. Or, for that matter, Billy Joel. Not even Stevie Wonder or Alicia Keys or, well, you get the picture. But that doesn't mean that, when we see the inviting sight of a piano and empty seat, we don't feel the urge to sit down, and do the show *right* there. Fortunately, for those of us who lack the knowledge of the keyboard classics, help is at hand in the form of 'Chopsticks' – that gentle, lilting paean to human existence . . . sorry, uncultured rattle down the black keys. If you haven't bashed this number out to a stunned silence in a hotel lobby, you haven't lived.

Chorizo

We like sausages. We like Spain. If only there was a way of combining the two together. Readers, welcome into your home the joy of chorizo, the cured red sausage where chilli and paprika add a bit of kick that, if the pig had shown it earlier on, it might not have ended up on your plate. Normally, of course, if you added slices of chopped sausage to a dish, pig is exactly what you'd been called. But, somehow, when you say 'it's a chorizo and feta cheese salad', suddenly you sound like a cultured, cosmopolitan culinary genius. *Viva España!*

Chris Moyles

'The saviour of Radio One', according to the man himself. 'DLT in Waiting', according to the late John Peel. They're both right, of course, which explains both the DJ's huge popularity and his almost universal loathing by everyone else involved in the media. But, while the fashion police are clearly expecting us to listen to Indie FM or Radio Grime, the fact is that, in the safety of their homes, the nation are setting their alarm clocks to wake up with Moyles. And, yes, he may not be someone you'd invite home to meet your parents, but he is still by far the funniest and most entertaining thing on the radio in the morning. If you don't believe us, have a listen when Scott Mills stands in for him on holiday. That's your future, radio listener: enjoy the good times while they last.

Christina Aguilera

Pop music aimed at fifteen-year-old girls is best avoided by thirty-something men in public, particularly when those singing it are not much older themselves, and could probably do with a wash. We know we should probably be more critical of Christina (and we are going to call her Christina, and none of that X-Tina rubbish), but you can't argue with a succession of top-grade filthy pop songs: 'Genie in a Bottle', 'Dirrty', 'Ain't No Other Man'. And as for 'Beautiful', it even brings a little tear to our eye. If only there was a way of banning Pop Idol types from attempting (and failing) to cover it.

Christmas Cards (with Cuddly Animals)

Here's an idea, why not dress a kitten up in a Santa's outfit. How cute! What about a puppy in a pixie outfit? Adorable! Or maybe mice in scarves out carolling! Sweet! Oh yes, it's that yuletide taste lobotomy again. You might as well string them up on the wall while you're at it.

Christmas Decorations (the Naff Kind)

What's the point of having a Christmas tree that looks like it just stepped out of the pages of *Grazia*? Keep your Philippe Starck designed Christmas tree, tastefully toned white lights and abstract art cards. Nothing gets that 'ooh, isn't that festive' feeling better than a real tree, with a carpet-apocalypse of pine needles, tinsel in migraine-inducing red, green and gold and a life-sized Father Christmas figurine that looks like he might well have an ASBO. Ho, ho, ho.

Christmas Tree Chocolate

Christmas tree chocolate, like its near relative Easter egg chocolate, is made of special, special stuff that no one except the Secret Brotherhood of Chocolatiers knows about. It's tastier than normal chocolate, partly by dint of it having been hung like a good pheasant in a centrally-heated room until it's all light-brown and powdery. After eighteen hours of Bacchanalian gluttony there really is nothing finer.

Chucking a Sickie

There is, it has to be said, still colossal inequality in the workplace. Most of the women we know are tragic workaholics who wouldn't take a morning off work if you called in a tactical nuclear strike on their flat and hid their season ticket. As men, though, we're under no pressure to turn up even on a good day. Nobody wants us to come in and spew up all over the glass ceiling. It's a terrible injustice really. Sometimes we feel really bad about it, in those quiet few minutes between popping out for a fried breakfast and some Lemsip and coming back for *Trisha*.

Chuggers

You have got to admire their tenacity – surely, after the hundredth person has pretended to be on the phone or examined their shoelaces, you would think the Charity Muggers would get the message and go and do something more rewarding than stand there with their be-sloganed luminous tabards tirelessly trying to raise money for Anorexic Miners or Save The Syllable as you hurry off to get lunch or to get to the office. But no – they persist in the misapprehension that your average man in the street will decide to give an average of £12 a month to a charity just because a stunning Swedish student is falling out of a T-shirt and laughing coquettishly with her glistening pouting lips as she chews the end of the charity biro suggestively and then touches you tenderly on the arm, compliments you on your English accent and explains in a thick Svedish accent how you could really make her day. How shallow do you think we are? Shame on you. Where do we sign?

Cirque du Soleil

Banish all images of sawdust, exploding clown cars and a ringmaster with a big whip. Cirque du Soleil is to the traditional circus what *Pretty Woman*'s Julia Roberts is to an escort working in the red light district of Wolverhampton. Expect corporate sponsors, expect slick production values, expect a huge live orchestra, expect the

Royal Albert Hall, expect multi-lingual clowns, expect believing (just for a moment) that man can fly, expect to pay West End theatre prices and also expect a residual feeling that maybe, just maybe, you would have preferred to see a slightly flabby Russian juggling troup and an air of menace and slightly desperate-looking staff selling over-priced kazoos and plastic 'spinnable' plates (with a free stick).

City Shorts

Crueller than hotpants for one simple reason: we delude ourselves that we can actually wear them. Whilst your typical size 12/14 woman would never dream of turning up to work in hotpants and heels (without getting sacked), somehow it seems okay to wear the bastard cousin of Bermuda shorts. But it's far from OK. In fact, it's very wrong. Basically, it's like wearing a billboard announcing you're pear-shaped.

Cod

We know we shouldn't. We know they're being over-fished because of bastards like us. We know that our grandchildren won't have a clue what we're talking about. But, let's be honest, when you want fish and chips, it's got to be cod. Haddock? It's got bones in. Hake? How can you order a fish you don't even know how to pronounce? Plaice? If you're happy to wait fifteen minutes while the fryer digs one out of the freezer. The cod, by contrast, is always there waiting for you – it's already dead, it's already cooked: what possible good are you going to do by turning it down and letting that fat fuck behind you in the queue snaffle it up instead. It's not nice but it's the truth – cod is dying out, so get your quota in while you can.

Cola and Mentos

If you don't believe us then check out www.youtube.com. For the price of a packet of Mentos and a cheap own-brand multi-litre of cola, you can create a spurting jet of sugary foam up to twelve feet tall. Simply remove lid, pour out about a cupful of cola on to the ground, chuck in a tube full of Mentos and stand back as science becomes fun. DON'T TRY THIS AT HOME KIDS as the ceilings, walls, carpets and all furniture within fifteen feet will be ruined. NO, REALLY.

Coldplay
Alan McGee described them as 'bedwetters' music'. Noel Gallagher accused Chris Martin of looking like a geography teacher. They're hugely successful and, thus, almost by definition, liking them is best not admitted in public. Yet, for all that their lead singer is a prat – and God only knows what he was up to calling his daughter Apple – the fact remains that they have shifted a severe number of records, which means many of the people who look cool by slagging them off must have at least one of their CDs in their collection. We recommend the 'I-prefer-the-debut-album-before-they-got-really-huge' line, if you must keep up your attempt at credibility.

Collecting After Dark Postcards
The craze for these completely black postcards emblazoned with the words 'London After Dark' or 'Rome After Dark' probably started in the pre-digital days when a photographer came back from a particularly strenuous assignment to capture that special nocturnal atmosphere of Piccadilly Circus or the Colosseum and realized in the darkroom that he had left the lens cap on and all he had was a bunch of unexposed film. Not knowing how to explain himself to his boss the next morning, he craftily dreamt up this canny marketing ploy, which was then seized upon by manufacturers worldwide. We love them and have the whole set.

Comment Whore (Being a)
In normal life, people commenting on your pictures is a bad thing (oh sorry, I didn't realize that was taken *after* your pregnancy), but online it's all about the ad libs.

Basically, if every picture on your online profile doesn't have at least fifty comments, you're nothing, you're nobody. Of course, it's egotistical narcissism gone mad – but who cares when someone just posted 'OMG so Hot! U R Sexy!' on your holiday snaps.

Competitive Bingeing

Luckily, before the madness of competitive dieting lays waste to womanhood, another competitive sport kicks in. Olympic bingeing. 'I will if you will' is actually the shot-gun at the starting line of a massive scoffing race. An eating orgy can be triggered off by the simplest of things, like the waiter asking if you want to look at the dessert menu. Unspoken glances are exchanged. If one of you nods, it'll turn into a free-for-all. Weirdly, considering that yesterday you were smugly gloating about your asparagus detox, once the binge begins, the more sumo-sized your stomach is, the more kudos you get. 'Mine's bigger,' you scream, sticking your belly out and smearing nutella round your face like a crazed calorie-warrior. It'll end in broken dreams, and a broken pair of weighing scales the next day.

Competitive Dieting

In this size 00 world, having a body big enough to con-tain your internal organs is a heinous crime. Which means licking your way round a lettuce leaf for lunch. But the only way to find the motivation to bypass the biscuit tin is to set yourself in deadly battle with your best friends. Because when breaking point comes (after about three hours) and you're about to snort a soufflé, the only thing to talk you back from the binge ledge is a call from your friend. Naturally, the conversation will turn to 'so, what did you have for lunch?' (Like, who has the spare calories to talk about politics?) And her answer will ring round your head louder than if it was on speaker phone: 'Oh, I just ate a ryvita, I was in a rush to get to the gym.' Which is female code language for: 'Spit that cake out you fat cow and get back on the steamed fish and vegetables.' Why?

It's not that women are scared of being fat. It's that they're scared of their friends being thinner.

Competitive Shopping (Food)
'We're vegetarians.' 'Well, we only shop organic.' 'Really? What about the food miles? We only shop for locally sourced vegetables.' Honestly. Shut up the lot of you and have a kebab. Now *that's* locally sourced.

Computer Top Trumps
It's all about knowing which question to ask. Sure your brother-in-law has just bought himself one of those sleek little laptops that you've wanted for ages, but it's bound to have a weak spot if you look in the right place. Be lateral: ask about hard disk size, or how much video memory it has, something like that. There's bound to be one feature that the ugly clunker you've 'borrowed' from work can beat the new one with. Just don't ask what it cost. Not if there are womenfolk within earshot. Competition is one thing, but nobody wants to see another man cry.

Concocting Elaborate Excuses for Being Late (When You've Overslept)
Honesty is certainly not the right policy. Where did that ever get anyone? You can't exactly walk into a vital office meeting and say, 'Sorry I am late, but I woke up with a hangover from hell and just couldn't be assed to get out of bed and, quite frankly, the promise of a repeat performance with the slapper I picked up last night was much more appealing than sitting here listening to you tossers run through some totally pointless projections about the pro-rata take-up of wheatgerm in the Toddington area.' Far better to concoct something – entry level excuses might range from 'The alarm clock didn't go off' to 'The car wouldn't start'; intermediate liars may wish to select from 'There was a tailback at the Hanger Lane gyratory system' or 'The traffic lights failed AGAIN in the Town Centre'; or you may wish to go for gold with 'Four lions escaped

from the local zoo and I had to help capture them', 'A UFO landed on Peckham Rye' or just 'I was just leaving the house when the next door neighbour's dog grabbed my car keys and ran up a very tall tree in the garden and sat on a branch growling until I could coax it down with a combination of Guatemalan animal hynopsis techniques that I picked up on my gap year and a large tin of Pedigree Chum'.

Conferences

Conferences have a habit of bringing together all the very worst elements of the industry you work in – all under one corporate Travelodge meets airport departure lounge atmosphere. There are usually at least seventeen people who you have spent the last three weeks ignoring calls from, five mind-numbingly boring seminars from self-important industry figures who like the sound of their own voices, an overpaid keynote speaker whose one-size-fits-all motivational speach you have heard before and a trade fair area with tinpot companies pushing their 'solutions' to everything from database management to office beverage dispensers. Why bother going? Because if you're skilled at the art of conferences, you only select those taking place in interesting locations (preferably overseas), you go to none of the seminars (but make sure you ask for an electronic copy of the notes to bulk out your Conference Report) and basically hang around the bar most evenings (after a hard day's sightseeing, waterskiing or just sleeping), network like hell and aim to come back with at least one job offer. All at your present company's expense – perfecto.

Control Top Tights

The payoff: a smooth and sexy silhouette that has every man at the party checking you out. The price: your marsh-mallow belly crisscrossed with red crease marks that look like a biblical plague of hives you can probably see from space. The victim: the only person that has to see it is the bloke you go home with, and he's the *last* person you need to impress.

Conversations About the Weather
Gosh, we were just sitting down to write this entry and we thought that autumn has started very mildly this year but, that said, it won't be long before the nights are drawing in and you'll be grateful for that extra layer you put on. Who'd have thought it, though – there is already talk of a white Christmas and it wasn't that long ago we had a hosepipe ban in London. Lucky we were able to get away to the Dordogne for a little month-long break – the heat over there you wouldn't have believed and it was actually hot enough to fry an egg on the patio. Did you see the forecast for today? Scattered showers, you say? Oh well – we must remember to take galoshes and waterproofs in case we get caught out in the open. Actually, we think we might take a scarf and gloves as well – it is jolly windy today and there is always a draft in the Garden Centre Coffee Shop. We thought it would be a good moment to get our spring bulbs in before the frost starts to bite.

Cop Groupie (Being a)
No, he's never fired a gun. Yes, that CS spray probably *does* sting a bit. No you *can't* have a look at his truncheon. Are you satisfied now? Just let it go.

Corner Shops
Why make the journey to the Mecca of a supermarket when there's a shop stocked entirely with baked beans right on your doorstep? The trouble is, corner shops only come in two varieties. One, the type crammed full of the most outlandish rubbish you never knew you wanted, and two, the type who's shelves are so bare it looks like it's just survived a nuclear holocaust. Either way, they'll be tinned produce – the cockroach of foodstuffs. But who wants pineapple chunks for dinner? Or chick peas in brine? The only consolation is, you get to hear all the local gossip from

the 'corner shop man' (you never get round to asking his name) and you can sleep easy knowing that you're not contributing to Jamie Oliver's fee.

Crashing Over
Put simply, there's no such thing as a clean stop out. Staying out and not getting home is dirty in at least three ways: one, it's dirty in the sense of bad behaviour; two, it's dirty in the sense that you haven't got any spare clothes with you; and three, well, we're never lucky enough for that sort of dirty, alas. Of course, sleeping on someone's couch with a coat as a blanket seems extremely rock'n' roll at two in the morning. It seems less so at three thirty when you wake up freezing cold and with a spring in your back. Likewise at four thirty, five, five twenty, six, six fifteen and six forty-five, when you finally give up with the whole sleep thing and attempt to get GMTV on the telly instead. And as for turning up at work in the same clothes you left in? If your work is rock'n'roll, then that, by definition, is rock-'n'roll. If it's not, then it's just a bit smelly.

Crisp Linen Sheets and Plumped-up Pillows
Some people like to be quite ritualistic about this – stripping the bed in the morning, airing the mattress and the pillows and then, after a hard day at work, returning to remake the bed with crisp starched linen sheets, linen pillowcases and a linen duvet cover. Properly made with 'hospital corners', there is something tantalizingly naughty about it – evoking images of the sultry heart that surely must beat under the starched bosom of Mary Poppins. A deep long bath and then the total joy of slipping into the slightly chilled sheets (even on a roasting summer's night) is pure heaven.

Cruise Ship
(**Shaggy Dog Story** continued) . . . it was a nice cruise ship, and sailed all round the world: the Caribbean, the Mediterranean, the Canary Islands (if Ronnie Corbett was

telling this, you'd get an aside about his holiday at this point). Anyway, the star turn on the ship was the entertainment, which featured a brilliant magician – let's call him Raymondo. But Raymondo wasn't happy, because the other star turn on the ship was a parrot . . . See **Parrot**.

Crying at Work
Sir Alan Sugar would blow his testosterone-fuelled top if he knew just how much we enjoy a good old weep in the work loos. Crying yourself to sleep over that bitch everyone else calls the boss is just no fun. Much better to *totally* lose it at your desk, accidentally snot on the only copy of the annual report and then run to the toilet in a manner that suggests you've been driven to suicide. Then, in time-honoured tradition, a co-worker will follow you and spend the next hour 'talking you down' by agreeing with all your grievances and throwing in a few of her own. It's a win-win situation: your manager has to be nice, or risks looking like a bully, you get to bond with fellow battered employees and you usually get a nice cup of tea and a biscuit thrown in. Until the next wave of redundancies that is . . .

Cushioned Loo Roll
Loo roll. We know we should buy the recycled variety, but, sometimes, isn't it just a little bit scratchy? Do you remember the days before we were worried about the environment, when you'd happily wad up with a peachy pink 4-ply from Andrex? Well, dear reader, this soft paradise can be revisited thanks to the 'I'm sorry darling, they've run out of recycled, this is all they had left' scam. Your partner won't admit it, but they'll be secretly pleased too.

Cut and Paste
There have been many technological breakthroughs that have made life a whole lot better. The toaster. The mobile phone. The pause button on the video. But no one should be applauded more than the man who invented the concept of cut and paste, thus saving the Western world from

ever having to do any proper work ever again. We'd love to know how that train of thought come about. Was the guy a work-shy student? *If only I didn't have to write that essay? And have to make notes from all those dull library books. Hang on, what if I invented a word processing feature where I could just copy whole chunks of someone else's work and transfer it into my own . . . ?* Actually, what is more likely is that someone else had the cut and paste idea, and Mr Cut and Paste just cut it out and pasted it as his own.

Cutting People Down to Size

We all have colleagues who hog the limelight and could do with a bit of humiliation every now and again – a simple but subtle way of making them look stupid is to plant a well-aimed but hidden kick under the table at the soft underbelly of their office swivel chair when they are chairing a meeting. Get it right and you can end up kicking the all important height adjustment lever and watch them sink gracelessly out of sight so they end up looking like a small child playing 'let's pretend we are in an office'. Preferably film this on your phone and then bung it on www.youtube.com and send a link to your colleagues. You may, of course, get fired but we think the risk is worth taking.

Daily Express **Headlines about Diana Death**

It must be a laugh working at the *Express* – most offices have a dress-down Friday, but they probably have slow-news Diana days instead. With incredible regularity they have the ability to take a total non-fact and translate it into a HUGE HEADLINE – if, for instance, the coroner of the Diana Inquiry has a bit of a chest cold and has to curtail proceedings early one day, we get treated to DIANA DEATH JUDGE HEALTH SHOCK or, if someone at the inquiry says 'gosh – what a lot of stupid and totally unfounded murder conspiracies there are about Diana, which have no truth behind them at all and actually are very scaremongering and damaging to this inquiry', we get treated to a DIANA MURDER 'PROOF' SHOCK, and if there actually comes a cry-wolf time when the *Daily Express* really did uncover a huge Diana-based exclusive, like DIANA ALIVE AND LIVING IN SURREY, then the world would probably ignore it. It is interesting, though, seeing how much they can drag out of a car crash in which the driver was pissed and two out of the three people who died weren't wearing seatbelts.

Death Metal Bands (Publicity Photos of)

Some facts about Death Metal: (1) you will never find any Cannibal Corpse tunes on the karaoke machine, (2) when teenagers who listen to it grow up and become milkmen, none of them will whistle old Morbid Angel songs (3) only girls who are a dress size 20 or larger pretend to like Death Metal (4) the Internet is full of Scandinavian Death Metal bands' photos, each one of which is funnier then the preceding one. If you click on one, you will click on all of them and almost certainly waste a whole afternoon of your life. What are you waiting for? Quick! To the computer! We'll wait here until you come back.

Debt

We're not great at maths, but we think we've got this whole credit card thing sorted by now. It's free money, isn't it? Basically, we put the new shoes on the card, and then we can pay them off at the end of the month, or not if we don't want to? And then we can go and buy another pair of shoes next month? Brilliant! And if we keep doing this, we get to join that exclusive club, credit card max. And then we do have to pay a bit back, otherwise they won't let us buy any more shoes. Hang on, unless we got *another* credit card . . .

Decaf, Skinny, Soya Latte to Go

Oh, go on then, get a vanilla shot too. Or why not go for a chai tea latte? Hey, and is it fairtrade? Hope that cup's biodegradable and recycled. Jesus, did you just put a *real* sugar in there? You'll need a degree in hospitality and food hygiene by the time you get to the till just to work out what you've ordered. And that's before you factor in the skinny, wheat-free, gluten-free muffin. Sadly, this is what happens when the corner caff with its trusty builder's tea is replaced by new-fangled coffee shops like Starbucks.

Deepak Chopra

You know he's spiritual gorgonzola yet *still* you find yourself hovering round the self-help section of Borders perusing his wares. The temptation to purchase *The Path to Love* proves too much for you. Then, at the counter, *by mistake* Oprah's *O* magazine slips into your basket as well. Surely more spiritualizing than one woman can handle? Well, come the apocalypse, the two of them will probably morph into 'Chopra Winfrey' – a sponsored second coming sent to save the world.

Deluxe Rabbit

The Rampant Rabbit is so 1990s. Now it's all about the Deluxe Rabbit – a vibrator so complex, with so many knobs (excuse the phrase) and technical antennae that you could probably pick up Sky Plus on it. Unfortunately the only drawback to a sex toy that looks as though it's about to explore the final frontier of your orgasm is its size. Yes, the designers (obviously men) got so carried away with the girth that it virtually needs a health warning. One slip and it could accidentally perform an illegal hysterectomy. Really, the penis might seem primitive compared to this mechanical monster, but at least you don't need paramedics to help you dismount.

Dennis, Les (in *Extras*)

The pure unadulterated brilliance of this thirty minutes of televisual genius didn't come from the exemplary performances of Ashley Jensen, Ricky Gervais or Steve Merchant, but from the extraordinary watch-through-your-fingers performance by Les Dennis as . . . er . . . Les Dennis. Akin to watching someone self-harming whilst sporting a rictus-like grin, it was as cringe-making as anything we have ever seen. Les Dennis's shameless self-parody was knowing but angry and breath-takingly poignant – it left you with one big question spinning round your head like an elusive *Family Fortunes* top answer: was he in on the joke or not? The answer is irrelevant, but you can sense Gervais and Merchant brilliantly pushing Les as far as he would go and, here's the brilliant bit, knowing that his quest to regain his 1980s celebrity status would mean he was totally unable to say no to anything they asked him to do. Scorching.

Dismantling Sweeties
We are spoiled for choice here – we love undoing all that hard work that has gone on in the factory – whether it is unrolling a liquorice allsort (having removed the centre first), dismantling a Bourbon biscuit (being careful not to crack either biscuit and to leave the chocolate stuff intact), cutting the jammy centre out of a Jammy Dodger or just sucking the chocolate coating from a Revel, we love this sweet deconstruction derby.

Disney Toothpaste
Dental hygiene is one of those dull necessities that all of us have to endure, and none of us enjoy. Every adult in the Western World is obliged to risk losing a fingertip to excessively-wound floss before squeezing some sort of evil white minty chemical muck onto a toothbrush (well, unless you're the Prince of Wales, in which case some poor flunkey does all that for you. And God bless you, sir!). It's all a terribly dull chore, and it's impossible to make it fun. But what's that in the back of the medicine cabinet? Some princess toothpaste? And it's bubblegum flavour? Gotta be worth a go! And it is, it's delicious! Of course, when your little treasure realizes that she's run out of her special dentifrice and has to use your crummy adult stuff there'll be tears, but it's worth it. Oh, that taste!

Disposable Nappies
Yes, they're bad for the environment. Yes, we know that eight million of the things are thrown away in the UK every day. Yes, we're more than aware that so long will they take to decompose that, even after the earth has been obliterated by an asteroid in 2097, there'll still be bits of that Pampers you threw away in 2007 floating around in space for several light years – shite years? – to come. But let us say this, green people. When we've got something that's bad

for our environment at three in the morning, we're going to deal with those noxious fumes as quickly as possible. If you want to come over and muck in (muck out?), you're more than welcome. But, otherwise, put a sock in it.

Disrupting Meetings

Being in a meeting is great – firstly, it wastes lots of time when you could be doing boring work, secondly, you can pretend to colleagues later that important things were decided but that you can't tell them 'yet' and, thirdly, you can play all sorts of weird status games that will show up the weaknesses of your fellow committee members. Bring a small mountain of computer printouts to the meeting. If possible, include some old-fashioned fanfold paper for dramatic effect. Every time the speaker makes a point, pretend to check it in one of the printouts. Pretend to find contradictory evidence in your printout and tut openly.

Doing Absolutely Anything Apart From the One Thing You're Actually Meant to Be Doing

Imagine, dear reader, that you've got a big project on – to pluck an example out of thin air, suppose you are writing a Christmas humour book and the deadline for delivery is fast approaching. You'd imagine, perhaps, that you wouldn't waste any more time than was strictly necessary, particularly when your more organised co-writers have finished their bit and are making noises about swapping notes and handing things in. Yet, in such circumstances, isn't it fascinating how anything, and we mean *anything*, is more interesting that sitting down to write. Surfing for stuff on the web. Making yet another cup of tea. Doing the washing up. Really, who thought doing the washing up could make you feel dirty? We say, if you want a clean house, write (or rather, don't write) a book.

Doing DIY with a Hammer

Why is it that, as soon as you pick up a hammer in the privacy of your own home, you suddenly feel like a serial killer.

Probably because the walls are screaming, begging for mercy from the damage you're about to inflict on them. The thing is, you'd never delude yourself you could handle a power tool (OK, you did once. But five hours in A&E cured you of that little hobby). But the humble hammer looks so harmless. How bad could it get putting a picture hook up? you ask yourself. Only the destruction of an entire wall and a lawsuit from the neighbours can answer that. But for one, powerful moment, with hammer in hand, you felt invincible. And that's what DIY is really about.

Donny Tourette

It's Paul Kay in the Vindaloo video doing an impression of Richard Ashcroft pretending to be Liam Gallagher doing an impression of Ian Brown acting as the gangly Britpop guy from Singstar on the PlayStation. Hair by Motley Crüe, sunglasses by Mike Read, fragrance by Lambert and Butler. No wonder Peaches Geldof went for him, it's the same reason Paula went for her dad. But why do *we* like him so much? The way he threw his own bag on the floor and then had to pick it up again before going into the BB house while doing that funny horizontal flicking-the-Vs thing that made him look like he was carrying two very tiny bowls of soup? The way he got his funny little suit wet in the hot tub but kept his rollup dry? Well, of course it's all of those things combined with his puppyish eagerness to do anything for our attention. What a shame he's been in *Big Brother* already. He's almost ready for it now . . .

DVD Recorders

Blessed with even more clutter-generating power than their tape-based predecessors, these silvery knights of the television stand virtually *order* you to collect whole seasons of terrible programmes you'll never watch, mostly with ad breaks intact, which will stack up in a corner of your front room gathering dust reproachfully until you see sense and take them all down to the council tip. DVDs, you see, unlike VHS tapes, can't be recorded over when you have an emergency because your sister's popped round for a coffee and *Cash in the Attic* is on. Consequently, your collection of tat will grow and grow in the way that collections of tat, irrespective of their technological underpinnings, have done since the Neolithic era.

Drinking Tonic Water Neat

Maybe it is all that quinine, or the delightful sticky tingly feeling you get on your teeth afterwards that does it, but a huge glass of tonic water with crushed ice is a perfect pick-me-up. If you have drunk too much and people might think you are secretly an alcoholic, you can always fill the bottle up with water and then leave the top unscrewed. 'Oh dear,' you can say the next time a gin and tonic is called for, 'it has gone flat – I had better pop to the shop to get some more'.

Driving a Better Car than Your Dad

You know when you were little, and going for a drive with your parents was a Big Expedition which involved your Dad messing around under the bonnet for hours 'fine tuning' the engine and then waxing the whole bodywork before ushering you into the back seat with strict instructions not to put your sticky fingers on anything? Good. You remember also how he bought a slightly higher-up-the-range car every two years and how you cringed when he enjoyed asking people 'what are you driving at the moment' just so he could show off a bit? Good. Now you are a grown-up it's payback time – just picturing his face as you casually drive over on a Sunday in a top-of-the-range BMW SLK is a joy in itself, but the actuality of it is even better as he opens the door and goes from red to green and then pretends to feign short-sightedness. Perfect.

Drunk Texting

First we lose control of our tongues, then our legs and then what's between them. Tragically, though, thumb functionality remains at 100 per cent throughout. Mobile phone network coverage is almost total in or around most popular bars and nightclubs too. In most UK cities it's easier to text an ex and tell them that you can't live without them than it is to find an unlicensed minicab. It's hard to say which is the more dangerous.

Eating a Secret Extra Portion while Preparing Food

You can almost justify this secret grazing as being essential to the culinary experience, but then again you can almost justify most things in life. It doesn't stop you knowing that cooking five kebab skewers or five stuffed chicken breasts when there are only four of you sitting down to dinner is just plain naughty. Not quite as bad as five slabs of chocolate cake, but you get the drift.

Eating at Supermarkets

There's something fundamentally brilliant about having a meal at a supermarket. You've gone there to buy food so you can take it home and cook it, when the thought suddenly occurs – stuff it! Why don't we have supper right here, right now? With a fantastic ringside view of, well, everyone else doing their shopping, you can munch your way through a selection of freshly cooked ready meals you turned down only minutes earlier for being too fatty. Do remember to at least *pretend* to do some shopping: if you're going to the supermarket just to eat, then maybe you should reconsider your priorities.

Eating Breakfast at Your Desk

Anything non-work you can do at work is always a pleasure, so why not bring your morning routine into the office? And, seriously, who is going to challenge you over eating breakfast? It's the most important meal of the day. It's going to make you more productive. Are they honestly going to confiscate your bowl and tell you 'you should have eaten that earlier'? Exactly. Of course, if you're knocking up a full fry-up in the office kitchen, you may be taking things a little too far. And, if you're thinking about making gloopy porridge in the microwave, just remember, you might have a full stomach, but you won't have any friends.

Eating Food in Front of the TV

We know we should be sitting down and having supper at the table. It's better for your digestion, not to mention a good bonding moment for the family, where you can discuss what's been going on all day. But, having said that, *EastEnders* is on, so maybe we can bond by watching that and balancing our supper on our laps? It might not be quite de rigueur etiquette-wise, but getting the food into your mouth and not down the sofa, all the while without taking your eyes off the screen, is something of an art form.

Eating Ice Cream as a Late-Night Treat

Falling asleep in front of the telly and waking up at midnight is a strange sensation. You are suddenly very awake and aware of the task that lies ahead of you of putting the house to sleep – we find the perfect craving-filling snack to have is a huge finger-scoop of ice cream to keep you going. No cutlery, no washing-up, no clues for your other half – just a big handful and a lot of licking clean afterwards.

Eating Ice Cubes

Maybe it is a need to connect with the animal inside us all (and we are not referring to any Richard Gere-related urban myths here), but nothing beats shotgunning a can of lager and then eating a hand-full of ice cubes in swift succession. Make sure you really crunch them for the full effect. According to our dentist, chewing ice is a terrible thing to do to your teeth which, seeing as we never bother going to the dentist anyway, makes it weirdly more enjoyable.

Eating Paper
Paper is, after all, only a different version of wood, so chewing paper shouldn't be frowned upon any more than chewing pencils or matchsticks, but somehow it is. Maybe it is the tell-tale little corners torn off books and newspapers that annoy people, or constant chewing, but the proponents of this habit cite the joys of deconstructing the different fibred layers of cardboard and of sampling different qualities of paper in a way that is almost akin to wine buffs or truffle hunters. Apparently the corners of this book are especially tasty, but don't chew the page numbers off as this may cause confusion.

Eating Sandpaper
It feels very bad to be eating granules of broken glass glued to a sheet of rough paper, but there is something rather sexy about the rough feel of one side and the smooth side of the other all at once.

Eavesdropping in Restaurants
If you've been to a restaurant with one of your gentleman callers more than once, you pretty much know what he's going to say. You will, of course, already have eaten before leaving the house, so as to give the impression of a daintily birdlike appetite at the restaurant, so the only remaining reason to accept such an invitation is the likelihood of tuning into a subtly hissed argument between two of the other diners. More entertaining than any soap opera and, unless your companion is one of those ghastly cheapskates who insists on going dutch, it's all absolutely free!

eBay Counters

It's one thing obsessively checking how many hits your blog or MySpace page has had, but it's a different realm when you're even monitoring your offcasts on eBay. A sign of modern times it may be, but seeking validation on a web page that represents the public face of your entire persona (and posed-within-an-inch-of-your-life pictures) is understandable. But that used rug on eBay? YOU DON'T EVEN WANT IT. Why do you need approval for it? But, sadly, you do. Even your rejects must be highly desirable objects to the general public. Yes, it's nuclear-sized narcissism – but your therapist can deal with that. In the meantime, how many views are logged on the counter. What – only thirteen?!? You may have to report fellow eBay users for lack of attention to your mammoth sized ego.

Eddie Irvine

Just what is the source of multimillionaire playboy Eddie Irvine's appeal? His anachronistically stylish approach to Formula One racing, which has, of late, been largely dominated by IT boys? His Irish lilt and Owen Wilsonesque looks? Or the fact that he was 'too sweet' for Pamela Anderson? We may have originally tuned into 'The Race' to shout 'You go girl' at the nice one out of Atomic Kitten, but we came back the following week for another fix of laid-back multimillionaire charm. What a lovely word that is. Let's all say it together: 'Multimillionaire'.

Egg and Bacon Croissant

Can't decide whether to go for the Full English or the Continental option for the first meal of the day? No problem – choose both! Simply empty one part of the clichéd English breakfast experience into the sexy little Continental croissant and, hey presto, culinary magic. Actually, it is even simpler than that – just ask those nice people at Pret à Manger and they do the whole thing for you, thus allowing you to eat something that looks very palatable indeed instead of a home-grown concoction which, we suspect, will look more like a closeup from *Extreme Celebrity Facelift*. Whatever will they think of next? Maybe someone could combine a Chinese with an Indian and deliver up to the grateful public a Chicken Chow Mein cunningly served in a Keema Nan envelope. Actually, that sounds rather nice.

Elderflower Cordial
A huge slug of this gloriously viscous liquid in a big mug of hot water with oodles of ice cubes is a taste sensation. Hot, cold, viscous – what else do you need in a drink?

Electric Toothbrushes
Apparently some people use their electric toothbrushes as an emergency holiday vibrator if they've forgotten to pack their real one. You won't read about that here, though. Oh no. We wouldn't dream of such a thing. Especially as we've got a special little flightcase for our Rabbit.

Email Kisses
Nothing divides the sexes like their approach to email: for a man, email is essentially a telegram, shorn of the requirement to tip a breathless young boy when it arrives. Sentences are short STOP convey only the information required STOP and the only adornments permissible on a manly email are Excel spreadsheets listing teams for the paintballing or a jpeg of a kind lady administering oral love to a donkey STOP. For a woman, by contrast, an email is a little letter which not only supplies the information requested but also contains many other niceties of polite social discourse, such as enquiring after the correspondent's health and offering opinions on the current crop of reality show hopefuls. If a man puts a little 'x' after his name at the bottom of an email, it means he wants sex. If a woman puts a kiss at the bottom of her emails, all you can infer for certain is that her keyboard is working properly. And she wants sex.

Emmerdale

Emmerdale, older readers may remember, used to be called *Emmerdale Farm* – a genteel soap where people called things like Amos would sup pints of Black Sheep and watch the world go by. But then the 'Farm' bit got lost and it all started getting exciting: a Lockerbie-style plane disaster cleared out most of the characters. Plots got silly, but at least it was *fun*, unlike *EastEnders*. And in came proper tabloid-friendly actresses, such as Patsy Kensit, Linda Lusardi and Lisa Riley. OK, so maybe not Lisa Riley. The fact that you could be watching Channel 4 News instead makes it all the more enjoyable.

Empty Calories

All the best stuff is made of empty calories. Beer. Wine. Sweets. Fizzy drinks. Butter. Hamburgers. Hot Dogs. KFC. Pizza. Crisps. Chips. Even lard! Ask yourself this – would life be worth living without these mysterious non-foods? (If you don't get an answer straight away, here's a clue: it's no.)

Equilibrium

Does the world need another feature-length car commercial that's three parts *1984* to two parts *The Matrix*? Well, if it's as chock-full of kung-fu, gun-fu, sword-fu and, for all we know, toe-fu as *Equilibrium*, then the answer is an emphatic yes. Tooled-up Brit stalwarts Sean Bean and Sean Pertwee provide gruff manly backing to a solid ninety minutes of signature brooding from Christian Bale. Sean number one gets shot right through the poetry and doesn't bleed at all. Sean number two gives it plenty of Big Brother and Christian works his eyebrows like they're going out of style. Brian Conley's in it too. Yes, *that* Brian Conley. Plus there's an annoying little kid who makes the lad in *Omen 2* look like the Milky Bar Kid. The story, if story is what you want, is about some sort of futuristic copper who kills upwards of 200 people for having the wrong sort of wallpaper but then gives it all up because he likes puppies. The whole thing unfolds like *Ultraviolet* with the colour turned down and you'll reach the final credits unsure whether to watch it all again or go out and buy an Audi. Perfect.

Estate Agents, Time-Wasting
Call it divine justice, but taking time-wasting off the web and into reality is even better in the pleasure stakes. 'Oh yah, I'm a cash buyer looking to spend over a million.' Not only do you get to see how the other half live, you have the unique experience of an estate agent being nice to you. Just on the off chance you *are* some oligarch's filthy-rich mistress.

Eyebrow Eating
Leave your eyebrows to grow to a good length and then have a good old tweezing session in front of the mirror. Make yourself look absolutely beautiful, of course, but that is not the aim of the exercise here – make sure you are meticulous at keeping the tweezed hairs to one side and then eat them one by one. We don't know what hair is made of but each little hair makes a satisfying crunch when you carefully bite through it. Honestly.

Failure (Other People's)

As that nice Gore Vidal once said, 'It is not enough to succeed. Others must fail'. Oh yes. Deep down we are all fiercely competitive beings and although winning a major new piece of business for the company, a major promotion, a whacking payrise and a gleaming new company car are all exciting things per se, they take on an even greater degree of importance and excitement when you realise that none of your colleagues is getting the same treatment. Back of the net!

Fake Tan

It's the easiest thing in the world to chuckle at Chantelle and write 'you've been tangoed' over her wedding pictures in *OK!* We're all quite happy to go on about Dita Von Teese and her flawless alabaster skin but, really – does Dita ever go swimming? Or get asked to make one of those fruity bedroom videos by her boyfriend? Well, yes, she probably does, actually, but if something's light-coloured it tends to look bigger and there are *some* bits of us that candidly don't need that kind of help. Given the choice between a tube of Lancôme Flash Bronzer and looking like that marshmallow man out of *Ghostbusters*, we're going with the David Dickinson option. Just don't, whatever you do, have a St Tropez on the day of your wedding. The photos will look like an experimental production of *Othello*. Trust us.

Family Picture Screensavers

Aww, isn't he cute. No he isn't. No one at work is the remotest bit interested in seeing a blurred picture of your ickle nephew, and they definitely don't want it in widescreen Technicolor on your computer screen every day. Which is what makes it so much fun. Create your own family slideshow – complete with snaps of every cat you've ever owned. Every colleague who comes to your desk will be forced to make small talk complimenting you on the utter cuteness of everything associated with your personal life. And, let's face it, it's the only time something nice and positive is going to pop out of their mouth. So why not milk it?

Fathers for Justice

There are plenty of pressure groups to choose from nowadays: Fur, Homelessness, Smoking, Cars . . . you can find all sorts of stuff that someone's against. Or, in some cases, for. Fathers for Justice are easily the best, though: for a start, they dress up as Batman and climb up things. No one else does that. Not even Batman nowadays. And the best thing is that what they're fighting for is the right to drag a bunch of unappreciative kids round a museum or a zoo or something. If they were climbing up a crane to *avoid* the occasional weekend of expensive ingratitude, you could probably understand it. They're like no other men on Earth, and we love 'em for it.

Fearne Cotton

Fearne assures us that her rise in the nepotism-riddled British Broadcasting Corporation, elbowing phalanxes of Attenboroughs and Dimblebys for the prestigious *Diggit* presenting job, was nothing to do with her family connection to former BBC controller Sir Bill

Cotton. We believe her. We think it's all due to her incipient fruitiness, and her ability to shout loudly enough to connect with sugar-rushing kids while dressing sluttily enough to connect on an entirely different level with their dads. We'd like to see Fern *Britton* present the Disney Show in the morning and still fit in a lingerie shoot with Maxim in the afternoon. Well. Perhaps that's a bad example.

Fellating Hotdogs

This is a guilty pleasure with a dual function – taking one's time to caress the bun, to lovingly squirt a spicy mixture of ketchup and mustard up and down the length of the gleaming sausage, to grasp it and eat it very sensuously, is a mighty good way of winding up the opposite sex and, secondly, it is actually rather good practice. Maybe go easy on the mustard though. Ouch.

Fez, a Tiny One with a Plastic Strap

It is amazing how much fun you can have with a small plastic hat and a piece of elasticated shoelace. Put it on your cat and it looks like Tommy Cooper with whiskers, put it on your dog and he looks like Tommy Cooper with huge drooling fangs, and put it on yourself and you look like Tommy Cooper with an enormous face. Go one – try it yourself – yes, that's right – 'like that'.

FIFA 07

When you were young, you probably dreamed of playing for England. (Unless you're Welsh or something weird like that.) As you matured, you realized that might not be practical and scaled back your ambitions to just managing the national side. Even that ostensibly quite modest ambition seemed less and less likely to be fulfilled as exciting management opportunities at B&Q distracted you from your destiny at the pinnacle of the Beautiful Game. Rejoice then, that an Xbox 360 is an entirely affordable luxury for a deputy regional sales manager and that *FIFA*

07 is perfectly designed to exorcise those lingering dreams and make it clear, beyond all shadow of a doubt, that you have all the tactical savvy of Graham bloody Taylor. It's worth a couple of hundred quid just to know for certain that you made the right choice back when you were fourteen and it was either new boots or a packet of Lamberts.

Filling Water Bottles Up with Tap Water

There was a time, of course, when the nation didn't go round perpetually hydrating itself. And yet now, if we're not swigging from Volvic every twenty minutes, the assumption is that death can't be far away. It can't just be us who are pained at the thought of shelling out for a bottle of water – it's water, for God's sake! It comes out of the bloody tap! Which is why we reuse our expensive water bottle (really, the more expensive the brand the better) and top it up with tap water. We get the kudos of looking cool: the water company don't get any more of our cash. Perfecto all round.

Flirting (Cynical)

There are two ways of getting your computer fixed. One is logging a code magenta call with the Helpdesk that will be actioned within ten to fourteen days unless the call is flagged as urgent by your line manager, in which case it will be upgraded to an ochre alert situation (response time twelve to twenty-four months). Or you can wait until the IT geek is walking past your desk, lean forward so your keyboard acts as a sort of alphanumeric Wonderbra and ask him in a little-girl voice if he wouldn't mind coming over and having a look because you think the television part isn't working with the typewriter part while twirling a lock of hair between your fingers (response time three to four seconds). Once you've mastered this simple procedure, you need never again concern yourself with the workings of a computer, car or kettle.

Football Celebrations

There's only one thing better than your football team scoring a goal, and that's your football team scoring a goal and doing a hilariously well-worked celebration routine. Rumours of taking cocaine? Step forward Robbie Fowler and pretend to snort up the touchline. Stories of bashing a colleague around with a golf club? All yours, Craig Bellamy, with the pretend 3-wood drive into the crowd. Any accused of being exceedingly dull? Raise your hand, Alan Shearer.

Football Phone-Ins

You've seen the match. You've heard the manager's thoughts. Now it's your turn . . . If that isn't a cue that the animals are about to be let out of the zoo, we don't know what is. But the 'phone-in', that classic radio programme filler, becomes even more compulsory listening when football is involved. Maybe the producer advises the caller to leave all perspective behind before they go on air? Maybe it's just that certain teams have more moaning fans than others? But, really, fans of Chelsea, Manchester United, Liverpool (is it just us, or is it always Liverpool fans), what do you actually have to complain about? You win things. You want sporting suffering? Try supporting a team like Kidderminster Harriers or York City. You do realize that, as you bang on about how it is your 'right' to be 'champions', the only thing you actually do 'deserve' is the rest of the nation united in laughter at your myopic misery.

Footballers' Cribs

What is it about footballers and rap culture? For some reason, the fact that they knock a ball around for ninety minutes once a week makes them think that, even though they play for Blackburn, they're suddenly Mr Bling. Fortunately, television people have persuaded the more extrovert of these types to let us see how a man with absolutely zero understanding of interior design can spunk fifty grand a week on his home. Hilarious. We could pick many out but here are just two: Gary Neville, failing to find Becks a wooden spoon in his spacecraft sized kitchen; and Jermaine Defoe, whose girlfriend had twisted his arm into loading up their kitchen with *six* different ovens. No, we can't think of six different types of ovens either.

Foreign Trains' Sanitary Arrangements

If you have ever travelled across Europe and felt the need to do 'number twos' then you will know exactly what we mean when we say that the whole experience can be summed up by two words – 'shelf' and 'track'. Whoever designed the sanitary arrangements decided that to save water the whole process would be reduced to, crudely, inviting your customers to do a poo on a little metal shelf and then simply allowing them to throw a lever that releases the said poo (with the minimal amount of water accompaniment) onto the speeding track below. We were never very good at physics or biology or even personal hygiene at school, but we do know that we wouldn't want to get a job as a railway track maintenance operative in Poland, Germany, Russia or parts of France. That said, it is quite fun to play executioner to your poor excrement and to release the lever to consign it to certain death below without so much as an urgent phone call from the Home Secretary to send news of a reprieve.

Foreigner

We bought *The Best of Foreigner* for £3.99 at a service station and, by God, it was brilliant. Track one – 'Cold as Ice': fantastic. Track two – 'Waiting for a Girl Like You': genius. Track three – 'I Want to Know What Love Is': Kleenex all round. Tracks four to twenty-two – admittedly not quite so good, but let's not dwell on the negatives, what about tracks one to three? Early eighties American soft rock doesn't get much better than this. It may not sound much, but have The Killers got three such killer songs you'll be listening to in twenty years' time? Have they got one? Exactly.

Free Newspapers

In the old days – you know, ten years ago – the concept of the free newspaper was that weekly local advertiser shoved through your door that was just perfect for lighting a fire. Now, though, whether it's *Metro* or *The London Paper* or *London Lite* or whatever, all that has changed. They're like your normal newspaper! Except you don't have to pay! No, we don't understand how they can make a profit either! If only the rest of the world would follow suit, it'd make mornings so much more pleasant. Just imagine it: reading your free newspaper, on your free train ride, washed down with a free coffee and free bacon sandwich. We say: someone give Starbucks the newspaper magnates' numbers, and let's get this party started.

French Maid TV

There's no clear reason why certain outfits are automatically sexy (Anne Summers Nurse) and some just aren't (Westminster City Council Traffic Warden). It's probably just about the level of effort made: if someone's trying to be sexy then they probably will be. Even if they look like a paramilitary Jade Goody in the cold light of day, a Saucy French Maid outfit will activate strange atavistic triggers in your brain that make you feel all . . . ooh . . . *fruity* and that. Imagine, then, the sheer fruit power of up to three French maids, with the occasional saucy nurse popping by to help out. There's supposedly some educational content tucked away in there somewhere but, candidly, we barely noticed. Unlike any other Carry On-style saucy maid ribaldry that may be available in the Internet, French Maid TV is 100 per cent free and will miraculously download itself to iTunes when you're not looking. As an added bonus, French Maid TV isn't remotely rude, so you can safely peruse the podcast at home or at work without substantially endangering your job or marriage. You might be thought rather sad. Tragic even. But you'll still be married and employed at the end of it all. Assuming you were in the first place.

French Toast

Yes, yes, yes, it bloats you up something terrible, but bread's great, isn't it? It's hard to imagine how it could be any better, but it can: soaked in egg and then liberally anointed with million-calorie-an-ounce maple syrup and you transform the humble loaf into *cuisine*. You can always offset the thigh-thickening properties of this ultimate continental breakfast by doing what the French do and just have a delicious and nutritious glass of wine for supper.

Friends Re-Runs or the One that We're Watching Even Though We've Seen it Sixteen Times Already

We're aware that *Friends* finished quite a few years ago. We're aware that we've seen every single episode several times over. And yet, when you're flicking through the channels for something to watch, why is it that yet another repeat of Chandler, Monica, Joey, Phoebe, Ross and Rachel is so irresistible? Are the jokes really that funny? Let's be honest – third time round, they raise, at most, a half smile. Are there any subtle sub plots you can only pick up fourth time round? Not quite. What we're talking here is the televisual equivalent of comfort food, or perhaps, more specifically, cold takeaway from the night before. And hey, we know how good *that* can taste.

Friends' Sisters (Fancying)

Some archetypal relationships are sexy by definition. Boss and secretary; girl and uncle; shepherd and sheep. OK, so maybe the last one is just us. But one that we know *is* universal is the fancying of your friends' sisters. We think it's to do with the fact they're unobtainable. If the sister is older, then she's going to put you in the same bracket of irritation as her younger brother – she's never going to take you seriously. If the sister is younger, then you've got your friend playing the older brother 'If anyone messes with my sister . . .' card. If it did happen, it'd probably bugger your friendship up permanently and, let's face it, which is more important, sticking by your mates or a furtive fumble with his sister? Our thoughts too – see you later, brother.

Gap, US Size 8

Quite honestly, the people at Gap deserve a Nobel prize for services to women's self-esteem. After a thoroughly disheartening trek around the other high-street shops, where you even had to ask for a shopping trolley in size 20, such was your inability to fit into anything, Gap comes as a welcome oasis of relief. In the magical realms of Gap world, you actually fit into a pair of size 8 jeans. And you even had to ask the assistant to get that dress in a 6 (OK, you didn't ask – you got a piano out and sang it with a show tune). It's as if all the coat hangers are dancing in jubilation with you. Why, you're almost a size zero. And you know, what does it *really* matter that they use the American size system and that a size 8 is really a size 12? After all, your partner won't know when you casually leave the size label hanging out of your clothes, giving you plenty of ammunition to call him a fat fascist when he next suggests that eating an entire packet of digestives might not be a good idea . . .

Garage Calendars

Calendars have a primary and highly useful purpose: to let you know what day of the week it is, and to mark down any future events you might have. In a garage, however, where a 'ready Thursday' approach to timekeeping is more prevalent, such date knowledge is seemingly redundant. Fortunately, calendar makers made sure that this part of their business didn't slide by introducing the concept of naked women into the design. It is not uncommon to see a garage calendar hung up with the wrong month showing, because the workers like the look of that particular model: not uncommon either for an old favourite to adorn the wall for years. And you thought being stuck in 1975 was just a figure of speech.

Gay Men Fancy You

We're as modern as can be, us lot. We're assuming that you are too: that's why, when we look at gay men, we see them as men first and foremost, rather than otherworldly creatures with a keen eye for interior design. And we all know what *men* are like. We're animals. We'll shag anything. Luckily, when it comes to our dealings with the opposite sex, the natural recalcitrance of the female lends balance to the equation. Unfortunately no such natural protections exist when there are no women present, so what's to stop every gay man in Britain chasing you around the room as if it were some bicurious Benny Hill sketch? Well, apart from your comparatively poor personal hygiene, terrible dress sense, flabby midriff . . .

Genesis

It doesn't matter whether we're talking the prog rock seventies version, featuring Peter Gabriel with a lawnmower on his head; the corporate eighties version, with Phil Collins taking over the vocals; or the desperate nineties version with that guy from Stiltskin clinging on for dear life. There has never been – and never will be – a time when Genesis are cool. Even so, 'The Lamb Lies Down on Broadway' is a work of genius. And who can resist singing along when Virgin decided to play 'Turn it on again'. Again. Just don't expect us to back you up in public on it, that's all.

George Bush's Command of Eng. Lang.

In the eighteenth century, the aristocracy used to pay to be taken on guided tours of Bedlam Lunatic Asylum to laugh at the mental defective. That was wrong and morally abhorrent. In the nineteenth century, people used to visit freak shows and laugh at the two-headed man or the bearded lady. That was even worse and totally unacceptable. We could never counter anything like that so in the twentieth and twenty-first century, we have to content ourselves with watching videos on YouTube of the most powerful man in the world giving press conferences. We should take George Bush Jnr very seriously, as he is the most powerful man in the world and he holds the future of this planet in the palm of his hand. Very seriously indeed. So is it wrong to look at Internet sites that juxtapose his image alongside those of chimpanzees? Probably. Is it wrong to read comments like 'I just want you to know that, when we talk about war, we're really talking about peace', and then to spit your TV dinner out all over the floor? Totally. And howsabout: 'For every fatal shooting, there were roughly three non-fatal shootings. This is unacceptable . . . and we're going to do something about it'? And then, finally, when asked about the similarities between himself and Tony Blair, he said, 'Well, we both use Colgate Toothpaste.' None of this is funny at all, so let the poor man alone with running the world. Shame on you.

Getting Ready to Go Out

Find miraculously ironed shirt in wardrobe and slip it on: forty-five seconds. Put suit on: sixty seconds. Look in mirror and convince self that stubble is 'rugged' rather than 'scruffy': fifteen seconds. Excellent. You're ready. You now have a solid fifty-eight minutes of hanging around the bedroom tutting ostentatiously and saying 'I think I preferred the other one' as your other half's blood pressure soars to life-threatening levels. Priceless.

Gillette Fusion

How many blades is it physically possible to get on a wet razor? We only ask, because the old days of one or two blades are long gone. Even the triple blade is looking a little feeble these days. Four, five, six, where is this razor madness going to end? And why can't we resist falling for the sales patter and buying in, even though we know that, deep down, another blade can't really make that much difference. Can it?

Girlfriend's Inability to Set the Video (Laughing at)

Look, for the last time, how bloody difficult is this to explain? Choose the programme you want, turn on the dvcr machine here with this remote, select AV2, press enter, from the drop-down menu select the channel you want, the time the programme starts/ends, where you want to record it (DVD, Hard Drive or Tape), press enter, turn the power off and then step back and congratulate yourself. Got it? Good. Now your turn . . . This is where the fun really begins as your significant other selects the wrong remote, inadvertently turns the Surround Sound system on and leaps in the air as the opening strains of Motorhead's *Greatest Hits* drown out her screams at +1250db, recovers, switches Sky on then off, tries to tell the machine to record something that happened two years ago and then finally throws the remote at you screaming, 'Why can't this be straightforward?' Hilarious.

Giving Her Lingerie

Every woman, irrespective of her tonnage, wants to feel desirable and perhaps a little bit naughty once in a while. Which is why the gift of very uncomfortable pants is perhaps the Greatest Love of All. As an added bonus for the gentleman benefactor, many popular lingerie chains now have beautifully produced glossy brochures and elegantly designed websites wherein one might peruse the various styles of very uncomfortable pants to their best advantage and if, by chance, some of the photographs tend to display very attractive young women in states of undress, that is just a sacrifice we will have to make to ensure that we select the perfect gift for our wives or partners. Imagine, an uninterrupted hour in front of internet sauciness and *she can't touch you for it*. You'll never clear your history again!

Glass of Wine (with a Midweek Meal)

It's more or less compulsory to have a couple of drinks on a Friday night, either at home, or slumped on the sofa in your trackie-b's waiting for *Ugly Betty* to start. The slope starts getting slippery, though, when you think to yourself 'Well, Thursday's *nearly* Friday.' Once you've crossed that line there's no turning back. Wednesday is nearly Thursday, and you probably do need a small one on Monday evening to get over the shock of the first day back at work. That only leaves Tuesday really, so you might as well have a drink while the other half is watching *Life on Mars*. As long as you're not drinking at lunchtimes as well, you're probably OK. Well, maybe just *one*. If it's a *special* lunch. Like a Friday or something.

Global Warming

OK, so it's some heavy shit going down. And, yes, we're probably all going to be dead in twenty years' time because we're still insistent on driving to the supermarket to pick up our New Zealand lamb, rather than chewing away on mouldy courgettes we've grown ourselves in the back garden. But global warming – it's not *all* bad, is it? Is it just us who are thinking 'great! I can sit outside the pub in January? Enjoy an alfresco coffee in December? A New Year's Barbecue?' Let's face it: your grandchildren are going to get it anyway, so you might as well pass us the paraffin and get that chicken going.

Glossy Fashion Mags (for Women)

Honestly. Is there anything better? Big thick shiny magazines full of quizzes about sex, articles about sex and women telling you all about how much they like sex, interspersed with adverts for perfume, shoes or (for all we care) spanners, which all seem to involve pictures of gloriously fruity young women with their kit off. Plus, if you pick the right issue (the article runs about every third month in every womens' glossy), there's a piece called 'Are your boobs normal?', which just consists of loads of photographs of knockers to suit every taste. Perhaps they weren't expecting that many fat men to read *Top Santé* but, quite honestly, mine are loads bigger than most of them.

GMI

Forget DIY, these days it is all about GMI, or 'getting a man in'. We know we ought to put up those shelves ourselves – it's not that difficult and it'd be a lot cheaper – but one quick phone call to a 'handy man' and it's job done. GMI is a lot easier for the fairer sex to indulge in than for men – said handy man will assume they've been called in because of a lack of basic carpentry skills. If it's a bloke making a call, then you'll have to deal with the fact he knows the real reason he's been phoned: you're a right lazy bastard.

God Bothering (in Emergencies)

Richard Dawkins might feel all smug about his Olympic atheism and how he never has a biblical moment which requires a one-to-one with old beardy in the sky. But us weaker souls will pimp our principles out at the slightest emergency. Need to get to the hospital sharpish? Suddenly, we're swearing on our Old Testament that evolution never happened and promising Jesus Our Lord And Saviour that we won't be rude to call centre workers *ever* again if, just this once, we get there in time. On a plane that has the *slightest* bit of turbulence? Straight away we're crafting a crucifix out of the coffee stirrers and muttering the Lord's Prayer fast, so God won't notice we've forgotten the words. The more serious the situation, the more extreme the bargaining. Yes, you will sacrifice Fluffy the moggy, as long as you land with all your limbs in one piece. Weeks later, when God and his dullard commandments are forgotten as you return to your default cynical agnosticism, it's only the sudden death of the cat that has you mouthing 'Sorry, Big G' up at the sky.

Grand Theft Auto

Computer games, like most forms of entertainment, offer us an idealized view of the world to which we can escape when the unutterable grind of real life gets too much. That makes sense when you're portraying some sort of science fiction superman handing the smackdown to a group of colour-coded aliens intent on colonizing the Earth, less so when you're cast in the role of some sort of multiskilled combat hoodlum who just wants to make enough money to get to the next bit of Liberty City. Everyone likes an anti-hero, though, which is why *Scarface* posters outsell *Dixon of Dock Green* ones by over two to one. When your Mundano is stuck in a traffic jam, and Heat radio is only playing Meme Traders, all you want to do is get home and play GTA.

Green & Black

If Bono had ever experienced a moment of self–doubt, he'd binge on Green & Black. It isn't gluttony if it's fair-trade: it's affirmative action.

Gruesome Birth Stories

These conversations usually start fairly innocuously with a few details about the midwife and the problems with breastfeeding but soon morph into a kind of maternity version of Monty Python's competitive Yorkshiremen sketch. 'You think that was bad but, by the time the third baby was delivered, the walls of the room were covered in blood, the doctor has passed out on the floor, I was having a heart massage, the babies were all in intensive care and my husband was being interviewed on Channel 4 news.' We are suprised there isn't a reality TV show called something like 'When Foetuses Go Bad' or 'Celebrity Baby Nightmares –

Live' which would show it all in gory detail. Sounds like terrible dumbing down and rubbish television, but we would SO be there like a shot.

Green-Shifting

It's like downsizing – but with more stuff to buy. Because, ironically, in a bid to halt our consumer-fuelled destruction of the natural world, you'll probably have to do a bit of shopping. At the very least buy a few trees. The new eco-lifestyle, as outlined by its spiritual leader, David Cameron, is all about spending your money in the right way – say, like installing a wind turbine on your Notting Hill mansion. Start by threatening to grow your own organic produce in the garden – then settle for ordering a deluxe organic veg-etable box online. You've saved a local farmer *and* you can whip up a nice roast.

Gun Porn

There's a tragic incident involving armed police on Britain's streets. Again. The newspapers are full of detailed analysis and comment. Why, then, are our eyes drawn inexorably to the helpful graphic of the Heckler and Koch MP5 at the side of the page? It's like *Look & Learn* never folded. Weapons were probably the first arte-facts designed by mankind and have, over the millennia, had more creative genius applied to them than any other class of object. No wonder they look good. The minute someone designs a food mixer that looks half as good as a Stealth Bomber, we'll stop playing Gears of War and take up baking.

Gym Playlists

Look, when you're working out you can't be listening to Nick Drake. Sadly, the treadmill *demands* pure, filthy cheese. We're talking 'Dontcha' by the Pussycat Dolls. We're even talking golden oldies like 'Two Can Play That Game' by Bobby Brown. Yes, really. But the problem comes not from the utter credibility bypass happening in your eardrum, but from the vehicle of your shame. The iPod playlist. Gone are the days of hiding your secret CD stash under the bed, safe from the prying eyes of menfolk who measure the merits and whole moral make-up of a person by what music they listen to. The iPod is a pocket-sized billboard for your musical taste – or *lack* of it. And finding Britney's 'Toxic' on your shuffle list is seriously going to make him question your suitability as a life partner. Until he sees the *buns of steel* you got working out to the the audio-tat in question . . .

Haddock in Beer Batter

Beer and batter combined? Which genius thought of this? Can we have his phone number? If it's haddock in there, then great: but, of course, if cod then even better. See **Cod**.

Hag Fag (Madonna)

Fag Hags, by definition, revolve around the sun of their gay chum. The Hag fag's role is to cackle with laughter as he tells witty jokes. He wears skintight gold leggings, she applauds his audacity. He sleeps with the barman and his male model friend, while she goes home to a night curled up with her dinky pet dog. Unless you're Madonna. More gay man than any gay man on the planet. A woman whose entire life serves as the unofficial guide to being fabulously queer. Like a transcendental, transsexual, trend-bothering Queen of Queens, Madge out camps, out sexes, out shocks and out fabulizes her coterie of admiring gay followers on an hourly basis. Really, this is a woman who should follow the yellow brick road, not Kabbalah.

Hairbrush (Using as a Microphone)

Men might use tennis rackets to play air guitar along to their favourite records. Women rely on the more traditional hairbrush as microphone model. Who's got the better deal? Put it this way, who would you rather be – Madonna or Mark Knopfler? Exactly. The hairbrush is a highly versatile instrument, but we find it works best with the classic power ballad, particular the ones where you get to wig out like Mariah or Whitney. Turn the stereo up loud enough that no one can actually hear your voice, and wail away. Singing into the mirror is particularly enjoyable, as is falling over backwards on to the bed just as you hit that high note. All the more enjoyable when your partner is downstairs, impatiently waiting for you to 'get ready'. Just make sure that you don't leave the door open – if you do, you'll never live it down.

Hairy Legs

She's got legs, those acute observers of the human species, ZZ Top, once noticed. And, indeed, women (Heather Mills McCartney half excepted) do. One of the attributes of said legs, of course, is that they grow hair. As on much of the female body, this is considered unattractive, and thus begins an endless routine of shaving in the shower to keep the pins as pristine smooth as possible. But, sometimes, isn't it nice to take the ZZ Top approach to shaving, and just, well, let it grow a little? It feels rebellious, naughty and like you ought to wear your jeans. It's also hassle free and a guaranteed argument winner with your boyfriend – if he starts to complain, fling him your BIC and tell him to sort his face out. That'll either shut him up or win you a smooth-chinned boyfriend. Either way, you can't lose.

Handsome But Dimwitted Barmen

There are probably some bad things about globalization, excessively cheap air travel and the expansion of the EU, but, offhand, we can't remember what they are. Certainly one of the best things is the apparently unceasing stream of Goran Visnjic lookalikes applying for work in our local All Bar One. They may be PhDs in Vilnius, but their halting English and non-transferable qualifications give us a limitless supply of rugged dreamboats we can giggle at without any fear of being understood. Delightful.

Harry Potter, Reading with an Adult Cover

It's a difficult balancing act. We want to read the latest Harry Potter on the train to work. Yet we're over twelve years old and don't want our fellow passengers to think that our reading ability is so stunted that we're only able to manage a children's book. Fortunately, J. K. Rowling's publisher has come up with a elegant solution – adult covers. Farewell, brightly coloured cartoon pictures. Hello, moody black and white photographs of steam trains. Do they do the same for *The Very Hungry Caterpillar*?

Hat Wearing

For centuries the hat was an everyday item – a bit like a pair of pants, but for your head. Now it's a fashion item. Blame Pete Doherty, if you want, with all his catwalk-inspired court appearances wearing a fag out of the corner of his mouth, a trilby on his head, and a guitar thrown casually over his shoulder. As you do. But the fact of the matter is, it takes a lot of effort to sport a hat that casually. You need to practise your 'hat confidence'. Which, in essence, means zoning yourself out from the fact that you look like a right idiot and pensioners on the street are staring. But, if it blows off, you're on your own. The hat is a cruel master like that.

Having 100 Per Cent Feedback on eBay

Trading on eBay is a bit like swapping stuff in the school playground or being a drug dealer – one bad transaction and your reputation is shot (possibly quite literally, in the case of the drug dealer) – so when you are one of several hundred sellers offering IPOD NANO VERY CHEAP BRAND NEW, you want your glowing feedback to shine out and attract bidders like wasps to a jam sandwich. So what if your 100 per cent rating is made up entirely of feedback you have deliberately generated in an elaborate long-time fraud operation biding your time for the big day when you offload 400 iPods at bargain basement prices, bank all the cash and then close your account. Shame on you.

Having a Bath in the Afternoon, with a Cup of Tea, Listening to the Radio

Many things feel indulgent and pleasurable just by virtue of doing them in the afternoon – having breakfast, making love, enjoying a nice hot bath. The latter is particularly enjoyable when accompanied by a nice cup of tea and the radio. Sheer unadulterated, uninterruptible me-time. If the ends of your fingers don't go wrinkly, you haven't been in for long enough.

Having a Breakover

An unspoken law is that, as soon as you break up with someone, you must have a radical life and looks makeover. A new hairdo will no longer do. Well, it might – but as long as it suggests you've relaunched into a different stratosphere of leagues since the split. Because plodding along peddling the same old you that was deemed unacceptable is, well, unacceptable. Upgrading yourself, whilst in the midst of a Krispy Kreme devouring depression, can be difficult, though. (Just look at Britney after the K-Fed split. Becoming the third member of Right Said Fred surely wasn't part of the plan.) The rule is: new body, new hair, new wardrobe. All by the weekend. This way, the new-supermodel-you can spend Saturday night giving the two-fingered salute to the rigor-mortis-ridden corpse of your relationship. The whole experience is, of course, a triumph of hope over experience. Come Saturday night you'll be sobbing into your Chardonnay, a loser in life *and* the war on wobble.

Having a Celebotomy

Remember when you used to be intelligent? You know, those heady days when you could debate Darfur without mentioning George Clooney? Now it's as if Max Clifford is performing a slow and painful celebotomy on your brain through the pages of the red top rags. You wanted to visit that new exhibition at the Tate Modern but *I'm a Celeb'* was on. You tried to recite the premise of Kant's *Critique of Pure Reason* but the story behind Kate's cocaine hell slipped out instead. You honestly thought you understood the situation in Iraq, but then it turned out that you knew more about politics in the BB house. One day you'll wake up, look in the mirror and see Chantelle staring back. Which is a pretty scary thought.

Having a Cleaner

We all moan about how little we get paid, how menial some of our responsibilities really are and how strict our bosses are at times. The irony is, of course, that more and more of us employ cleaners for little more than the minimum wage, ask them to clean our loos and leave slightly strict notes if the bed-making or dusting isn't quite up to scratch. Hmm. This isn't, perhaps, the socialist ideal we dreamt about when we were at Uni, but it does enable you to pretend once a week that you are back at home where everything was done for you or, in fact, pretend you are living in a hotel with maid service. All you have to do is to place a large cardboard sign on your front door knocker saying 'Please Service This House', leave a massive pile of ironing in the kitchen, the dishes in the sink, the loo seats up, the beds unmade and the house in general disarray and return eight hours later to domestic harmony. Shocking. Really. No really. Sorry, but you've missed a bit.

Having a Good Side (in Photos)

How is it that one side of your face resembles Kate Moss on the catwalk, whilst the other is the bastard child of Shane McGowan and Vanessa Feltz? It's like God got bored half way through the job and decided to finish up with any old spare parts knocking around. Still, no one understands this when you find yourself on holiday, making diva demands as some unsuspecting German tourist kindly agrees to take a snap of you and your other half. NOT THAT SIDE, you screech, with a disgusted tone that people normally reserve for suggestions of swinging. Two hours later, you get the perfect shot. Only to discover the lens cap was still on. Ho hum. Hold the contract with Models 1. For now.

Having a 'Long Lunch'

One of the best perks of working is the ability to 'go on a long lunch' every now and then. The way you pipe up and say it as you're walking out of the office suggests an important meeting. Better still is the early-warning system. 'I'm having a long lunch on Thursday – is that OK?', you ask your colleagues. What can they say? 'No problem', of course. 'Go about your very important long lunching business,' they concede with good grace. So what would happen if you told the truth – if you booked your skiving slot in with utter frankness? 'I'm just going to doss around for a couple of hours on Friday lunch – I might even go shopping and have a manicure? Do you mind?' 'No, feel free – we'll just sit here like chimps and do your work for you.' Really, the 'long lunch' is the nano-version of the sickie. Everyone knows what you're up to, but honour amongst work time-wasting thieves means that no one can ever call you on it. Except the boss. But he'll be too busy out on a long lunch of his own to notice.

Having Stupid Computer Passwords

The great thing about passwords is that you never have to reveal them to anyone at all. EVER. So, on the basis that NO ONE WILL EVER KNOW, you can take revenge on your workmates by making your computer password something like MYBOSSISATOTALIDIOT or FORFUCKSAKEIAMBORED. Every time you type it in you can smile inwardly and laugh at your LITTLE SECRET. Until you are off-sick and the office manager calls you urgently on your mobile to say that a temp urgently needs to access your desktop and needs to know your password. Doh!

Hayseed Dixie

Hard rock? By a bluegrass band? With a cheesy pun of a name? (Hayseed Dixie – AC/DC, do you see what they did there?) On every letter, the Dixie should be an absolute aural disaster. Yet somehow, when you hear someone twang a banjo along to 'Ace of Spades', it's difficult not to raise a smile. Like the 'hilarious' album titles (*A Hot Piece of Grass*? *Let There Be Rockgrass*? *Kiss my Grass*? We've got the joke now, guys), Hayseed Dixie are fantastic fun for about five minutes, before it all starts to wear off. Just remember to listen to it in small doses and you'll be fine.

Headphones (Not Plugged in)
Wearing headphones on a train, plane or bus but not plugging them in to anything or having the volume set to mute means that you can listen to everything people are saying without them suspecting a thing. Genius.

Helping Self to Things from Neighbour's Skip
In this 'makeover', 'chuck out your chintz' and 'ground force' culture, neighbour's skips are much more likely to contain rich pickings than the dead dogs, sodden roof insulation and broken televisions of yesteryear. The trick here, though, is to wander by a couple of times and clearly identify your target and then come back at midnight or very early morning and swiftly remove the rocking-chair, pine planking or butler's sink and, without looking back, walk off confidently and swiftly. Try not to help yourself to anything from people's skips who you know or you might face embarassing moments next time they come round to dinner. 'We used to have a chair just like that but it got death watch beetle – where did you get yours from?' Um.

Hen Nights
It's hard to find anything wrong with eating too much, drinking cocktails with improbable names and flirting with sailors. Some people do, though, apparently. It seems to be mainly the staggering down high streets dressed like hookers and cackling like witches they don't like. Well, when it's *their* last single mate getting married and leaving *them* as the last turkey in the shop then perhaps they'll understand

how a slow comfortable screw against a wall is the only thing that can numb the pain. Well, that or a cocktail.

Hiding CDs

Let's say your partner has just bought a CD that you absolutely loathe. For two weeks said CD – let's call it *The Fratellis* for the sake of an example – is on heavy rotation in your house to the point where you wonder whether the relationship is worth continuing with. Dear reader, let us save your marriage by introducing to you the delights of hiding the CD. There's only one place the CD should go and that's back in a CD box. But not in it's own CD box – oh no, another one, slipped in behind the CD already there (a CD your partner loathes and would never reach for is particularly recommended). Add in the classic diversionary tactic of accusing your partner of never putting CDs back in the right boxes, and perhaps this will be a lesson to them once and for all. Evil? Maybe, but then, so are the Fratellis.

High Definition

There's something about technological advances with the word 'high' in them. Thirty years ago, we got all excited about high fidelity, and now it's the turn of pictures, not sounds, with the launch of high definition. Have you seen high definition? It absolutely rocks. It's so sharp and crystal clear it leaves you with the thought that maybe your eyes aren't good enough quality to be watching this stuff. In fact, it's so brilliant there's only one problem: once watched, your normal television will never seem quite good enough again.

Highlighter Pens (Over-Using)

Is there actually any practical purpose to highlighter pens? The correct answer, of course, is no. Made from boiled-down eighties towelling socks, they exist purely to waste time, to give off the appearance of doing work, when in fact you're doing no such thing. Essentially colouring in for office staff, they can turn a dull-looking document into a more attractive-looking document – as long, of course, as you consider fluorescent yellow and pink and green attractive. But still, though, exactly the same document as before.

Holiday Beard

Because you're not just on holiday from *work*, you're on holiday from all the things that make life hell – like *washing up* and *shaving*. Besides, if we remembered to pack our razors there would be a massive spike in the birth rate every May. Once we've removed the usual deterrents, like crippling tiredness and a laundry-strewn bedroom, looking like Popeye's nemesis is the only thing that keeps the Mrs off.

Holly Willoughby

Holly Willoughby is successfully following the Cat Deeley model of going from cute children's TV presenter to glossy grown up Saturday night star. God only knows what she thought when she got Philip Schofield as her TV 'husband' on *Dancing on Ice*, but maybe Tess Daly pulled rank and refused to let Vernon Kay work with her, just in case. Because, while Cat Deeley has that Beyoncé air of unavailability to her, and Kate Thornton can never quite shake the dinner lady of presenting tag, Holly has just the right mix of curvy good looks and girl next door availability to maintain your interest, and, despite your better judgment, watch almost two hours of clumsy celebrities going arse over tit on the ice.

Holy Toast

We love the simplicity of this naughty product. Basically, it is a plastic stamper that you secretly stamp on to a piece of Mother's Pride before chucking it in the toaster. When it pops up, bring it to the table and, hey presto, the face of the Virgin Mary has appeared on your toast. Best served to unsuspecting maiden aunts or religious relatives. 'Jesus

Christ Almighty,' they will exclaim. 'No,' you can reply, 'I think you'll find it is the Virgin Mary'. Ad lib to fade. . . .

Home and Away

Hold me in your arms, Don't let me go, I want to stay forever, Closer each day – ALL TOGETHER NOW – Home and Away.' With a theme tune this lyrically sophisticated and the lurking suspicion that one day Fisher and Alf might accidentally strip to their trunks at the surf club, tuning your TV in and your brain cells out at 5.00 p.m. every weekday is life's way of telling you there is a God.

Homemade Soups

Everyone gets struck down with the domestic goddess virus at times. But a particularly nasty strain is when the wholesome natural food bug kicks in. I know what, I'll make a soup, you think. And by that, you're not talking about heating up Covent Garden Soup's finest in a saucepan. You're talking no holds barred, coal face of the kitchen, ten hours hard vegetable preparation labour. The odd thing is, it costs £30 in organic ingredients, takes at least three hours to make and ends up tasting like sink water with a few floating carrots. Much easier to have nipped to the corner shop, bought a tin of Heinz tomato soup for £1.50, spent five minutes bringing it to the boil and then spent the rest of the afternoon in the pub.

Home Office (Getting a)

A lot of people wring their hands and witter on about 'work/life balance' but, given the extent that our personal lives have invaded the office these days (ordering stuff from Amazon, surfing for porn, photocopying our nether regions etc.), it's only fair that we bring a bit of work home now and then just to even things up. Of course the last thing you want to do is plonk yourself in the middle of the sofa with a laptop while everyone else is watching *Saturday Kitchen*. That's no fun for fans of PowerPoint presentations *or* washed-up chefs. Consequently, your only real option is to finally ditch all of those cardboard boxes of junk you haven't unpacked since you moved in and turn the box room into a home office. There you will find the peace you need to really focus your mind on ordering stuff from Amazon, surfing for porn and (once you get your scanner working properly) photocopying what's under your dressing gown.

Hoovering Up Things that You Shouldn't

We are sure that the instruction books (not that we read such pedestrian publications) for Hoovers and Dysons and other vacuum cleaners state that no solid objects should be vacuumed up for fear of damaging the machine and invalidating the guarantee or some such corporate anti-consumerist twaddle. We see this as a challenge and the fun to be had sucking up conkers, paperclips, marbles, ash (wait for it to cool a little or the machine will literally melt) and, the *pièce de résistance*, gravel, beggars belief. Who'd have thought you could have had so much fun with a vacuum outside of the bedroom?!

Hotel Rooms, Adding Drinks on to Other People's

It takes a while to master the fine art of feeling like a proper hotel person. But it's worth persevering: once you've got it, you've got it for life. No one is going to challenge anyone with an air of confidence to them – they're simply not going to do anything to upset 'sir' or 'madam'. So, when you sit at the bar, order a champagne cocktail and are asked for payment, all you have to do is dismissively say 'Room 351'. The barman will say 'very good, sir', even if he can see your key for Room 243 lying in front of you. He doesn't care – as long as he's got a number, his job is secure. Whatever you do, don't feel bad about the free drinks – someone else is just as likely to do the same thing to you.

Hotpants

Topshop might stock them, but really they belong to the interior vision of a psychedelically bad nightmare. In a way, finding yourself walking down the street in a crop top and hotpants is far worse than strutting your shame naked. It's all about lines of contrast. Even a really bad naked body can look merely like an unidentified land mass. But the cruel cut of a pair of hotpants is like a road map signposting saggy bum cheeks. Men may watch that Kylie video where she's wearing those gold hotpants, slack-jawed with appreciation. But women simply register shock and awe. Not even a lifetime on the treadmill, simultaneously exfoliating, could get us anywhere close. In a way, though, when fashionistas announce that hotpants are the must-wear item of the summer, really they're just softening us up for city-shorts. After a bum-cheek-bothering item, suddenly mid-thigh doesn't seem too bad.

Hughmima

See **Tomkat**. Actually, don't bother seeing TomKat, because they've split up now, haven't they?

Humumga

What you get for under a tenner is a large plastic stick to throw for your dog. Doesn't sound like a bargain or a guilty pleasure, but what we didn't tell you was that the plastic stick is actually shaped like a Jim Carrey-in-*Mask*-mode bright red tongue. So when your obedient mutt is trotting back with tail wagging seeking approval for his brilliant fetch-and-retrieve behaviour, you are actually more likely to be bent double laughing at how preposterous he looks. Shame on you and shame on the makers of Humunga.

I'm Fine (Said Moodily)

Saying 'I'm fine' in slightly strained tones is the modern equivalent of a suicide note. The subtext is, 'I'm about to shoot myself, like you care. My whole life has gone to shit. So why are you even asking me these dumb questions?' Literally, it's as if the words 'How are you?' are two fingers in the eye of every miserable, pathetic little aspect of your life. Obviously, the zombie look in your eyes as you spit the 'F' word out will elicit the response, 'Are you sure?' To which, through gritted teeth, you spit out 'Yes. I'm. *Fine.*' God help anyone who comes back with a 'Well, you're obviously not. . .' Those poor souls can expect to be on the business end of your oncoming meltdown.

Iceberg

(**Shaggy Dog Story** continued) . . . it was a big iceberg and, just like the Titanic, the ship was badly damaged and started to sink. Raymondo, along with the rest of the crew and passengers, struggled to escape. As the ship went down, he leapt into the sea and hoped for the best. As luck would have it, an upturned table bobbed past, which he hauled himself on to and used as a life raft. Exhausted from his efforts, he passed out. When he came to, the ship was no more, and no other survivors were in sight. Well, there was one. For on the opposite corner of Raymondo's makeshift life raft sat the parrot. For two weeks they sat there, bobbing up and down on the open sea, not speaking to each other. Until, finally, one day, the silence was broken. The parrot looked across at Raymondo and said . . . See **Punchline**.

Ignoring All Traffic Signals (If You Are a Cyclist)

There is a little known European law that states that a cyclist can break any road regulation and traffic safety bye-law without fear of prosecution as long as they are cycling after dark on a bike with no lights while listening to an iPod and not wearing a helmet. Sounds dangerous to us but what do we know? STOP PRESS – you can now cycle on the pavements as well, in case of congestion on the roads – what a marvellous innovation.

Ikea Hating

It's Sweden's answer to purgatory for men. Worse than spending Saturday afternoons in solitary confinement. Worse, in fact, than slowly amputating a leg with a blunt spoon. And it's *so big*. Cavernously so. The kind of dimensions that not only suck up an entire day, but take your will to live, and possibly your marriage, with it. And for what? A pine bookshelf that slopes to one side, and a wine rack you didn't even want. But the real stroke of evil genius is how the store is a gift that keeps on giving. If you've managed to survive the hell of the checkout system then chances are assembling your wares at home will finish you off. No doubt the instructions will be undecipherable and one of the essential parts will be missing. If it all goes disastrously wrong, though, and you end up with a bed that looks like a spaceship, rest assured you can probably sell it to the Tate Modern as an art installation.

Imagining What Your Colleagues Look Like Naked

Liven up any meeting or confrontational 'in my office now' situations by imagining Mr Gill from Accounts with a huge tattoo of John Maynard Keynes across his buttocks or Mrs Horne from Sales with her enormous unclad bazookas hanging low over a pendulous stomach or, for light relief, that total stunna from Reception bending over to pick up a dropped package, and all your meetings problems have dissolved at once. Just remember to chew the insides of your cheeks very carefully to avoid any tell-tale guffaws or giggles, let alone lustful groans.

Inevitability of Britain's Inability to Deliver Large-Scale Projects on Budget and on Time

Imagine if we had a Space Shuttle. Imagine, for one laughable minute, that we could somehow raise the money: obviously the Government could never manage it, but perhaps we could afford a moderate-sized space programme if we organised a whip-round at a City wine bar on Bonus Day. Imagine the sheer quantity of Local Government officials who would have cousins or Brother Masons who would need a taste of the budget before we squandered any of it on *engines* or anything. Even if we bought an American one and painted a Union Flag on it, *something* would go wrong. German cars are the most reliable on Earth, but Ken Livingstone buys a fleet of special buses from Mercedes that take up twice as much road as the old ones he's replacing. They cost a million quid each, so they must be very, very good, but they develop the strikingly un-bus-like habit of bursting into flames in the middle of the West End of London as soon as we take delivery. It's *almost* as if he was taking some duff stock off the Krauts' hands and was expecting a non-exec. directorship in return when he retires from his current job. As if. The very idea. And that's just the stuff we *buy* – we haven't even touched on the multi-million-pound IT system for the NHS which is less powerful than a Sinclair Spectrum, on Wembley Stadium or on the rolling disaster that is the Millennium Dome, all of which we've somehow managed to make a right royal mess of. Let's face it, we used to be top nation but these days we can't be trusted to run a bath. Still, you slip me a share of the money you've put aside for soap and I'll quote you on the best bath you ever had.

Insectilix Lollies

Fancy an alcoholic lolly laced with Vodka? Course you do. Fancy a little extra crunchy treat as well inside it? Um . . . not sure? Go on – it'll be lovely. The vodka flavoured one contains an edible Chinese scorpion, the tequila variety comes with a specially bred edible worm and, if those don't tempt you, go for the refreshingly minty one chock-full of edible ants. All for £3.95 each – a novelty snack combined with crustacean exploitation – hard to say no to.

Intensive Conditioning (Hair)

Science tells us that our hair is merely dead tissue. But that's quite a boring, depressing message. Instead we'd rather believe the shiny, somewhere over the rainbow, dreamspeak of the giant cosmetics companies. 'Instant repair – 3 minute molecule mask' their ads promise, with the swish of a glossy, highly alive, ponytail. No matter that you spent the last ten years with your hair stuck in an ashtray soaked in beer, punctuated only by the occasional dose of industrial strength bleach. Not to mention the punishment meted out by nuclear-heated straightening irons. No, all the damage can be reversed in just a couple of minutes. Simply plonk some white goo all over your head and you'll be re-born with the hair of an eighteen-year-old Swedish supermodel. And quite possibly the bone structure too. Hell, why not smear this stuff all over your bank account while you're at it. And if it could repair the damage done there, that really would be a miracle.

Internet Questionnaires

Whether you're of the *My Guy* and *Jackie* generation, and ticked boxes to find out what your mum should embroider on your snood so you could catch Nik Kershaw's eye when he blew through town, or the *More* and *Minx* set who are less about needlework and more about determining the right intimate piercing for that dream date, you know that a good questionnaire is an almost irresistible temptation. And, like marijuana or chlamydia, a temptation is all the better for being shared. Once you've ticked all the boxes in 'Which type of stockbroker is right for you?' in *Tatler*, it's impossible to let anyone else have a go in case they think your answers make you look a bit dense. Hence the beauty of the infinitely editable *tabula rasa* of the Internet, where your answers can always be edited after the fact and, if you have ticked Mostly Cs, meaning you will definitely sign a Pre-Nup by mistake, you can always explain that you're too mature for this kind of thing nowadays so it must be an entirely *different* danielradcliffefan69.

iPod Nano

Your truly embarrassing gym playlist – the musical equivalent of being caught wearing fluoro lycra cycling shorts – is a hundred times more shameful if it's on an iPod Nano. Or worse, the iPod Shuffle. It announces the fact that your extensive music knowledge doesn't extend beyond ten albums.

Jack Nicholson, Doing Impressions of

We're not great at doing impressions. Fortunately, the realm of celebrity has been kind enough to supply us with a small array of stars that even the most un-Bremner-like can pass off to the vague amusement of our friends. But among the ranks of Jimmy Savilles and Andy from *Little Britains*, one stands out. Who wants to be an ageing DJ or a comedy character when one can be Jack? For a split second, as we put on the shades, pull our hair back and wheeze 'Jack Goddam Fucking Nicholson', shout 'You can't handle the Truth!' or grin manically and scream 'Here's Johnny!', we are caught in the thrill of being the greatest film star ever to have walked the earth. If only we could do a decent impression of his amazing way with women, we'd be completely sorted.

James Hewitt

Let's not talk about Harry. Let's just talk about Leslie Phillips. He just *pretended* to be a louche posho and look how much we loved him. It follows, therefore, that James Hewitt is even cooler. Even if he will insist on signing up to one low-rent reality gawkfest after another . . .

Jamie Oliver

Are we meant or love or hate Jamie Oliver at the moment? It changes so quickly, it's difficult to keep up. He's saving the nation's children! Hurrah! He's getting two million for his Sainsbury's ads! Boo! He's helping deprived kids get a start in life! Hurrah! Oh no, he's getting his drumkit out again! Boo! He's doing his cockney mockney routine! Hurrah! He's sticking up for dinner ladies! Boo! Oh hang on, we're getting it the wrong way round now. You see how difficult it is? We say, avoid looking out of touch and play safe – hate him in public, love him in private.

Jamie Oliver Recipes

Your signature dish is spag bol. Or chicken korma. And has been since you were a student. Then Jamie twirls into your life, grinning gormlessly from the pages of a glossy supplement, challenging you to chuck something into a dish and come up with a three-course gourmet feast. With his cheeky-chappy charm, he makes it look so easy, like it's the culinary equivalent of white van man: stupidly simple. Suddenly you find yourself wandering through the aisles of Sainsbury's, wimpering piteously, as you clutch hold of your torn-out recipe, trying to locate South American fragranced fern. Then some sub-human sales critter directs you to another store, and so you go on hunting for the holy grail of gravy ingredients. Until, 'quite by chance', you stumble across an Iceland. One day you will be a great chef, until then it's frozen pizza for dinner. Again.

Jazz Hands Dancing

Some people have rhythm – they tend to be known as 'women'. Others are slightly more lacking – technically known as 'men'. Fortunately, for those moments when you have not yet drunk sufficient alcohol to blot out the self-awareness that your clumsy, disjointed off the beat movements are not considered dancing, there is the opt out clause of 'jazz hands'. Essentially, it's palms out, fingers stretched as wide as they can go, and a bit of a waggle.

Yes, it's a bit naff, and probably not best advised if you've gone to watch Metallica, but otherwise it's a mirth-inducing piece of displacement activity to distract people away from what your feet are (or aren't) doing.

Jazz, Pretending to Like
Here's the big secret about jazz. No one, literally no one, knows what is going on. Even the people who play it don't know what is happening – they just call making it up as they go along 'improvisation', as if this makes it better. Once you know this, you have the opportunity to sound smart and sophisticated at any social gathering – safe in the knowledge that no one is going to challenge you, as they have no idea what you're talking about either. Sprinkle your chatter with words and phrases like 'juxtaposition', 'behind the beat' and 'playful use of time signatures'. Pick random sounds to make up genres: be bop, ba-tra, hip quip – and watch as the sophisticated girl with the Gauloise makes a beeline for you. And if she asks what 'Bitches Brew' is all about, just laugh and say, 'Honey, not even Miles Davis knows what "Bitches Brew" is about.'

Jeremy Kyle
Daytime television shows are guilt inducing instinctively, because you have to be dodging work for whatever reason to be watching them. But at least with some of them you finish the programme feeling as if you've learnt something. With *The Jeremy Kyle Show*, the only thing you're left with is the sense that you should go and wash your hands. The show kicks on from previous British discussion shows by the virtue of Kyle acting as some sort of moral policeman: firstly, he's got the whole range of PC Plod weaponry of lie detectors and DNA tests to back up his opinions; secondly, rather than holding back and being impartial, the Kyle form of interrogation gives both barrels to those he feels deserves it. It's great telly, but maybe we're missing a trick here: why don't we kill (Kyle?) two birds with one stone and throw him some real-life criminals and terrorists for

our entertainment? *The Jeremy Kyle Show – Live From Guantanamo Bay:* now that'd really be something.

Jingles
Essentially filler bits of adverts for radio shows, jingles never quite get the credit they deserve, particularly when they are irresistibly catchy and stick in your head, sometimes years after the DJ has hung up his headphones. For us, summer and Peter Powell go hand in hand, and at the first burst of warm spring sunshine, we can't help singing 'Summer Radio on the Pete-Peter Powell Show'. When we hear 'Wake Up Boo' by the Boo Radleys, we still expect them to sing 'Wake up it's a beautiful morning, Chris Evans on your radio'. And how can 'Ooh Gary Davies, Ooh Gary Davies, Ooh, Gary Davies on your radio' stop a smile spreading across your face?

Joey Barton
For all the overpriced, overpaid footballers in the world, there are a few who still make it all worthwhile. Step forward Manchester City legend Joey Barton. Joey has had his fair share of problems – a liking for the liquid refreshment; a brother put away for murder, which rival fans occasionally remind him of – but he still makes you smile. Mooning at away fans who are winding him up. Celebrating a goal by picking up the corner flag and 'knighting' the scorer. And best of all, his stunning literary critique on all those World Cup autobiographies – 'Went to Germany. Played shit. Here's my book.' Mark Lawson couldn't have put it better himself.

Jokes about Samantha on *Sorry I Haven't A Clue*
Recently voted the second-funniest radio programme ever, behind *The Goon Show*, this antidote to panel games, *I'm Sorry I Haven't A Clue*, is notable for many things (including, of course, Humphrey Lyttleton, Barry Cryer, Tim Brooke-Taylor, Grahame Garden and Colin Sell on the piano) but we prefer it for the filthiest double

entendres ever underwritten by the licence fee. The silent Samantha, who is there to keep the score, has been the butt of Humph's ribaldry for many years and it just gets filthier and filthier. We know that we should be grown up and not laugh at innuendo but we just can't help it. Our favourite schoolboy snigger moments include 'She's looking forward to going out for an ice cream with her Italian gentleman friend. She says she's looking forward to licking the nuts off a large Neapolitan', 'She's popped out to visit an old gentleman friend of hers who's a notorious curmudgeon. However, she finds that if she butters him up properly she can sometimes get him to splash out' and, finally, 'In her spare time, Samantha likes nothing more than to peruse old record shops. She particularly enjoys a rewarding poke in the country section'.

Jonathan Ross

At the end of the working week, there's nothing finer than a relaxing evening on the sofa with a nice glass of wine. Or six. Even those of us with the renal fortitude of Shane MacGowan might find themselves drifting off for a well-earned sleep around nine-ish during some ill-conceived Dawn French vehicle about vicars or nurses or some such. Waking up with a start to see Jonathan Ross kissing Russell Brand or tickling Matt Lucas is very much part of the tipsy Friday night experience. The only way you can be sure if it's a dream or not is waiting to see if your mum turns up naked to bring them a tray of cherryade. Either way, it's the only way to round off the week.

Jordan and Peter

They are the council estate Richard and Judy. All churlish banter and back-chat – but with more fake tan and fewer clothes. Proof that even celebrity couples operate on the same level as civilians. To say Peter Andre – the pop equivalent of an Oompa Loompa – is pussy-whipped is the understatement of the year. His self-respect is wedged between Katie's huge mammary glands, begging for air and destined never to see the light of day again. But considering he was living with his parents in Cyprus in the fame 'Where Are They Now?' file beforehand, maybe it's a better place to be.

Kaballah

Ask yourself this question: do you really seriously want to meet celebrities? Of course you do. Are you willing to pay double price for your mineral water from now on? Yes? Then welcome to Kaballah. It's as packed with famous people as AA but the membership requirement is one of those silly friendship bracelets you used to wear at school rather than a wrecked liver. You know it makes sense – in the long run it's cheaper than buying *heat* every week.

Kate Beckinsale

Apparently, if you watch *Underworld* all the way through, there's some sort of sub-plot about vampires in it. True *cineastes*, though, are unlikely to get through the first ten minutes of Kate slinking around in her spray-on vinyl suit. That, and a couple of squares of kitchen roll, is all most of us will need.

Kate Moss

For decades now, the fashion elite have *inexplicably* eschewed the use of models that looked like women in their shows in favour of models that resemble pale young boys. Kate Moss is no exception. On the other hand, she's minted, she knows where you can get some drugs and, if you ever *did* cop off with her (and let's face it, if dice-headed no-mark Pete Doherty can, who can't?), there's every chance that she'd bring along one of her posh Primrose Hill mates for a bit of three-in-a-bed sauciness. The Perfect Woman.

Keeley Hazell

Every generation, Paul Simon once sang, throws a hero up the pop charts. And every micro-generation creates a top topless model who claims Page Three as her own. The latest in this long tradition of Samantha Fox, Linda Lusardi, Melinda Messenger and Jordan is young Keeley Hazell, pneumatic as necessary but with a comely girl next door look about her, sort of an adult version of Rachel Stevens. Unlike her predecessor, Jordan, Keeley has so far opted for the Kate Moss school of silent modelling, which we wholeheartedly recommend. Models should always be seen and not heard – as soon as you hear that council estate English coming through, the sophisticated image you've created in your head is sadly shattered.

Keeping Things in the Loft

In most houses, the loft is a repository for things that you don't need, you don't want to look at, but for some reason you can't take to the council tip. For houses where the loft has been converted into a little bed-sit for your husband's interfering mother, that goes double.

Keira Knightley

There are few celebrities who women seem to have it in for more than Keira Knightley. Accusations normally include suggestions that she can't actually act, how thin she is and her seemingly innate inability to close her mouth. And we haven't even got on to her role in *Pride and Prejudice*, on which any Jane Austen fan can (and will) give you a lecture longer than the film about why she wasn't the right choice for Elizabeth Bennett. The fact that, as a man, none of this seems to bother you, and you still fancy her anyway, only serves to rile women further. Be careful when you get *Pirates of the Caribbean* out on DVD, that's all we're saying.

Ken Bruce

There may be many DJs out there who steal all the headlines and the glory – Terry Wogan, Chris Evans, Chris Moyles – but is anyone out there really any more listenable than Ken Bruce? Spinning discs on Radio 2 for as far back as we can remember – he was there when our parents made us listen to it, and, no doubt, he'll still be plugging away for our grandchildren, like some DJ equivalent of Dorian Grey. Yet, somehow, his patter of bad self-deprecating jokes and even worse flirtations with the travel lady has withstood the test of time. Indeed, like a mature cheese, we'd go as far as to argue that they've actually got (marginally) better with age. We passed him once in the corridor at Broadcasting House and were so excited at seeing him in the flesh, we were too dumbstruck to say hello. True story.

Kendal Mint Cake

Originally developed to help butch men with beards climb mountains and, indeed, still advertised today with a quote from Everest-conquering Sir Edmund Hillary, this confectionery bar in its no-nonsense packaging has the consistency of chalk mixed with parmesan but tastes as though it contains an illegal degree of sugar. But what it does offer above and beyond other sweets is the feel that you have crunchy snow beneath your feet, there is a challenging ridge ahead and that in the far distance there is a strange sound that could, just could, be a hungry yeti wailing. Even if you are just stepping off the Clapham Omnibus.

Kerry Katona

It's pretty hard to remember how Kerry Katona came to our attention: *Wife Swap*? Atomic Kitten? *Crime Watch*? Something like that. Now we only see her on those bizarre Iceland adverts that look like a particularly luxurious version of the 'before' table in *You Are What You Eat*: all frozen sausage rolls and GM-free cola-style drink. Her appeal stems principally, if we're being candid, from the way that she exemplifies endangered adjectives like 'Rubenesque' or 'Busty'. Well, that and the way she fizzes around her well-stocked dining table like someone who knows where all the (really cheap) drugs are hidden.

Keyboard Fastidiousness

Unfold a good thick paperclip and very slowly scrape all the gunky fluffy stuff out from between the computer keys. If you are feeling particularly frisky then dismantle the mouseball as well and scrape the paperclip along the tracking wheels. Ooh, stop it – that's just too much!

K-Fed

Hollywood's least favourite rapping rodent. But truly the most brilliant villain ever to emerge from a trailer park. Literally, every time Britney stepped out of the house a whole nation mouthed 'He's behind you!' Kevin arrived in Britney's life, not so much like a knight on a white charger, but more like Roland Rat riding a JCB gold digger. Amazingly, as is always the case, what Kevin lacked in looks, charm and talent he more than made up for in the sperm donation department. This is a man who only has to look at a lady through the bottom of his Bud bottle and she's knocked up. Survival of the fittest? It appears evolution is looking to propagate genes that can bodypop and look good in a white wifebeater. Poor Britney never stood a chance. Hopefully, K-Fed will be forced to use his million dollar divorce settlement to pay child support to the entire lap-dancing populace of Las Vegas. Because, let's face it, the only way his rap album is going platinum is if he markets it as a dartboard.

Kicking Your Legs in Joy

One of our friends tells of how she and her sister used to share a bed until their teens. Part of the fun was to lie down very, very still and then on a given signal both of them would kick their feet up and down as fast as possible until they both fell back exhausted with laughter. For scientific purposes, we have tried it out and it really delivers – your legs are weak with the effort (like climbing a tall tower with a spiral staircase on an Italian holiday) and it is impossible, truly, to still be in a bad mood as a result. It clears away the cobwebs and you even sleep better. Probably looks a bit daft if someone walks in, though.

Kissing Girls (to Wind Boys Up in Clubs)

It started in the glory days of Acid House. The fact that everybody in Britain under the age of thirty was either on Ecstasy or in a chess club made the world, and especially nightclubs, a much friendlier place. Friendly as everyone was, boys kissing boys doesn't really work for anyone. In the first place, their stubble might Velcro together in a terrible way and, in the second place: eeeuuww. Girls kissing other girls, though, made perfect sense. For a start we always used to hold hands in the playground anyway, so it's not such a leap, and once we saw the reaction we got from the first generation of boys raised on porny VHS it was just too rewarding not to do it again and again until, before we knew it, there was a cameraphone picture of us in *Zoo*. Which is a great achievement, we keep telling our mums.

Knocking Off Early

The ability to access your work email from home has made the twenty-first century a skiver's paradise. Chip off at four and be home in time to answer a couple of mails before teatime, maintaining the illusion of industry. Add to this the advent of the blessed BlackBerry, making long afternoons in the pub effectively invisible to senior management, and office life will never be the same again. *Someone* must be doing all the work. Poor buggers.

Larry David

Larry. Larry, Larry, Larry. *Curb Your Enthusiasm* is so brilliantly funny – it's the ones who profess *not* to watch it you should be worried about. But treating the star of the show not as a hilarious comic creation but as a role model for how you should live your life is perhaps something you should keep to yourself. Whether it's complaining about service in restaurants, hiring a prostitute so you can drive in the car-pool lane or affecting racism to skip jury service to watch a sports match, we say, let Larry get the laughs and keep the grumpy old man thoughts to yourself. Otherwise, it's likely that someone else will be having the last laugh.

Lawn-Mowing

A long-time male preserve thanks to the sheer slog of lugging a stone-age machine round the garden, the art of lawn-mowing is now available to all thanks to the new fangled Flymos that float their way between the flowerbeds. But in terms of who actually does the grass-cutting, it's still very much a case of one man went to mow. The reason why is simple, really: this 'contribution' – along with manning the barbecue – means we avoid all the real hard work in the garden, like digging, weeding and pruning. That and the fact that when we buy a house with a garden the size of a football pitch, we want there to be no argument about who gets to drive the 4×4 grass cutter around.

Leaving Your Wife/Girlfriend/Female Flatmate to Deal with Workmen

We know it's pathetic, but when it comes to men coming into your house to fix things, it really is best to find a way of letting your lady do the talking. All the workman wants is an ogle and a cup of tea with three sugars. If he's got a man to talk to, he's only going to take out his disappointment by conversing with you about plumbing or electrics or any proper sort of man stuff that you should really know about but don't because you went to university to do a liberal arts degree rather than getting a proper job. And while you can talk at length about Hegel or Karl Marx, you are quite frankly out of your depth when it comes to discussing changing a plug. The more he sprinkles the chat with phrases like 'it's not that difficult really' and 'have you really not got a spanner?', the more your sense of self-worth and masculinity shrivels up, to the point where you are reduced to feeling 'I am not a real man so I deserve to be ripped off by this alpha male'. Trust us, make your excuses, and hide in the pub until he's gone.

Leggings

The younger, wilder, harder-to-wear sister of black opaque tights. Tights that partied so hard they lost their feet, but none of their ability to keep a landslide backside in place. The legging took on summer mini-dresses and won. It meant that you could spend all night in the pub, just fake tan your arms and face when you got in, and *still* wear a wisp of material the next day. It meant you could take a Tardis to the 1980s and come back in black leggings and neon stilettos for a night out, rather than having a WAG-attack and flaunting your corn-beefers to the innards of Boujis (or the Brewers' Arms). The legging was an unmitigated triumph. Until you asked the opinion of a man. A tight, however thick, is still a (very) distant relation of the stocking, and therefore acceptable. The legging, however, will always look to men like you're going in for a varicose vein operation. And is *never* sexy. But who cares what men think?

Let Me Entertain You

A bit like dating your cousin, daytime TV and the talent show is one of those match-ups that should be banned by law. The fact that the show is hosted by Brian Conley (the poor man's Paul O'Grady?) should only make matters worse, and yet, and yet . . . somehow the show works. The stroke of genius is that the audience are the judges – once 50 per cent have pressed the buzzer, the act is off – however short their time might have been. Suddenly, watching a bad juggler is transformed as you watch to see how many seconds of his appalling routine the audience will let him get away with. If only this was true for all TV shows . . .

Licking Things

It's the saucy postcard of tongue movements. Even the most innocent lick makes you feel like you're starring in your own *Carry On* film. Slurping an ice cream: 'Ooh, I say!' Licking cake off your fingers: 'Naughty, naughty!' Which is all well and good until it's your mother inadvertently doing the tongue teasing. Licking things is also a selective sport. Lips are good. Other places are better. But deliver a wet one on someone's cheek and you've veered dangerously into freak territory. Sometimes, only a lick can reflect the primitive animal desires stirring within you. Like when you get carried away and lick the the pictures of Daniel Craig in *heat*'s 'Torso of The Week'.

Lighting Your Farts

Best not tried alone, as you will invariably end up setting fire to your trousers, burning your fingers and having some tricky explaining to do. Trust us – we know. This home science experiment is a marvel – as a group of inebriated friends stand around and ignite the methane expelled from their bowels by clever use of sphincter control and lighter manipulation, it feels great to be alive and proud to be human and living in a sophisticated society. Girls truly don't know what they are missing out on – who wants to talk about sex, shopping and relationships when you can shoot a large smelly flame out of your arse instead? Now that, my friend, is the future.

Lindsay Lohan

Or Li-Lo, as we like to call her, all chummy like. Well, when you've seen someone's ladyparts on your computer screen, it seems churlish not to dispense with formalities. Our Lindsay is a proper firebrand (or 'firecrotch', according to Paris Hilton's friends), which is great, because we want our celebs to have fun and give the two-fingered salute to their publicist's demands for decorum. After all, without her and her partying ilk, we'd be left with deadly-dull celeb-droids like Jennifer Aniston.

Listening to Music When You're Meant to be Working

It helps me relax. It helps me concentrate. It puts me in a creative mood. There are many reasons for having music on when you're trying to work, but let's face it: your parents were right when they told you to turn the radio off when you were doing your homework. All the reasons for listening to music while working are bollocks. How can you concentrate when someone is singing at you? The human brain (well, ours at least) is a simple thing and cannot cope with two such tasks at once. All that happens is that you stop thinking about what you're meant to be doing and start listening to the music instead. Or you end up adding the lyrics into the report you are writing (*'In conclusion, my recommendation to the board is that I Want To Know What Love Is'*) And yet. Despite the fact that we know all of the above, we still go ahead and put the CD on anyway. Hell, we're even doing it ourselves as we type: it's

Air, it's got no words, so we can . . . oh, who are we trying to kid?

Lists

1. They're a great way of ordering things. 2. As long as by 'things', we're talking top ten records or greatest films of all time. 3. Of course, it's all a bit Nick Hornby, which is exactly why we don't shout about enjoying it. 4. Though secretly we know that Nick is right. 5. *OK Computer* by Radiohead. Well, it's compulsory that it's got to feature somewhere.

Live Television, Being Able to Pause

This just does our head in. Picture the scene: you're watching *EastEnders* when the phone goes. But rather than miss the duh-duh-duh ending, television has now advanced to the point where you can pause the transmission, spend ten minutes yakking to your brother, then press play on the telly and carry on where you left off, missing absolutely nothing. How does that work? How can you stop something that's live? What's next – pausing that car in the road so you can pull out? Freeze framing that rain shower so you can get to work without getting wet? It may just be us, but it feels as if the space-time continuum has been broken. It's only a matter of time before the dinosaurs find the 'hole' and end up being transported into your back garden. One can only hope that, by then, technology has advanced to the point where we pause the T. Rex's advance and rewind it back to the Lost World.

Living the Playboy Lifestyle (While Your Wife is at Her Parents)

There are countless motives for your wife to spend the weekend at her parents. It's not just unreasonable behaviour. Not nowadays. She probably even told you. One of them could be ill or something. It's hard to say when you're not actually listening. Anyway, the minute she's out of the house it's more-or-less compulsory to stock up on beer, sausages and slightly racy DVDs and spend forty-eight hours in your dressing gown, like some kind of suburban Hugh Hefner. There will inevitably be a degree of contrition when she gets back from her dad's funeral to find you slumped on the sofa surrounded by spent beer cans and tissues, but that's a small price to pay for a pleasure you're too drunk to measure.

Local Radio Adverts

The thing about radio, a friend who works in the 'biz' once told us, is that it is one of the most creative mediums as it forces the listener to use their imagination. If only it forced the people who come up with local radio adverts. Truly, they are the all expense spared commercials, with no one strong enough to tell the local welder or curry-house owner that perhaps they shouldn't narrate their own ads. Or write their own scripts. Or come up with their own puns. Of course, there might be some sophisticated double bluff going on here – a so-bad-it's-good ad will stick in your mind. But it's more likely that 'When dinner is a worry, ring us for a curry, we'll deliver in a hurry . . .' tells you everything you need to know as to why this restaurant owner didn't make it in advertising.

Local Weather Forecasts

The point of these, it has to be said, is never exactly clear. We're bright people, we can work out which part of the country we live in, locate that on a national weather map, and thus work out what it's going to do tomorrow. And yet the powers that be insist on giving us a double dose of meteorology. Strangely, despite our best intentions, we are unable to avoid watching this second forecast. Is it because we think that there might some peculiar local weather system that the national forecaster might have missed? Is it because we feel more homely by seeing the name of our own town on the map? Or is it because we are too lazy to move from our sofas and turn the television channel over? Quite.

Loch Ness Monster (Retaining an Open Mind About)

Things are always changing their names. Peking's called Beijing now for no reason that is clear. Ditto Bombay and Mumbai. Marathon and Snickers. Caesar and Mr Dog. Latest in this long line of rebrandings is the replacement of the term 'nutter in the pub' with the more politically correct 'cryptozoologist'. Cryptozoologists believe that there's an enormous dinosaur in Scotland which has seemingly missed out on several mass extinctions which have occurred in the last sixty-odd million years. If that were to be the case, two other things would be true: first, the thing would have to be suffering from a serious eating disorder because there really aren't enough fish, Ryvita, or delicious nutritious shakes to support an animal of that size in Loch Ness; and second (assuming that we are looking at a family group rather than one immortal dragon), the creatures would by this time be more inbred than the population of the Scilly Isles and would have developed six heads, nine fingers and one of those silly yokel accents. Two words: 'Chinny' and 'Reckon'.

Lock-Ins

Twenty-four-hour drinking is all very well, but when it's legal to be drinking late, it's not half as fun as when it's not. Is there any finer moment in the life of a drinker than when the bell for the last orders has gone, but the landlord tips you the wink and allows you to stay on drinking behind closed doors? For one split second it's as if you've been transported back to prohibition America and you're in an illegal drinking den. Of course you're not, you're drinking watered-down lager in a shithole in Streatham, having to make small talk to the barman you don't really like but are pathetically grateful to for being allowed to stay on. But even so, the thrill of pulling one over the state and getting drunk at the same time remains.

Looking for CDs whilst Driving

If cars had black boxes like aeroplanes, what do you think their tapes would record in the seconds up to a crash? Oh my God, the gears are stuck? Why is the steering locked? What was that bang? If we're going to go, we're fairly sure our final words are more likely to be something along the lines of 'I'm sure that Arctic Monkeys CD is in the glove compartment somewhere . . .' Ordered people have all possible CDs laid out on the passenger seat next to them. We are not ordered people. Our CDs are in the door, the glove compartment, the back seat or on the floor. By the law of sod, whichever CD you want to listen to is the one that's just out of reach – leaving the driver with a dilemma: is it worth risking death to secure a quick blast of Kasabian? Probably not, but we both know you're going to give it a go anyway.

Losing on eBay

On the surface of things, eBay is a place to buy and sell items. Nothing more, nothing less. But subliminally it's a swirling tour through the subconscious of your already battered self-esteem. Your personal profile includes a section titled 'Items you have lost' – frozen in cyberspace for you to recriminate over. Because what it's really saying is: you have Lost; you are a Loser; LOSER! Naturally, the only way to soothe your shattered ego is to bid recklessly, wildly, on anything, whatever it takes, to WIN. Which explains the Elvis gnomes currently decorating your front garden . . . but, hey, at least you won. And after all, that's what counts.

Lost (Putting Up Fake Theories on Messageboards)

Is this cruel? We're not quite sure. It sure as hell is fun, though. As all those desperate nerds debate whether it's a dream or a snowstorm or an interruption in the space-time continuum, drag the Losties even further away from the truth (the writers are just making it up as they go along) with a few hokum theories of your own. Dress it up with a little bit of fake cred ('A friend of the writer told me this last week . . .'/'I found the shooting script in a bin and you'll never guess what it said . . .') and then give the messageboard both barrels. All I can say is, look for the frog in episode three. Go back on line a week later: we guarantee they'll still be discussing the amphibious implications.

Lost (Watching on Video to Skip Past the Endless Adverts)

How do you make a programme that lasts roughly forty minutes squeeze into a television schedule that requires a whole hour of transmission? Welcome to the world of excessive advertising. A world where some smart arse in a suit decides it is reasonable behaviour to put advert breaks into the programme *even before the opening credits have rolled*. A minute and a half of action (most likely a recap of the previous show's episode) and bang! another five minutes of Cillit Bang and Persil Automatic. We don't have to put up with this, and we won't. Record the programme, watch the blurred ads spin past on very fast forward in a matter of seconds, and enjoy the warm glow of both regaining twenty minutes of your life and sticking it to the man at the same time.

Lurking

There are many delightful activities that the Internet has delivered us over the years, from downloading your favourite TV programmes to having your credit card details stolen at the touch of a button. But perhaps no joy is better than lurking, the twenty-first-century equivalent of having a crossed phone line. Whether it's a chat room or a messageboard, why humiliate yourself by offering an opinion when you can sit there anonymously for hours, sitting in on what everyone else is saying until, with a leaving flourish, you finally reveal yourself – 'you are perhaps the dullest people I have ever come across. You know nothing about what you are talking about whatsoever.' It's bad, but it feels so good.

Lush Soap

Soap used to mean Carbolic (for schools and hospitals) and Pears or Simple Soap (for the home environment), although there were some maiden aunts who had that disgusting lavender soap, but luckily we didn't have to visit them very often. Soap was, pure and simple, something for getting dirt off your body – a purely functional product – but these days soap is sexy, sultry and up-for-anything. Visiting the Lush soap-erstores is a sensory delight and feels vaguely like you are entering a forbidden zone of self-indulgence and erotic sensuality. With soap names like Demon In the Dark, The Full Minty, Miranda, Rock Star and Ooh-La-La, all of which sound vaguely like adult films, bathtime has never been so much fun. Throw in a Ballistic bath ball or two and maybe even a MMM (Marshmallow Melting Moments) and it all feels like Willy Wonka has come over to scrub your back.

Lying About the Number of Boyfriends You Have Had

They always say a lady should never reveal her age but maybe there are other things best kept quiet about as well. . . . When you are all loved up and lying back in a post-coital bliss and the new boyfriend bravely says to you 'how many boyfriends have you had?', the implication is quite clear – what he means is 'how many men have you slept with and I hope I am the best' You are faced with a terrible dilemma – do you tell him the truth on both counts (i.e. I lost track at twenty and you're about average) and risk him getting very cross indeed, or lie as well as you can ('only two before you but they were boys and you are my first proper man') and risk him feeling that you are already planning the flowers and the seating plan. Either way, you are screwed.

M&S Pyjamas

Size 18. In blue. With a furry rabbit motif. It's the kind of look that would make Dita Von Teese choke on her nipple tassels. But, on the plus side, they're extremely comfy and act as the best contraceptive known to man.

Make-Up (Practice Runs)

While men can twiddle about with computers for hours, women like to mess around with make-up. Who knows what men think mending the hard drive will transform them into, but for women it's quite simple: that new blue Rimmel eye shadow will turn you into Kate Moss with one swift application. For a big event, the rule is your whole make-up routine has to be shaken up. A new look, a new image, an entirely new you – one who Select model agency will probably want to book – has to emerge from the innards of your make-up bag. This always involves a trial run, which will inevitably involve you strutting round the house looking like Siouxsie and the Banshees at a time when you're usually in bed with only an anti-wrinkle cream to protect your skin's dignity. The trial run is always an unmitigated success; ambitious, edgy, out-there, but ultimately deeply sexy. You are a supermodel-turned-rock-wife. On the night it's a different story. In the bright lights of seven o'clock, you look like Courtney Love in a serious drugs phase. Panic washing off of the offending face paint ensues. You look bare-faced and revolting, in an over-scrubbed way. But nothing some trusty old Elizabeth Arden brown eye shadow and a slick of Eight Hour Cream won't solve. Again.

Making Tea Upwards

It's like the concept of paying it forwards. But with bad karma. Well, except for your career. Making cups of tea for your boss, or anyone who holds a more senior position, isn't called sucking up any more, it's called a promotion initiative. Obviously, you don't make a round for the 'little people'. That would totally send out the wrong message. Pity the most junior member of staff who needs to brew up for hundreds in order to make tea upwards. Or worse, the MD, who can't even use the 'making a cuppa' excuse for a five minute skive. That *is* a glass ceiling.

Making Up Stories about How Your Train Was Late

Just occasionally, your morning ride into work might arrive at the time that it was meant to. But just because they've done their job properly for once doesn't mean that you should be inconvenienced into having to turn up to work on time. Your boss knows your train is shit. She's not expecting you for another fifteen to twenty minutes. We say: enjoy yourself. Use your bonus time to full effect – have yourself another coffee or second breakfast. And ready your line about 'points failure' for when you finally decide to rock up for duty.

Making Yourself Sneeze

There is something joyous about sneezing but even more so if you have made it happen deliberately. Sticking a cocktail stick or maybe even a key into one nostril and stimulating the hairs inside should do the trick. It is also good to try and beat your personal record – we are up to about forty in one sitting, and it feels good.

Male Mascara
Brandon Flowers from indie-rock band The Killers did it. As soon as he slapped on the mascara and eyeliner, and looked rather damn sexy as a result, the line between men and women did an involuntary back-flip. But wait a moment, just imagine: 'Eh, Frank, I've got you some Rimmel multi-lash to try when you've finished grouting those tiles.' And here's the problem, what's the point in hooking a whole generation of teenage girls on androgynous, adolescent boys who can sport face paint and look sexy, when those very same boys will grow into balding, beer-bellied blokes who look like a serial-killing tranny at the slightest hint of eye make-up? It's morally wrong to cruelly raise their expectations like that. So, if you're a skinny-hipped sex god, lay off the eyeliner. You girlfriend will only leave you when you grow up, the band doesn't work out and you're forced to re-train as a builder.

Marie Antoinette (the DVD)
You've watched it over twenty times, and even though you can't recount a single line, you've redecorated the bathroom in gold leaf, had a chandelier fitted in the airing cupboard and served a meringue fancy for supper.

Meet The Fockers
There is one defining moment in this 2004 sequel to the Stiller/De Niro vehicle *Meet The Parents* that makes you love it and hate it in equal measures. When De Niro's cat flushes Dustin Hoffman's cat down the chemical toilet you cringe at this predictable plot line and seen-it-all-before slapstick routine but actually all concerned play the scene with such sincerity and truth that it is side-splittingly funny. I suppose that's what you get when you cast proper actors – the same scene with Owen Wilson and Vince Vaughan and it would have gone for nothing.

Memory Sticks
Why is that floppy disks or CDs have never given us any sense of satisfaction but that latest gadget of data storage, the

memory stick, we can't get enough of? Is it the design – small, cute and eminently loseable? Is it the fact that you can get them to fit on your key ring? Is it the sheer number of porn videos, sorry, important documents, that you can get on to them? That's all a plus, but the real key, of course, is that ours has got a little flashing light on it when you slot it in the computer. Top banana – you can't beat that in our book.

Messageboards

You're an interesting person. You've got a lot to say. Some of the things you say might seem a bit controversial for the average dinner party or long-distance car journey, though. How are you going to get all of those politically revolutionary, socially controversial and frankly bloody fruity ideas out of your system? Of course! The magic of the Internet! Converse freely on a wide range of topics with people from across the globe, or more probably across the street. Godwin's Law, formulated by renowned Internet smart-alec Mike Godwin way back in the 1990s, states that 'As an online discussion grows longer, the probability of a comparison involving Nazis or Hitler approaches one.' What Mike fails to point out is that, long before anyone's mentioned Nazis, somebody else will have gone off at a tangent about Grange Hill, or which flavour Aero is best. And that's in a discussion about Bird Flu. Messageboards are, put simply, the best way to discover the opinions of overfed social inadequates like us.

Michael Winner

Well, yes, obviously he's an oleaginous old cheeseball, and he hasn't made a good film since. . . . well, candidly, he's *never* made a good film. But one look at him tells you he knows how to order a good dessert. We'd go out with him just for a bite of his profiteroles.

Michel Houellebecq (Re-reading the Porny Bits in)

Oh, come on. You can crack on that it's a literary novel to your mates in the Book Club, if you like, but they put those pictures of birds in their pants on the cover for a reason.

MILF

One of those acronyms it's best not to admit knowledge of in public. Short for Mother I'd Like to F***, the name designates a more mature form of sexual fantasy – a porn version of 'yummy mummy': 'cummy mummy', if you will. Basically, it's website shorthand for any model over the age of, well, about twenty-two – the bored housewife brought bang up to date for the twenty-first century. With the emphasis on the word bang.

Mineral Water

From all the fuss, you'd think that tap water had been re-classified as a grade A toxin. That taking one accidental sip would have you doing an Alexander Litvinenko. Really, with all the rogue agents attributed to the national water supply, it's a surprise you don't get home and find that the kitchen sink has been cordoned off with large yellow and red hazard signs stuck on your tumblers. Who's been spreading these nasty rumours? Well, the finger of suspicion has to point to mineral water suppliers. Because the solution to all your dehydration-induced problems comes in one handy bottle with a flip lid and a cleansing picture of mountains. At a quid a pop. So your poor, fragile little system might be saved. Just don't worry about the mountain of plastic bottles about to detonate the world.

Minty

A proper East End rough diamond, what makes Minty (of 3a Albert Square, E20) unique is the fact that he is covered from head to foot with an attractive greyish stubble. This ensures a thoroughly exfoliating experience for any girl lucky enough to be invited back to the kebab-strewn Playboy mansion he shares with his best pal, co-worker and frog-faced Dennis Waterman impersonator, Garry. Despite his apparent lack of ambition (he's a mechanic in Walford, where no one owns a car unless it's a cab they're about to be banned from driving), he seems to be worth a few bob. Certainly misguided Aussie gold-digger SJ took him for a few bob, rather than opt for West End bar work like every other Antipodean of marriageable age. Other than this secret trust fund, there really is nothing else right about him. Still, compared to everyone else in *EastEnders*, this great cuddly loofah of a man is an absolute dreamboat. More Minty, please!

Mobile Phone Games

Mobile phones are useful for many things. Ringing people up, obviously. Sending text messages. Storing all your addresses. Taking photos. Acting as an alarm clock when you're a dirty stop-out. What they're not useful for is playing games. That's just a distraction, and not a very good one at that. I mean, solitaire? We still can't figure out how that became a computer game freebie staple. Yet, somehow, when drawing up a shortlist of potential games, some bright spark must have said, 'Oh, what about solitaire? I've got that on my computer. It's great fun.' Well, indeed. But only if your definition of great is squinting at cards that even Ronnie Corbett would consider microscopic.

Monkey-Picked Tea

'Oh, I could murder a cuppa tea.' 'Let me see – we've got Earl Grey, P G Tips and Monkey Picked.' 'Sorry???.' 'Yeah – it's very rare Chinese tea and is picked by trained monkeys. No, really.' From our perspective, a nice fresh brew with just a hint of animal exploitation sounds a bit worrying, but actually, before you write in to complain, the monkeys enjoy the job and do get suitably rewarded for their labours. Just a passing thought, though – do they use humans dressed as monkeys to advertise it? See also **Weasel Coffee**.

Moobs

It's a national disaster – men are growing boobs. And like the horror of climate change, it's more than a storm in a D-cup. Apparently it's women taking the pill and inadvertently pumping female hormones into the water supply that's to blame. Let's not think of how that journey happens, because frankly it's way too gross, but suffice to say our continuing onslaught on the environment has created a metrosexual apocalypse. What's next? The builder coming round in a Wonderbra? Your husband sporting nipple tassels to 'spice things up'? Rugby players wearing sports bras? But before you can say 'nice pair of tits love', fear not – the poor lambs are losing their bitch tits to lipo. Just as well: how off-putting to sleep with someone with bigger, better boobs than your own.

More to Love
Sadly, that greedy, self-serving sentiment that sees you stick two fingers up to sharing is a fast track to planet fat. But, boy, was the journey fun.

More to Share (Dairy Milk)
More to Share! So reads the strapline on the bumper-sized Dairy Milk bars. Sod off. Make that more for me. There is no room for communism when it comes to chocolate. Sorry, comrades.

Motorcycles (Buying Them when You're Forty)
You'll never see thirty-five again, the mortgage is nearly paid off and, realistically, you've gone as far at work as you're ever going to get. It's time to dust off those dreams you had to give up fifteen years ago. Once you realize you *can't* have a drum kit, though, second prize is likely to be a motorcycle. All right, you don't exactly look like a young Marlon Brando in your leathers; in fact, you look more like a pile of well-filled binbags. That's hardly the point. It's the freedom of the open road, the feel of the wind in your teeth and the unaccustomed thrill of raw power between your thighs. In fact, by the time your wife has read a couple of cautionary articles about comatose born-again bikers in *Closer*, you will have actually ridden your shiny red Ducati a couple of times and realized how bloody terrifying the thing is. You'll probably be quite relieved when she makes you sell it back to the shop.

Moustache Waxing

Waxing your legs is like the manual labour of womanhood – necessary and non-descript. Waxing your bikini line is almost classed as exotic – it doesn't mean you've got a pubic-beard, but instead suggests that you're good in bed. And then there's the 'tache. If you're brunette, it makes you look like a lost member of the Village People, and if you're blonde, it glistens in the sun most unbecomingly. Whichever way, it's a guilty secret that has to be exterminated in utter secrecy. Because no man wants to think he's dating a woman who's half-human, half-beast. For maximum efficiency, do the hairy toes at the same time. Then pretend it never happened. Until the stubble grows. Aghhhh!

Mutton Dressed as Lamb

Which is the more pleasurable sight – a young, gorgeous twenty-two-year-old, or a forty-five-year-old trying desperately hard to dress like a gorgeous twenty-two-year-old? Time, as Martin Amis once said, goes about its immemorial work of making everyone look and feel like shit. Whether some people are in denial about this, or just feel like giving time a helping hand, we're not entirely sure. What we are sure about is that seeing what they're wearing makes you feel either a) smugly young, or b) smugly sensible for deciding on changing out of that dodgy outfit at the last minute.

My Monopoly

For a mere £79.95, those nice people at Waddingtons will deliver to your front door the ultimate in egotistical delights – a Monopoly game in which you decide the name on each and every square. You may see yourself as a Mayfair kind of chappie and your significant other as a Sloane Square girlie, you may decide that your favourite curry house deserves permanent inscription or you may simply wish to embarrass your nearest and dearest by inscribing in perpetuity their annoying little habits by christening a square 'Kevin's Porn Stash', 'Mum's dirty washing pile', 'Dad's favourite lap-dancing club' or 'Grandpa's flatulent underpants'. The possibilities are endless and it even comes in a lovely silver special edition box.

MySpace Shoot (Doing One)

Just as you mastered MSN, there was a new, cooler kid on the block. MySpace – the cyber community centre where Murdoch not only owns your soul, but also your dodgy pictures. The truth is, you only joined when the current zeitgeist delivered you a dinosaur warning via carrier pigeon, and you never planned to get as far as 'pimpin' up your page'. But here you find yourself, on a Sunday afternoon, pouting into the camera, wearing ridiculous white shades and pretending you weren't around when old rave was new. So try hard. So now.

Nasal Hair (Trimming)

What evolutionary pressure determined that as men get older they will need coarse black hair issuing from their nostrils and merging with their moustache hair until their entire upper lip comes to resemble a burst mattress? Women seem not to require this key survival adaptation, which is a shame, really, because they'd probably like having something else to trim, wax or (say it softly) pluck. Newcomers to nose hair ownership may experiment with poorly designed and potentially dangerous electronic appliances whirling like miniature helicopters in the nostril, but the experienced nasal barber always plumps for the small scissor for sheer accuracy. When that rare magical synchronicity occurs and you can get the nail scissors, sole occupancy of the bathroom and five minutes' peace all at the same time, having a bit of a rhinal tidy up is man's second most satisfying solitary pleasure.

Nathan Barley

It's supposed to be a parody of witless style magazine writers, but somehow working on the staff of *Sugar Ape* magazine seems like the best job in the world. Some people watch it for laughs. We watch it for career advice.

National Enquirer

If buying *heat* makes you feel slightly soiled then buying the *National Enquirer* is like catching herpes. The clue to the contents of the magazine is in the fact that it's (virtually) printed on toilet paper. But still, come the witching hour in Somerfield, your gaze will be inexorably drawn towards the cover. Reaching out and putting it in your trolley is almost like an out-of-body experience. Are you really doing it? Yes, but you can cite temporary insanity in court later. It was Jen's furious calls to Angelina that did it m'Lord. If you rearrange the letters of the coverline, it probably says 'buy me' as a subliminal subtext. The really gross bit happens when you get home. You sit on the sofa, read it *cover-to-cover* and *really* enjoy it. How do you feel afterwards? Like you accidentally went dogging on a first date. But with less class.

Navy SEALs

Michael Biehn, the bloke who punched a Terminator, and Charlie Sheen, The Kinkiest Man Alive™, together on the big screen for the first time. And, realistically, the last. This testoserone-enriched gunfest is routinely aired at around eleven o'clock when you know you *should* be getting your jim-jams on and saying your prayers but its power to mesmerize with sheer firepower endures beyond the second, nay the umpteenth viewing. Joanne Whalley-Kilmer's in it as well, if you like *girls*.

News Junkie (Being a)

Whether it's fifty-two or fifty-five people missing in a mudslide in Guatemala, tragic as it is, it means bugger all to your life. Still, it would be nice to know for certain. Unsatisfied by the regular TV news, you flip over to one of the rolling news channels that honestly doesn't know any more but they keep telling you the same five facts over and over again until they start to seem like old friends. Then, before you know it, you've signed up for text alerts. And having improper thoughts about Kirsty Wark. Then it dawns on you. You're hooked on news. Then you forget about that and start wondering if Teletext is still going.

News of the World

Otherwise known as *News of the Screws* or *Screws of the World*. This is a Sunday paper that ranks a celebrity's dogging scandal as more vitally important than, say, World War Three. Indeed, should a nuclear bomb ever explode, expect the news to be buried on page thirteen in really small type that most *NOTW* readers wouldn't understand anyway. Because, in the long run, the fallout from what Jude did with the nanny is far worse than what an atomic bomb could create. Taking this lead, Prime Minister's Questions should really focus on the crucial issues. Who cares about Iraq when a page three lovely 'allegedly' got roasted? We demand answers. And quite a lot of salacious detail. Now.

Newspaper Diaries

Out of all the regular components of your daily read, the newspaper 'diary' is perhaps the least distinguished. Normally run by the graduate trainee before they rise to the 'proper' job of being a journalist, they are the resting home of second-hand pieces of gossip overheard at parties, good old fashioned bitching and stories that the news editor nixed for lack of supportive evidence. Sort of *heat* for grown-ups, and all the better for it.

Nibbling Warts

We know that nibbling our warts is dangerous and every doctor would advise us against it. So, even if we derive huge entertainment from it, we will stop doing it from now on. No really.

Nicholas Hoult (Illegally Hot)

You know you're committing a crime when you close the curtains in order to watch Nicholas Hoult in teen sit-com *Skins*. The phrase 'my hasn't he grown' doesn't even *begin* to cover his startling transformation. Going from being the chubby twelve-year-old star of *About A Boy* to a sexy seventeen-year-old stud-muffin has, by default, placed the entire female population on the sex offenders register. In a way it's horrible, just as your entire repertoire of sexual fantasies are hanging off his newly chiselled cheekbones, you get a gruesome flashback to him as a cute'n'cuddly child in the days when urban-bachelor Hugh Grant still rocked your world. What's that noise at the door? Oops, it's the NSPCC. Just don't get jailbait-tourettes and tell them how sexy he is . . .

Nicknames

At school, in the same way that your uniform was there to be subverted, so your name, painstakingly chosen by your parents, was there to be shortened, squashed or plain ignored for the hilarious moniker of 'Lardy Arse' or 'Ginge'. But, unless you're a professional cricketer (who by law have to change their name to one with an 'ee' sound – Freddie, Hoggy, Harmy, etc.), what excuse in the adult world do we have for still persisting in calling each other by nicknames? You're right, we should probably grow up. Swot boy.

Nigella Lawson

The guilt comes from how transparently obvious it all is. Posh bird. Bit of a shape on her. Dresses like she knows it. Can cook. Does things with a well-buttered spear of asparagus that Dita Von Teese couldn't even imagine. It's every council type's dream, isn't it? For those fleeting moments between John Diamond's sad demise and her hooking up with Archie Saatchi or whatever his name is, every man in Britain stood ankle-deep in his own saliva.

1980s Brat Pack Films

Maybe the producers were high on hair-spray, or maybe a rogue shoulder pad had pushed them into the vortex of eternal brilliance, but back in the 1980s they could really relax you into a state of inertia – without inducing a sugar-induced coma. Films like *Bridget Jones* can only sob into their cheese-addled scripts at the pure genius of giants like *The Breakfast Club*, *St Elmo's Fire*, *Pretty in Pink* and *About Last Night*. In a stroke of pure cinematic (OK, DVD) Viagra, you can learn about life, love and how to wear leg-warmers with a batwing jumper, whilst marvelling at what gravel-voiced Demi Moore can do with her eyebrows.

Nintendo Wii

When you find yourself in your pyjamas standing in front of your TV and a gleaming white box of Japanese electronics at 6.00 a.m. on Christmas morning with a sleek wireless controller strapped to your wrist controlling a computer-generated cartoon version of yourself playing tennis against your son (who is standing next to you similarly garbed) then you know that you've got it bad. Simply put, the Nintendo Wii is the Holy Grail of consoles and well worth pretending to work at the office whilst secretly pressing F5 constantly on your keyboard in an attempt to secure one of them in the seven minute window of opportunity on Amazon before they sold out. Imagine how bad that would be – you might actually have to do something else . . . like go to the park and play . . . um . . . tennis with your son.

Nipple Tassels

Well, it really is the icing on the cake. Nowadays we even have to accessorize our breasts. And master the skill of making the critters planted on them twirl round. Then there's what colour to choose. Red sequins can make the whole area look a bit, well, sore, whilst whip on a pair of black 'uns and it looks like rigor mortis has set in. It's hardly practical either, not like say, a Chloe Paddington, which is decorative but actually carries things around. No, nipple tassles are a hard and unlucrative look to work. Try them on your husband and he'll think you've gone mad, try them on a new man and chances are he'll think you're a hardened hooker and run a mile. The only bonus is, you can use them to block the sink when the plug goes astray.

Noel Edmonds (Self-Help)

It's hard to believe that Noel Edmonds, the man who brought us Mr Blobby, has now been entrusted with the spiritual enlightenment of the masses, David Icke-style – but in beige slacks. You'd think the 'rebirth' of his career with *Deal Or No Deal* was down to the nadir of television programming in the late noughties. But no. It's down to cosmic ordering. A kind of catalogue service for the universe. You simply place an order for something you want – a car, a boyfriend, George Clooney on Viagra with a sex addiction problem – and, hey presto, the FedEx of fairyland wings it over to you. Weirdly, this hasn't resulted in a 100 per cent success rate for *Deal Or No Deal* contestants. But it has made Guru Edmonds filthy rich. Guess they must have processed his form first.

Non-Egg Eggs

The most wholesome and complete food imaginable: fresh from the wrong end of a chicken and perfectly packaged for easy use. Unfortunately, it's not the original product that's under discussion here, so much as its key spinoff brands: the Easter egg, a hollow ovoid of poor quality chocolate tightly bound in tinfoil that is just itching to get on to your back teeth and make a crude battery out of your fillings; the Scotch egg, a hand-held gala pie that's constructed of equal parts of mechanically reclaimed pork residue and bread-free breadcrumb (albeit with a microscopic quail egg lodged at its centre); and, of course, the Ben-Wa Love Egg, the housewife's friend that makes the quotidian grind of housework fly by with its joyful vibration. A proper egg may be all very well when you're making a nice fry-up, but if you want oral electricity, the ideal real ale companion or some afternoon delight, the egg impostors are your best friends.

Non-Iron Shirts

The concept seems almost too good to be true. It is. Not, of course, that it stops you from casting all your fashion opinions to one side in order to buy a truly hideous work number that will spare you the grief of digging out the ironing board on Sunday night. Perhaps the phrase 'non-iron' refers to the lack of metal in the fabric? Because, as far we can see, they still come out of the washing machine pretty creased. Still, having paid your money, you're damned if you're going to actually iron the thing. A quick hold up to the light, a quick check of the label – it says it's non-iron, therefore I must be imagining those creases – and it's job (not) done. Just notice, gentlemen, that they don't try and pull this marketing con on the ladies.

Not Getting Up Till after Lunch
There is something about the British work ethic that means that even on weekends some people can feel a little guilty if one lies in to, say, after 9.00 a.m. You amateurs! We suggest that if you want to feel really guilty then try spending a day pretending to be a teenager all over again – get out of bed at about 1.00 p.m., stagger to the pub for a liquid breakfast and a huge fry-up, amble back in time to fall asleep under the *News of the World* in front of *EastEnders* and then stay up all night playing video games, smoking roll-ups, having sex and fighting. After all that you won't be able to look yourself in the face again. 9.00 a.m.? You muppet.

Not Keeping New Year's Resolutions
Making New Year's Resolutions are a total waste of time and they never last beyond 4th January (a bit like diets, battery operated toys and relationships that started in an Essex bar on New Year's Eve), but they are fun to dream up. In fact, maybe 2008 will be the year we stop writing whimsical humour-driven books aimed at a market of people unable to commit to a product that demands extending a four-second attention span into something that will assimilate a narrative arc and a coherent momentum . . . or maybe it won't.

Not Reacting in the Way People Expect
This, if perfected right, can annoy the bejeezus out of people. There was one boyfriend of mine who dumped me after

explaining in great detail why the relationship wasn't working and analyzing in great detail all my faults. He explained why, as a result of all of this stuff, yaddah, yaddah, yaddah, we shouldn't go out anymore. Although I was totally gutted, I just smiled and said, 'Oh well – I am not going to try to change your mind – I am sure you are right. Hope it all works out well for you.' No tears, no trembling voices, no pleading words demanding another chance to make it better – just reasoned understanding. God it made him mad. Works in all sorts of situations and is never less than blinding.

Not Remaining Seated Till the Plane Has Stopped Taxiing

We are all familiar with the plaintive cry of the stewardess, 'Could passengers please keep all electronic devices switched off and remain seated until the plane has stopped taxiing and the seatbelt signs have been extingiushed?' Er, no. Surely what they mean to say is 'As soon as the plane has shown any signs of approaching the terminal please can all passengers frantically fire up their BlackBerries and start checking messages and then immediately jump up and start rummaging around in the overhead lockers so they can perhaps force their way off the plane thirty seconds earlier than they would otherwise have done?'

Not Waiting for the Train to Leave the Station

You don't see this sign around much any more but, when you did see it, bossily placed over the flush mechanism, it was quite clearly a red rag to the bull. The trick was not just to flaunt it and allow your bodily fluids and excreta to cascade from the bowels of your train, but to choose your target very carefully. If you had a maiden aunt at Woking who bored you with stories of the Boer War on never-ending Sundays then flush as you approach her local station.

Novelty Pens

You're in a new Prada suit, trapped in a 1980s career girl time-warp, pretending that the whole downshifting revolution never happened. You're even wearing designer glasses, looking over the rims at the spreadsheets in a super-intelligent manner. You cut into someone's speech to make an acutely observed comment, and suggest a well-thought-out action plan. Everyone nods in admiring agreement and reaches for their pens to note it down. You reach in your pocket and then, by mistake, you pull out your favourite novelty pen. The one you bought on a boozy hen night. The one that has a mini naked man inside it. The one whose member increases exponentially to the angle of the pen. To record your moment of brilliance will mean at least a semi on his behalf. Nice work.

Nu Rave

When rave rebooted for the noughties, the whistle posse almost had our ears off. Trend predictors were getting their day-glo knickers in a right old twist about the rediscovery of dance. The kind you need to bosh three Es to enjoy. It would be like the summer of love all over again. But sponsored by *NME* this time. With souvenir T-shirts. And none of those nasty new-age traveller types holding free parties in fields. So what do we get instead? Neon leggings and a few middle-class white boys playing guitars their mummies bought them, accessorised with smiley faces and glow sticks. Come back The Shamen, all is forgiven.

Ogling

Any fashion student will tell you that the focus of male attention shifts every ten years or so: 50s, sweater girls, breasts; 60s, mini skirts, legs; 70s, dolly birds, melons again; 80s, bloody rah rah skirts, of all things, legs (albeit with legwarmers). And so on and so on. You can trace it back as far as Edwardian Gibson Girls or forward as far as the Urban Nudists you can see on every modern street. Honestly, we don't care. We'll look at *anything*. It's in our genes or something. We can't help it. We can't walk past New Look if they're changing the clothes on the dummies. So our message is this: girls, don't try too hard. You had us at hello.

Old School Reports

When you are grown-up, you can be very selective about how you expose your strengths and weaknesses to the world and you can become perfectly skilled at refocussing any situation to paint yourself in a better light. You can also look back on your schooldays with an equally selective manner and imagine yourself doing rather well at everything. Imagine the shock, then, when you go home one weekend and your mum hands you a large brown envelope, saying, 'We thought you might like these old school reports.' Imagine the horror when you start reading them and realize you were crap at English, pissed around in Maths and came bottom in French, along with having severe psychological difficulties which the school were considering getting outside specialist help to contain. From this pit of despondency, though, one happy thought sparks and catches fire – you are reading these reports from the comfort of a fulfilling well-paid job with a loving family around you, lots of friends and a life full of variation and stimulation, whereas the majority of the teachers who penned these barbed reports are still at the same school.

Organic Food Stores

Get this straight, you've not just walked into Planet Organic – you've walked into a whole new parallel universe of wellness. Just browsing the mung bean section will probably lead to instantaneous cell rejuvenation. By the time you're at the organic, wheat-free muesli section, you're virtually waltzing with wellbeing. Unlike other, down-market supermarkets, there are no stressed mums attacking you with their psycho-prams. No. Instead there are enlightened yoga teachers smiling beatifically at you as they waft past the 'how to build a yurt' book display. Funnily enough, for all the health foods available for purchase, you end up with a super-large bar of Green & Black chocolate and a litre of fairtrade wine. That's all right, though, organic, innit?

Original Features

Why do we all hanker after original features when viewing properties? Maybe it is the influence of the sublime Kirsty, Phil and Sarah Beany, or maybe just that we were all brought up in Victorian or Edwardian housing stock and want to replicate this sense of order and restrained design in our own homes? Whatever the reason, there is something rather satisfying (and dare we say a little bit sexy) about a well stripped combination of intact floorboards, skirting board, dado, picture rail and cornicing – not to mention the more 'specialist' tastes, for the discerning couple, of your corbels, your ceiling roses and your marbles surrounds. And let's leave all talk of the corbels, the butler's sinks and the dumb waiters before we come all over unnecessary on you and start applying for Grade II Listed status.

Owning a Guitar

Hey, look at me – I'm cool, I'm creative, I can fit into skinny jeans. Probably. Hell, I might even go on tour one of these days. You know, when I learn to play it. There's nothing more symbolic of an anarchic, rock'n'roll free spirit than the humble guitar, which is why having one gratuitously propped up in a prime location in your room is essential. Just make sure you hide the untouched 'Beginners Guide to Guitar Playing' manual. *You* know you're more David Brent than Pete Doherty, but you don't want to spoil your 'cred' and announce it to the rest of the world.

Parking in the Toddler Zone at the Supermarket when Your Toddler is Thirteen

We have all done it – cruised around the car park in vain at the MegaSuperStore in the pouring rain looking for a space that isn't half a mile away from the store, and then cruised around again in the hope the situation had changed and, each time we go round, our eye is caught by the pristine line of empty spaces for Toddler and Child right by the door. But, alas, your child is a recalcitrant teenager sitting in the back playing on a PS2 and shouting along to Eminem so, like a good citizen, you keep going and silently regret not having borrowed next door's toddler. But then something happens – each time you go round (with the rain getting heavier and heavier) your resolve weakens and, by the fifth time, you think SODDIT, swerve into the space and leg it into the store without so much as a backward glance. Of course, if it isn't raining and there are plenty of spaces just a few rows away then we would never do this . . . ever. Um.

Parking

What do you do when you see a spaceman? Park in it, man. What do you do when you see a space woman? Drive on until you find a bigger space that you might possible have a chance of getting in to. Boom, and if you must, boom.

It is a truth universally acknowledged that the larger the man's level of testosterone, the smaller the gap he feels capable of getting in to. No matter if the space is shorter than the car: that's not physically impossible, that's a challenge. Some men feel that unless the space is so tight they have to get in and out via the sun roof, they're not really trying. Do remember: should the unthinkable happen and you bump bumpers, resist the temptation to blame your partner's directions. That is, unless you don't mind them shouting 'it's because I've been told *this* is twelve inches' across the multi storey.

Parrot

(**Shaggy Dog Story** continued) . . . Now the Parrot had been round the world so many times on the cruise ship that he had seen Raymondo's magic routine more times than he cared to mention. And the parrot, who couldn't help himself, would sit on his perch and give away how each trick was done. *It's up his sleeve,* he'd squawk. *The Queen of Hearts! Look in his pocket!* Raymondo, who was not used to being upstaged, would come up with new magic tricks, but the parrot, who had seen everything, would always know how he'd done it, and would squawk out the secret. Anyway, one day the ship hit an iceberg . . . See **Iceberg**.

Partworks

'First issue £2.99!', they shout. Then, very quietly indeed, 'normal price £9.99'. Week by week, it builds into an impressive mouldering pile of magazines in the corner of your sitting room. Ahh, the Partwork: with a bit of cruddy plastic on the front which – we are assured – will one day form part of a scale model Saturn V rocket. Or a steam train. It doesn't matter much either way. You're not going to buy all of them. Just enough to earn you a withering look from your wife when she does the maths and figures out that collecting every single Police Academy DVD with a magazine glued to the case is going to set you back close to £300, while buying a box set of them at the supermarket probably won't cost much more than a tenner. Charles Dickens used to publish his books like that, you may be mildly bored to hear. Not with a scale model of an Aston Martin on the front, you understand, just a chapter at a time. We thought of doing this book like that but we couldn't think of anything to stick to the cover. Yes, we considered the thing you're thinking of but apparently WHSmith won't allow it.

Paying Bills Late

We hate bills. Well, of course we do, who doesn't? But this isn't the place to get us going about how we've spent £30 quid on calls but somehow BT has managed to sting us for just under one hundred smackers. No, this is the place to tell you about the joys of paying bills late. Firstly, it gives you control back – I'm not at your beck and call, British Gas, I'll pay when I feel like it (i.e. when I get paid). Secondly, it gives an otherwise mundane task a thrill – will it be the reminder this time? Can I last out till the final notice? Relive your student days with threats of being cut off and bailiffs coming round to beat you up. Laugh uproariously as the bailiffs do turn up and you tell them, 'It's all right, I can pay, I just can't quite be arsed.' Watch as the bailiffs laugh back and take your plasma TV. Ah. Maybe we should have done the direct debit thing after all?

PDAs

There are many weapons within a woman's armoury, but none is more effective than a public display of affection, or PDA for short. Everyone hates a PDA, of course, which is exactly the reason for doing them. If you ever feel like you'd like a little bit more space on the bus or tube, then they're almost foolproof. As a way of warning other women off your man, they work wonders. But best of all is the effect it has on your loved one – any time he shows interest in another woman, give him a snog to remind him whose he is. The rule of thumb is simple: the more he is pissing you off, the more you affectionate you become –

hugging, kissing, squeezing, saying 'I love you' in that squeaky, scary voice. Five minutes of that on a crowded train and he'll never be rude about your mother again.

Peeing in the Back Garden

This is a primal act best performed when legitimately out watering the garden – we particularly enjoying standing behind a strategically placed rosebush (although, obviously, not too close) and holding the hose in one hand and the . . . well you get the picture now, OK? Peeing outside has a freedom about it almost unparalleled and also allows one not have to worry about toilet-seat splashback, although, before closing, one should remind you of Confucious' saying, 'A wise man never pees into the wind.'

Peeing in the Sink

The fairer sex may carp, but then they've never had to deal with the writhing menace of a penis under pressure. After a fine night on the grog, with bladder pressures reaching an estimated 4,000,000 psi (estimated by drunken scientists), the comparatively short range marksmanship required of an in-sink micturator is a significantly more approachable challenge than the tricky long yellow of the traditional method. Once you've been tempted by the late night practicality of the sink method, it's a short hop to daytime sink-pissing. You can hook the little lord over the edge of the sink, leaving you hands-free for other vital bathroom activities like cleaning your teeth, or reading a book or something. You could go for a little practice now, actually.

Peeling Sunburnt Skin Off

It is almost worth getting sunburnt and going through all the agony that it entails just for the pure joy of peeling bits of your skin off afterwards – this is an illicit pleasure best carried out with a mate (in an almost gorillas picking fleas off each other way!) so those nice long strips of skin can be lovingly unpeeled from your back. Obviously the best way to end this would be to eat the skin, but maybe you are having dinner while you read this so we wouldn't dream of suggesting it.

Period Pants
In a world where women are expected to wear a sequined, crotchless thong just to put the rubbish out, there is no greater pleasure than that time of month when you can put your 'out of order' sign up. The dirty secret of your underwear drawer rises to the surface in all its grey, misshapen glory: the Big Pants. Quite frankly, if you can't tuck them under your armpits, you bring shame on womankind and the wonder of the curse. Getting the colouring right can be quite a feat – at least 897 boil washes to get that dishcloth look. But most important is the cut – they must intersect your thigh at the thickest point, and your belly at the most bloated curve. The Period Pant is essentially nature's way of making sure nothing unnatural happens.

Personal Ads in the *Guardian Guide*
All those single, brainy liberals. None of them with a shag. If the *Guardian Guide* small ads were a nightclub, it would be the best one on earth. As it is, though, it's just a terrific place to play 'what if . . .' when you've read the very funny bit about adverts and the film reviews but you don't want to read Charlie Brooker yet because you're saving that for last.

Personalized Number Plates
Walking up a street (sorry 'avenue') in Hampstead one day and seeing a Porsche hove into view with the numberplate NOT 1 swiftly followed by a second identical Porsche with the numberplate BUT 2 made us think that these things really really matter to some people. No matter how rich you are, you always want one extra way of telegraphing to the world that you are actually a little bit richer than the next person – a personalized number plate is a great way of doing this, although of course it does also send out the

message that you have no taste at all, but one suspects we have slightly different ideas of taste to 'those' kind of people. That said, can anyone honestly say that their eyes haven't wandered to those ads for personalized number plates in *The Sunday Times* Motoring Section, purely for fun, to see what they might have to pay for something fitting to their name or job or hobbies? LOS3R.

Pet Blogs

Honestly, they blog themselves. With their little paws. So desperate are they to share news of their day and their deepest most existential angst, they can fire up an iBook just with a flick of a furry tail. 'Woke up. Used the litter tray. Had a wash. Ate some Whiskas. Went back to sleep. For ten hours.' Ooh look, Tabitha the Tabby from next door just posted a comment: 'Just off for a nap. Had a nasty incident with a furball earlier, lol.' ARE YOU MAD? We know you love your pet, but blogging on his behalf is a step too far. It must stop now.

Pete Doherty

Millions of men have asked themselves this one question, over and over again. What does millionaire hottie Kate Moss see in poorly groomed Conference League pop monkey Pete Doherty? It's simple when you know his secret: he's a lightweight. He carries about as much cocaine around with him as the Prince of Wales does. He just pretends to do drugs because he thinks, in the adolescent dimness that afflicts a lot of no-mark musicians, that it makes him look Rock'n'Roll. It wouldn't, even if he did take loads of drugs. It would make him look council: coke used to be the recreational intoxicant of the glitterati about twenty-five years ago but now dustmen do it. It's about as groovy as Kerry bloody Katona. That's beside the point, though: if little Pete did have as much gear as he pretends to, he'd have been sent down for a ten-stretch years ago instead of just constantly getting community service for wasting police time getting caught smoking nutmeg and banana skins behind the bike sheds. So what does Kate see in him? The same thing we all see in Private Pike when we watch *Dad's Army*. He's a sad little boy who thinks he's tough but really just needs a cuddle. Or a slap, we can't decide . . .

Photoshop

Adobe Photoshop is the premier image-editing application for graphics professionals. It is also the premier image-editing application for unscrupulous internet dating enthusiasts. In February 2007 Adobe announced a free web-based version with all the tooth-whitening cheek-slimming hairline-filling power of its £400 bigger brother. Make sure you're wearing a red carnation, because no one's going to recognize you from our picture.

Pigs

Some animals we're not really that bothered about. Sheep, cows, donkeys, so what? But give us a field full of snout-nosed snortlers and we can't help ourselves. Pigs are cute, pigs are funny, pigs need to be greeted with a squeal of 'Piiiigs!' whenever you see one. Big ones, little ones, it doesn't matter – they're all brilliant. Piiiiiigs! And, yes, so we may end up eating them in a variety of different and delicious ways, but that doesn't detract from the sheer joy of shouting Piiiiiiiiiiigs!

Pink iPods

If you get caught listening to your gym playlist on a pink iPod, you might as well change your name to Jordan and swear undying love to Peter Andre.

Pink Tool Box

One of the biggest sellers on the high street for Christmas 2006 was the pink tool box – packed full of everything you are ever likely to use around the 'home, car or boat' – it looks like a Barbie accessory but is actually full-size. Clever that. Obviously designed by a man as a joke, but will look good gathering dust on the top of a cupboard somewhere until it can be conveniently 'lost' in the doorway of an Oxfam shop a little way away.

Planning which Relatives to Ignore when You Win the Lottery

With odds in excess of 20,000,000 to 1 AGAINST you ever winning something worth arguing over in the lottery, this is a total waste of time as a game but, then again, so is voting Liberal Democrat, but people still do it. It is best to start with a nice round number (we find £10,000,000 works very well indeed) and then start chipping away at it – £2 million for a London house, £1 million for a country house, £5 million to invest and £½ million for personal treats, leaving £1.5 million to use to break your extended family apart with squabbling, in-fighting and hatred. Perfect. Start with some real reasons for NOT giving people any share of your spoils (Auntie Marjorie is richer than Croesus and always gave me only a chocolate orange for Christmas, Uncle Leo owns four BMWs and three houses) and then move on to more spurious and much more fun excuses for creating disharmony (your brother once spat on your head from the top of a treehouse, your cousin has a fat pet, your nephew looks like Shrek in a certain light and your next-door neighbour still has that stepladder you lent him last Easter).

Playing Buzzword Bingo During Important Meetings

The only way to enliven meetings (other than release an oiled pig under the table during A.O.B) is to collude with a few select colleagues and have a good old game of Buzzword Bingo. For the unitiated, all you need to do is to visit our nice friends at http://isd.usc.edu/~karl/Bingo, download a randomly generated bingo card and take it with you to your next meeting. Mark the buzzwords as you hear them (or, better still, say them yourself!) remembering, of course, that the BINGO square is a free square. If you get five in a row (up, down, diagonally), shout 'Bingo!'. You've won! Typical words might include buy-in, spearhead, win-win, client-focused, fudge factor and something unlikely like extra-virgin olive oil. Of course you might get fired for shouting 'Bingo!' when you should be concentrating on the Chairman's end of year statement, but at least you leave the room as a winner.

Playing Spot-the-Tranny

Our mothers always told us not to laugh at other people's appearance, but we don't live at home any more and hopefully they won't be reading this volume so that's OK then. Let's leave aside the whole complex psychological reasons as to why men decide they want to live their lives (or part of their lives) dressed as women, and let's zoom in on why they dress so badly. There is a man who gets on the 8.08 every morning from a certain South London station (OK – Sydenham) who obviously thinks he looks the business and is convinced that he has integrated into society seamlessly. When he is standing in front of his mirror he sees Marilyn Monroe's hair, Keira Knightley's delicate features, Julia Roberts' shoulder-blades, Scarlett Johannson's cleavage, Beyoncé's tummy, Kate Moss's bum and Jane Russell's legs – all dressed up in Versace's finest frock and Mr James Choo's cutest shoes. What we see on the platform (in the brief seconds we glance his way before hiding behind our *Metro* stiffling our giggles) is a fat man with inch-thick pancake makeup with Julie Goodyear's hair, Les Dawson's face, Mr Incredible's shoulders, Dick Emery's cleavage, Jade Goody's tummy, Matt Lucas's bum and Jocky Wilson's legs – all dressed up in an old pair of flowery curtains. And that's on a dress-down Friday.

+1 Channels

Television scheduling for lazy people, we can only salute the likes of Channel 4 for spunking what must be expensive and limited channel space by reshowing programmes we couldn't quite get round to watching an hour earlier. Missed the repeat of *Friends* at 8.00 p.m.? Watch it again at 9.00 p.m. on E4+1. We worry that, in time, we're going to become so lazy that even an hour is not going to be enough, and E4+1+1 will have to be introduced. But we worry more that someone might decide to try to shake us out of our lethargy by replacing E4+1 with E4−1, to give early bird types a head start on what is going to be shown an hour later. So enjoy it while it lasts, and don't concern yourself with the biggest dilemma of all: E4+1. Is that E5?

Poker Night

Don't know the rules? Don't worry, nor does anyone else. As a game, poker is an impenetrable code only understood by friendless sociopaths. As an excuse to get a bunch of the lads round and smoke cigars until the Glade plug-in admits defeat, it is without peer.

Porn Movies, Watching the Free Five Minutes when Staying at a Hotel

We don't know who first came up with the idea of putting porn movie channels in a hotel, but, by goodness, they must have been mighty chuffed at their genius. For us, the free porn sample is right up there with the free biscuits as one of the perks of staying away. As soon as you get into your room, it is all but compulsory to switch your TV on and flick through to see what channels you've got: BBC1, BBC2, ITV, Channel 4, Channel 5 – oh that's not working, no change there – Sky News, Movie One, Movie Two, Movie *Porn*. Here is where a real hotel connoisseur comes into their own – establishments generally allow the passing flicker a one or two minute view for free, before adding the movie to the bill. The trick is to get as much of a free eyeful as you can, without overstepping the mark and thus (not) enjoying the moment when accounts ask why they're being asked to pay for 'Cum on Eileen 3'.

Porn Names

Who would have thought that what you decided to call your cat when you were four would come back to haunt you so many years on? But it is pretty much a given that, whether we are talking university or office, sooner or later someone is going to ask you what your porn name is. And if yours is Fifi Algernon, it's not going to make you sound sexy in front of the opposite sex. We're not sure if real porn stars get their porn names from combining the name of their pet with their middle name, but, put it like this, there's not many cats and dogs round our way called Krystal, Jenna or Faith.

Porn Stars, Exposing More of a Knowledge of in Public Than is Advisable

We're not really aware of what pornography is. We know it's something that other people might indulge in behind closed doors, but with no personal experience of it ourselves, we are not really in a position to comment. That, at least, is the line to take when your girlfriend is about. When you want to rile her, however, or when some other bloke is lording his feminist credentials, why not drop into the conversation a morsel of knowledge that only an intimate acquaintance with the Madame Palm material can produce? 'Who's this floozy?' asks someone, waving round a copy of *heat* magazine. 'Oh, that's Olivia O, she's trying to go mainstream after her starring role in Cumming Up 17.' You might want to thank irritating bloke for burning you the DVD at this point. (By the way, we made up Olivia O, rather than being stupid enough to namecheck a real porn queen like Briana Banks or Kyla Cole.)

Power Girl

Few of us continue to read superhero comics into adulthood. Those who do tend to be conspicuously nourished gentlemen who wear big hats and a great deal of black clothing. If they have girlfriends at all, they will inevitably date Rubenesque Goths. The comic reader does not dream of settling down with an alt-rock Dawn French, though. Oh no. He dreams of shacking up with Power Girl. With its all too frequent cosmic cataclysms and Stalinist revisionism, very few heroes survive for long in the DC universe. Those who do last tend to be the major stars that even men *without* a Terry Pratchett hat have heard of: Superman, Batman, Aquaman and a couple of other guys. Oh, and Power Girl. One look at a Power Girl comic will tell you why the DC staff love to draw her, and the fanboys keep buying her stuff. Imagine, if you will, Pamela Anderson. Now imagine she can fly. And beat you up. Feeling a bit fruity? Yes? Better buy a big hat.

Practising Your Signature

We don't expect anyone under the age of twenty to understand this entry but, just in case they are interested, let's start with the basics. Are you sitting comfortably? Great – let's begin. In the olden days – or B.C. (Before Computers or Before Chip and PIN) – people used to have to use PENS (Google Images will help you out here) to SIGN official documents and pay for stuff in shops by signing cheques. Cheques? Oh, please just try to keep up and I can go into detail later on. Anyway – part of being about ten years old was cottoning on to the fact that grown ups had something unique called a SIGNATURE that they scribbled on pieces of paper, and so most ten-year-olds started to cover sheets and sheets of paper trying to design their own signature that was, at once, cool/different/striking and noteworthy. The insides of desks, exercise books, the torn flap of wallpaper down the side of the bed, even the painted tiles in the upstairs loo, were all fair game for scrawling your name until you hit on the one that worked for you. That is all fine and dandy when you are ten, eleven, twelve even, but when you are in your late thirties and still experimenting with a signature makeover that maybe incorporates a comical little smiley face or an extra ambivalent loop under the 'n' or above the 't' then that is really sad. But fun.

Pretending Something Was in the Sale (When it Wasn't)

You can never have enough clothes but actually some blokes find it difficult to understand that and begin to resent their ever-decreasing wardrobe space as your clothes start encroaching on to their territory. Not only do they resent the space all our wonderful clothes take up but also they begin to hate the cost of it all. One great way to defuse this is to be very economical with the truth when it comes to any close questioning about such irrelevancy as the cost. If you can get away with saying 'it came from that smart Oxfam shop in Kensington High Street and was only a fiver' then you are better liars than we are but we admire your gall: but, otherwise, maybe just reply in a slightly disconnected manner, 'you wouldn't believe how much it was in the sale'. A clever answer this, because it doesn't actually say you bought it in the sale if you read it very carefully. It could actually mean 'I paid the full price of £200 but (here goes) . . . you wouldn't believe how much it was in the sale . . . yeah, 40 quid. I was robbed'. Works every time, though.

Pretending to Be Blind

Taking a route you know really well (beginners could try from their bedroom to the kitchen) and doing it with your eyes shut is a laugh-out-loud challenge. Probably not so laugh-out-loud if you try the advanced technique and start introducing street furniture and busy roads to cross but still a terrifiyingly good value way of kick-starting your day without caffeine.

Pretending to Be Out when You Are in

There are, of course, genuine occasions when answering the door is impossible or ill-advised – when you are naked, in the bath or dressed in your wife's little black dress to name but three – but we want to concern ourselves with those occasions when you just can't be arsed and decide to hide like a child and hope it all goes away. Situations like your Mum and Dad arriving on a suprise visit, a Jehovah's Witness in search of new souls or just a group of paparazzi and the Porn Squad asking you to help them with their enquiries. Don't make the mistake of twitching curtains or peeking through the letter-box before hiding (that is for amateurs) – our best advice is to just run upstairs very quietly, peep out from the spare bedroom and then, if you don't like what you see, just do something manly like hide under the bed until it all goes away. With a lampshade over your head.

Pretending to Like Your Colleague's New Haircut

As your colleague walks in after a lunchtime salon appointment looking like David Blunkett has styled her hair while wearing boxing gloves, you must stop choking into your baguette, put on your loveliest smile and say 'wow – it looks even better than I dared think!' Everyone one wins – she sees you as a supportive loving friend and you can have a great laugh later when she next leaves the room. Of course the downside is that, in the Emperor's New Clothes environment of most friendships, she has probably lied through and through about everything from how attractive your new boyfriend is to how nice your new haircut is.

Pretending to Listen

If someone is recounting some seemingly boring story to you at length, it is very easy to switch off and to get caught out when they ask you for a reaction or an opinion at the end of their monologue. There is, of course, a way round this – it is all a question of interjecting the right number of 'ahhs', 'mms' and 'I see what you means' into the mix. You may even have to listen every now and again to at least maintain the gist of what is going on if not the actual detail. If you get asked anything then we suggest you use catch-all phrases such as 'Yes it is a tricky one', 'Gosh – I don't know what to say' or, in extremis, 'Can you just run that last bit by me again?' Good luck . . . um . . . sorry we drifted off a bit then. What were we talking about?

Pretending You Can't Work the Washing Machine

When the little lady can't work the video, or a car or a zip, we're always there with a helping hand and a patronizing quip. That big white thing in the kitchen, though, it's terrifying: there are two dials! It's got water in it! Everybody knows that electricity and water Do Not Mix. Plus sorting out all the different coloured pants is a bit boring. Best leave that one to the Mrs.

Pretending You Haven't Eaten (When You Have)

We like food. If you've read some of the other entries, you might even get the sense that we like it rather too much. Yet however one likes ones food, sometimes you have to go the extra mile to get that extra portion. 'I would offer you some, but I suspect you've already eaten,' says a late-rising friend with a vat of scrambled eggs. 'Oh no,' you reply, subtly wiping the crumbs and tomato ketchup from your mouth, 'I only had time for a coffee.' At this point, of course, the friend knows you're lying, but, really, is he going to call you out? 'Right, well then,' he'll say, bitterly, 'grab a plate.' Just don't make the fatal error of saying, 'Oh don't worry about a clean one, I'll use mine from earlier.'

Pretending You Never Got the Email

'Bloody computer. It's been playing up for days, you claim. 'It's this firewall, it's gone mad,' you swear. 'Must have gone straight to junk mail by accident,' you argue. Funnily enough, as you make your excuses you actually start to believe that you are at the receiving end of a massive IT conspiracy. Then you remember. Oh yes, that's the message I opened the other week and couldn't be bothered to reply to. Oops. But really, there's nothing more annoying than having your inbox bothered by every casual acquaintance you've ever traded email addresses with. When will people realize: giving out an email is the equivalent of saying don't call us, we'll call you.

Pretending You've Eaten (When You Haven't)

We like food. If you've read some of the other entries, you might even get the sense that we like it rather too much.

However, even for us, there are occasions when we really don't want to take a knife and fork to what is about to be put down in front of us. It might be because we're on a diet (if you'd eaten what we've written about in the other entries, you'd want to diet too): it might be that what's cooking is not cooking for us (even though it is). Of course, we could be polite and say 'calf's liver? My favourite,' before enduring a tortuous half hour of that sicky feeling in the back of your throat as you try to keep it down. Or we could lie through our teeth and pretend we've already eaten. A bit rude, admittedly, if you've been invited round for supper, but not quite as rude, we think, as throwing up on the table.

Prince Harry

Honestly, we couldn't care less who his dad was. The fella's hilarious. Ginger hair, a Nazi uniform, excessive cocktails: he's a veritable Freddie Starr *de nos jours*. His brother can have as many teeth as he likes. Harry's *earned* the right to be king.

Princess Diana (Implausible Conspiracy Theories About)

Everybody likes a good conspiracy theory. The world seems somehow a better place if you can convince yourself that the CIA are very, very clever people who managed to publicly execute an inconvenient president rather than a thumb-fingered bunch of clowns who couldn't protect the most important man in America, let alone the rest of us. So it is with Princess Diana. If we can convince ourselves that Henri Paul was in the pay of the Bilderberg Group and that he decided the best way to terminate the slightly mannish-looking People's Princess was to have several shandies and then pile her very expensive car into a lamp-post *on purpose* then it means we can be less worried about having just the one after a round of golf and then spearing our not quite as expensive car into a hedge on the way home. Because if it was just an accident then it means drunk people really *are* terrible drivers and that buying a big German saloon car doesn't make you any safer. And we haven't even mentioned the White Fiat yet. Because who else had a white Fiat? *Columbo.* And that sounds a bit like *Columbus.* Who discovered *America.* Which is where the *CIA* are from. . . .

Problem Pages

The 'Dear Deidre' advice column in the *Sun* is quite possibly the ultimate nadir of good taste and human experience. Which is precisely what makes it so compelling. With headlines like 'Wild Threesome With My Boyfriend's Parents', it makes your little indiscretion last Christmas look positively virtuous, and is basically a licence to re-offend. In Deidre's world, distress under the duvet is always split into two camps: either 'he's not big enough to satisfy you' or 'every time you pop out to the shops you accidentally have group sex'. Either way, the message is clear: British women are absolute raving nymphos. Which, funnily enough, is a message white van man quite likes to read about. The advice is always firm but fair: at least offer to pay for his penis extension before you gang bang the bin men. But the real revelations are always reserved for 'Deidre's Photo Casebook' – a swinger's world populated by busty BB rejects having existential angst in their underwear. Not so much Schadenfreude, as youshuddanafreude.

Property Sites, Virtual Tours

Even though your budget registers in pence not pounds, somehow there's more fun to be had typing £million plus into the price search engine. For one simple reason: the virtual tour. More 'looking right down your toilet bowl', than 'through the keyhole', it's the nosy person's (i.e. every woman on earth) wet dream. 360 degrees? Yes, please. It's how men must feel when they happen upon a seventeen-year-old Russian supermodel getting filthy with a webcam. Property porn indeed.

Provincial Nightclubs
The big metropolitan superclubs are so awash with wannabe Big Brother contestants looking for a footballer to marry and Croatian waiters pretending to be millionaires that it's not all that easy to have any fun. A nice provincial club is a whole different mess of hairgel: remember the hormonal desperation of the school disco? It's alive and well and ready to give you a lovebite in any club in any market town in the UK. Pucker up, buttercup.

Pubic Art
After a good session of trimming 'down there', it is great to cut a picture of a famous world leader or personality out of the paper, spread some glue over his/her head or face and then arrange the mound of pubes accordingly – giving the aforesaid person a nice Hendrix afro or Saddam beard.

Public Schoolboys
Rich, probably. Stupid, possibly. Will run the world one day, most definitely. The venom that is reserved for those privately educated never quite goes away, but while your male friends might make unsubtle noises about their privileged backgrounds, is it just us who are quietly thinking . . . well educated, good manners, decent wonga, played rugby, nice body, good shag? (The same can't be said of public schoolgirls, of course. Despicable creatures. Should be avoided.)

Public Schoolgirls
Rich, probably. Stupid, possibly. Will run the world one day, most definitely. The venom that is reserved for those privately educated never quite goes away, but while your female friends might make unsubtle noises about their privileged backgrounds, is it just us who are quietly thinking . . . well educated, good manners, decent wonga, glossy hair, nice body, good shag? (The same can't be said of public schoolboys, of course. Despicable creatures. Should be avoided.)

Punchline

(**Shaggy Dog Story** Continued) . . . OK, you've got me. How did you make the ship disappear?

Punning

Show me a piano falling down a mineshaft and I'll show you A-flat minor. A prisoner's favourite punctuation mark is the period. It marks the end of his sentence. A bicycle can't stand on its own because it is two-tired. Terrible. Terrible. Terrible. But strangely appealing all the same.

Putting Tomato Ketchup on Everything

No one without a heavy life insurance policy would dare ask Gordon Ramsay for a bottle of Heinz classic tomato/vinegar/salt and emulsifiers combination, but at home it is a different matter altogether. If you or your loved one has spent hours in the kitchen preparing a beautifully balanced plate of food with a delicate sauce, it is very bad table manners indeed to secretly squirt a little bit of ketchup under the food to be enjoyed, but, that said, it always makes everything taste better.

Putting Weird Stuff in the Toilet

After you have flushed and just before you leave there can be a lot of satisfaction derived from leaving the next occupant of the cubicle a little present – we find it very funny to empty something that floats into the toilet bowl just to bemuse, perplex or worry them. We find a packet of Hula Hoops, some marshmallows or a few liquorice snakes should do the trick.

Putting Your Cat into Different Positions

Jack T, the son of one of the authors of this esteemed tome, has upwards of sixteen different positions in which he can carry his two cats, Leonardo Di Catrrio and Edward Tumnus – they range from 'Battersea Power Station' (which Leo excels at and sees him on his back with all four legs pointing skyward) to 'Rucksack' (where Mr Tumnus lies on his owner's back like one of Millets' finest) and, of course, 'Tie' and 'Belt' (you should be able to work these out for yourselves by now) and not forgetting 'Bazooka', 'Baby' and 'Parrot'. Hours of fun for a boy and his cat. If only cats could indeed talk.

Quote . . . Unquote

Who said that 'the Radio 4 quotations-based quiz hosted by the pedantic Uncle Nigel Rees is so twee, so boring and so excruciatingly old-fashioned that it is essential listening – if only to remind oneself that there are worse programmes than MoneyBox Live?' Um – let's see, was it Oscar Wilde, Graham Norton or Shakespeare? No, actually, it was us.

R&B Grinding

What is about girls dancing? One minute they're ordering a G and T at the bar and talking about soft furnishing, the next minute R Kelly's on and they're botty winding like its singles night at a Jamaican dancehall. Yes, R&B music somehow unleashes the inner slut in any woman. Which is most disturbing at a work do. Take Lesley, the portly divorcee in Bought Ledger, who usually spends nights out staring down the barrel of a bottle of white wine and adjusting her support tights. All it takes is a blast of the Pussy Cat Dolls and she's up, casting her Dorothy Perkins jacket aside like a stripper might toss away her thong. Did she just lesbo grind the receptionist? Afraid so. Is she sticking her bum out and suggestively slapping it? Affirmative. Please God, someone take that chair away from her before it sues for sexual assault. It's at times like this you could almost pray for a nice Cliff Richard ditty to come on and decimate the floorshow.

Radio Quizzes (Cheating Using Google)

Notwithstanding the shocking revelations about dishonesty underlying TV quizzes, the radio quiz remains strong. Whenever the drivetime jock asks us to guess the connection between 'Tutti Frutti', 'I Eat Cannibals' and 'Always

Look on the Bright Side of Life' we've got the station on speed dial and our mouths are already watering at the thought of a slap-up feast at a top local restaurant. The fact that always-on broadband access and the power of Wikipedia means that the answer is never more than a few mouse clicks away in no way dulls the keen sense of anticipation that this time might be the the time we actually get on air and are permitted the fleeting satisfaction of saying 'One Foot in the Grave' to the entire Three Counties area.

Rag Mags

Rag Mags were brilliant when you were a teenager. Every so often, a collection of hungover students dressed as nurses would rock up in your home town and, for a shiny fifty pence piece, would give you a badly photocopied selection of sick and rude jokes. That's education for you. We know we should have grown out of it, but when we are approached today we still can't resist buying a copy and chortling away at the puerile innuendo.

Rave Anthems (Old)

Just play us any record with that funny fizzing synthesizer noise and some big-lunged diva shrieking about ecstasy and we're twenty years younger and dancing in a field again. Show me the vitamin supplement that will do *that*!

Ray Lamontagne

Sooner or later everyone irons their own clothes. As long as you've got a housewife-compliant CD to take your mind off it, it's really not too bad. So, if the boys need some hip easy listening, there's Corinne Bailey Rae with her elfin look and Radio 2 friendly soul-with-stablisers sound. But, for the 50 per cent of the population that actually know how the iron *works*, she's a bit too much of a loveable pixie for comfort. Well, if you need inoffensive acoustic chillout, look no further than Ray: sounds like Ben from *X-Factor* jamming with the Eagles, looks like David Schwimmer disguised as Richard Chamberlain. If you've got a big pile of ironing to do, there's nothing better. Just don't tell anyone we said so.

Reading on the Toilet

Perhaps, in a glorious example of life imitating art, you are reading this very entry while resting awhile in the smallest room in the house. If you are, then you probably already know the sheer pleasure that a few minutes of undisturbed reading time can bring and need read this entry no longer. If you aren't, then we recommend you make for the brick privy forthwith (or one of those new-fangled 'inside' toilets, if you are really posh) and continue reading. Just remember: if you didn't need to go and just went to read, flush before you leave so no one thinks you're weird.

Reading XRRF & Passing the Jokes Off as Your Own

'No Rock and Roll Fun' is a brilliantly written blog that periodically makes insightful remarks about politics, the media and pop music. Girls don't read it. Which is why you can memorize a few *bons mots* from it in the morning and trot them out on a date that evening in order to give yourself the air of a well-informed Oscar Wilde *de nos jours*. Plus, if she rumbles you, she's probably not a woman after all so it's an excellent method of preventing yourself accidentally going home with a tranny.

Recordable DVDs

Do you remember when you were little and you wanted to record the *Top Forty* on Radio 1? Your options were either to put a microphone in front of the speaker or to stick sellotape over the little recesses on the top of a blank cassette. And then *Tomorrow's World* said that we would soon be able to record TV programmes to watch whenever we wanted. Of course they also said that we would all be flying to work on jetpacks, eating lunch in tablet form and living on the moon, so we didn't take it too seriously. But THEN IT HAPPENED and our rich friends had enormous video cassette machines with tapes the size of the yellow pages and they started to build up an extensive library of *Dr Who* episodes and the Test Card (when they had pressed the wrong button), and then that became old hat and some boffins invented the CD, which was amazing (although we sort of missed the hiss and fluff of vinyl), and then the DVD and then (cue 'Zadok The Priest' by Handel) – the record-able DVD – or DVDR, as we like to call it. The quality is near-broadcast standard and it all feels a little illegal (frankly) to be able to make perfect copies of anything, and it doesn't take much of a leap of the imagination to see how people end up infringing copyright. Shameful.

Rehearsing Your Exit Interview (Again and Again)
'And *another* thing . . .'

Relationship Advice U-Turns
The eleventh commandment was 'thy friends shall always date idiots'. But, unfortunately, you're forced to describe him as a 'really nice guy' whenever the aforementioned friend is in earshot. Which feels like the vocal equivalent of chewing on shards of glass. Until she makes the drunken late night call after they've had a major row. Before she's can even say 'what should I do?', you've launched into a two hour, vitriolic rant that can be distilled into three words – HE IS SCUM. The next day they're back together, more loved up than ever. Your response? 'He's a really nice guy.' Not so much eating your words as gagging on them.

Remote Control (Putting on the Television)
What's the point of a remote control? Well, it enables you, the television viewer, to switch from *Ugly Betty* to *What Not To Wear*, without having to physically leave your seat. A wondrous, energy saving device we're sure we're all in agreement about. Where there is slightly less harmony, perhaps, is where the control should live. The answer for anyone with a brain is straightforward – when not in use, it should reside on top of the television. The answer for those less mentally equipped – let's, for argument's sake, call them men – is

down the side of the armchair, on the coffee table next to another half dozen black controls to work the DVD/Hi-Fi/Digibox/MP3 Player/Light Dimmer/Fridge Freezer, or most commonly, that mysterious place known as 'Darling! Do you know where the remote control is?' The upshot is that, while *EastEnders* is starting, you're missing the first ten minutes as you're scrabbling around under the sofa trying to switch on the television. Leaving it on top of the television is both clutter free and practical, and the fact that it winds your partner up something rotten makes it all the more worthwhile.

Rewriting History

It's mashup culture! Remix the facts until they support your argument. She won't be carrying a Dictaphone, she always threatens to but . . .

Riding a Motorbike (Just So You Can Turn Up to Work in the Clothes)

If you've ever seen *Mad Max*, or played a violent sci-fi videogame, then you've had some sort of hankering for the twenty-first century armour of the Man with the Iron Horse. Even if you've just left a 125cc mimsy-bike in the office car park, the receptionist doesn't need to know that. Just swagger past her desk looking like the bloke from *Doom* and hope to God she doesn't give you a jiffy bag to deliver.

Rockumentaries

It's music television with a restraining order. Rock documentaries claim to go behind the scenes to illuminate the inner workings of our most troubled idols. Naturally, the idea is that it's 'all about the music', when in fact it's all about deviant groupie sex, body-reconfiguring amounts of drugs and any incidents that involve punch-ups, knives or first degree murder. The first five minutes establish that a) they did once write some good tunes and b) everyone is much better looking before the drugs. The next hour goes on to catalogue just how much heroin it's possible for one man to take and live to tell the tale. Better than a grainy clip of the said rock star fellating a guitar strap by mistake whilst playing the pubic hair of a supermodel are the pundits dredged up to comment. A coke-addled groupie whose heart is still in 1972, but whose face has 'done a Keith Richards' can always be relied upon for some remarkably obtuse observations. But, however tragic the ending, you still can't help thinking it's better than dial-a-druggie Doherty, the modern music industry's answer to rock rebellion.

Rotherham Shower
When pressed for time, a handy bottle of Jo Malone reaches the parts a shower just logistically can't.

Roy Chubby Brown
Not particularly funny, and hardly a style icon either, Mr Vasey's principal function in our world is as an irritant to smug *Guardian* readers who, on the one hand, despise his atavistic racist misogyny but, on the other hand, feel obliged to stand up for the colourblind Novocastrian's freedom of speech if you are bold enough to suggest a tactical nuclear strike on his gaudy Geordie mansion.

Running For a Bus (Kind of)
The last time you ran was 1984, and an egg and spoon were involved. Your best friend was also called My Little Pony. Cut to the future and the number 73 bus is careering towards the bus stop. It's late. It's dark. And it's very cold. Plus, the laws of public transport suggest that, should you miss this one, the next one will arrive at roughly the same time as the next Olympics. As you're madly calculating and processing all this information, a vague stirring starts in your legs. A twitch that threatens to break out into a trot. Then accelerates into a loping canter. Finally, you are actually *running* – like a whirling dervish of Sainsbury's carrier bags and corn plasters. At this stage the inhabitants

of the bus seem designated witnesses to the gross indignity of your gallop. Making it on the bus, or missing it – either way is guaranteed humiliation. No woman should ever be seen undulating with such desperate abandon towards a bus stop. And those kids sniggering at the back of the bus? Laughing at you, lady.

Rural Daydreams

For all the great points of living in the city – the murders! the muggings! the traffic jams! – there may be the odd occasion when you dream of a calmer, simpler life. As you stand there on the Tube, packed in like sardines, the countryside suddenly seems paradise by comparison: warm, glowing sunshine, the twitter of birds, the glass of cold wine in a country pub garden. Never mind that last time you visited it rained all weekend, the RAF decided to practise their low flying routines and the locals at the pub were so unfriendly you thought you might be in *Straw Dogs* by mistake – without the rural daydream to distract you, you'd be thinking about how that bloke's BO armpit is two inches from your face.

Russell Brand

The Artful Dodger of the screen may *look* like he's got more Cure records than sense, but every woman in Britain has at least briefly entertained the notion of tucking those skinny little legs into bed. If you're old enough to remember John Cooper Clarke, you've seen it all before, but his knack of bringing his ballbag into every conversation makes every Royal Command Performance an experience to be savoured.

Ruth Badger

When Ruth Badger (whose middle name is 'the') shot to fame during the compulsive 2006 series of *The Apprentice*, the nation embraced her as a butch role model – not since Margaret Thatcher had we enjoyed seeing people handbagged as much. We relished her encounters with that mad woman, Jo, with the oily Syed, with Paul 'The Tulip' Seed, who screwed up big time right at the last hurdle, and, of course, with the ultimate winner, Michelle Dewberry. Not to mention Alan 'You're a lightweight – you're fired' Sugar. It didn't matter, ultimately, that Beauty won out over the Badger – the Badger was OUR winner – the sight of her, after her triumph during the Estate Agent challenge, alone in the Limo shouting: 'The Badger on her own! Let loose!' and singing the Whitesnake classic – and now Badger theme tune – 'Here I Go Again' was enough to motivate us all.

Saddam Hussein, Watching Being Hanged on the Internet

How does this work? We don't believe in capital punishment (indeed, we'd go as far as to say it's the hallmark of an uncivilized society) – yet as soon as Saddam Hussein's execution was available on the Internet, we were right there to have a look. As we watched it for the third time in all its grainy, gory detail, we'd like to say we were so appalled at the brutality of the act that it reinforced our liberal views. However, if we're being honest, we can't quite deny the queasy enjoyment of seeing a brutal, fascist dictator deservedly getting it in the neck.

Sandals, Wearing to Work

Why is it that wearing trainers to work is very much not de rigueur, whereas sandals is somehow acceptable? We're not sure – to us, it's as if we're saying to the man: my body may be here, but hey! my feet are on holiday. In fact, one can't help escaping that feeling you got back at school of subverting the uniform – all of which, let's face it, makes it twice the fun. Just be careful if you're one of those slip-them-off-under-the-desk sort of people. It's one thing to push it with the sandal thing – to walk round the office barefoot is unlikely to get you a raise.

'Satisfaction' (the Benny Benassi Video for)

Take the postmodern 'living catalogue' metatextuality of *Fight Club*, add some power tools and some half-naked models who appear to have been dipped in Swarfega. Well done. You've got the 'Satisfaction' video. Once you've seen it, you'll never be able to hear the song again without experiencing at least a mild frisson of arousal. Which, after all, is exactly what Benny would have wanted.

Saying the Word 'Hot!'

Thankfully, some Americanisms never reach our shores. Take the word 'neat', or it's more saccharine little sister 'neato' – never quite caught on (well, can you imagine saying 'neato' to your local hoodie). But 'Hot!' – the LA way to describe everything from sexy men to new fashion looks – hasn't just migrated here, it's breeding like a Viagra-crazed rabbit. From Southend to Swindon there's a whole army of women who sound like they're guest starring in *The Simple Life* with Paris Hilton. Somehow, though, the world seems more glamorous when you describe Neil in accounts as 'Like, so HOT!' rather than merely 'really nice'.

Saying You Are in a Meeting

If everyone was in a meeting as much as they claimed they were when people phoned for them then quite clearly no real work would be getting done and the country would grind to a halt. Being in a meeting actually means either 'can't be arsed to stop gossiping with a friend in accounts' or 'there is an eBay auction ending in 4 minutes 53 seconds and I am poised to make a last minute offer', but we enjoying giving it as an excuse because it makes us feel all grown-up and important and also a bit mischievious. Sorry – gotta dash – I have a 4.00 p.m. in the boardroom . . . SkySports on the 50-inch plasma screen is so much better than watching it on WindowsMediaPlayer10.

Scarlett Johansson's Smile

Her pearly-white perfect teeth surrounded by that voluptuous pair of heart-shaped lips all combine to produce a smile that, were it made just for you, and maybe you like to pretend it is sometimes, could have the most tangible effect on your average bloke. It is that winning combination of innocence and pure bubbling-under eroticism that produces a back-of-the-net effect every time. Can you honestly say you haven't got to the end of *Lost in Translation* and wondered (almost aloud) why the people you met on your business trips in far-flung hotels looked less like Scarlett and more like Ann Widdecombe?

Scented Candles

What Valium was to the 1960s, scented candles are to the noughties, basically, enabling millions of fraught housewives to relax. We know it makes us look like we're psychotic new-age spinsters and we don't care. That's how stressed we are.

Scientology

You want to know why church attendances are down? Really? It's because modern religion simply isn't bonkers enough. Look through the Old Testament and it's all cherubims with four wings and four wheels, made as if from beryl stone, flying around and smiting the bejeezus out of people with some sort of Bronze Age death ray. Go into any C of E gaff nowadays and there's just some softly-spoken duffer trying to give you tea and explaining that the Virgin Mary was more of a single mother and that God didn't really kill thousands of non-Jews in the first couple of books of the Bible alone so much as give them a sort of holy ASBO. Not the Scientologists. You want crazy sci-fi? You got it, buddy: for a nation raised on *Aliens* and *The Terminator*, it's the only religion worth considering. Show me another religion with a little machine to test your personality. Show me another religion that is half as quick to prevent your bank account from getting over full. Praise Xenu!

Scissor Sisters

If, for any reason, you can't find any late seventies Leo Sayer albums, you could do worse than (legally) downloading some Scissor Sisters tunes instead. They're the new masters of squeaky-voiced glam disco, and as if that were not enough, there's always well-upholstered sex mascot, Ana Matronic, swishing her skirt around in the videos like a well-fed Stevie Nicks. There's this story going around that one of them might be gay, but we're not so sure. They said that about Sir Elton John, and he married that Russian bird in a video, didn't he? You can't fool us with those silly Internet rumours. You'll be trying to tell us that old one about Freddie Mercury next. Freddie could never have rocked that hard if he was good with colours. All the best records are by straight geezers: fact. Look at the charts today – Franz Ferdinand, Scissor Sisters, Mika, FischerSpooner. Pop music's never been healthier and it's all because of the pure red-blooded heteros in it. Scissor Sisters are just the latest in a long line of butch disco bricklayers.

Screen Wipes

Essentially wet ones for computer nerds, screen wipes sort out all the crud that has built up on your computer screen over the years. Which in the case of computer nerds . . . actually, let's not think about that too closely, shall we? A bit like a tube of Pringles, once you've started it's very difficult to stop the moist cloth cleansing habit from becoming a frequent, almost obsessive part of your day. Now, if only they could work out a way of getting crumbs out from under the computer keys . . .

Second Breakfasts

We all know how good a bacon sandwich tastes. But how much better does a bacon sandwich taste *when you've already had your breakfast?* Sometimes, one breakfast is simply not enough. Sometimes you need to (quite literally) go the whole hog, and max up your early morning munching with a second helping. In terms of getting caught, it's foolproof: your partner/flatmate/ cat will not witness breakfast two; your workmates just assume you missed breakfast one. The only person who knows just what a greedy lard-arse you're being is yourself. Now, stop making us feel guilty and pass the brown sauce.

Second Life

Entering this virtual world is a curious business, but once you get the hang of the Sims-like flat-earth world where you can fly, trade and build communities, it is rather soothing and dream-like. One user has even amassed sufficient 'Linden Dollars' (named after the laboratory that created this world) to be declared the first Second Life millionaire – unlike other attempts at creating these alternative worlds, the advantage of Linden Dollars is that they are fully exchangeable into real money. Of course lots of people who wander into Second Life head straight for the lap-dancing clubs and the sleazy bars and start chatting up almost-naked ladies who are probably obese lorry drivers from Rhyll, but that is probably part of the fun.

Secret Messages

Funny as it might seem, sometimes writing can be a bit of a bore. Until, that is, one discovers the joy of adding secret messages to the text. Contracted to ghost-write a book about Tolkien, this writer decided that the barrow-wight creature sounded a little too like Barry White to avoid adding in a succession of 'Walrus of Love' references. Kicking a literary rival can be another motivation. Take the spat between rival Betjeman biographers Bevis Hillier and A. N. Wilson. Hillier wrote a letter under the name 'Eve De Harben' (an anagram of 'Ever Been Had'), which not only appeared in Wilson's book, but included the acrostic 'A. N. Wilson is a shit'. Inspired stuff. Shame we're too much of a chicken to try anything similar ourselves.

Self-Help Books

Feel the fear and put it to one side while you make a cup of tea. The self help section of book stores is actually spiralling out of control. Do we really need to know the ten positive steps to being a productive person? Apparently, yes. The most disturbing aspect of the self help genre is the message that your life is a product of your thoughts. Which means that either you'll a) win the lottery and wake up in Cameron Diaz's body after a night with Brad, or b) your boss will come down with Ebola and the neighbour's house will explode.

Sex (With Knickers on)

That scanty pair of Agent Provocateur knickers might look like an invitation written in silk and black lace trim, but the fact is they serve as a noughties chastity belt. Modern sexual etiquette dictates that any activity taking place whilst pants are firmly on doesn't actually count. It's a bit like the phrase 'Did you drop your knickers?' If you didn't, then technically nothing happened. The fact that a sneaky, round the side swerve was undertaken is meaningless. Facts is facts. You kept your knickers on. So, if you spot a bunch of virgins having an orgy in their pants, rest assured it's as innocent as a Church gathering.

Sex Blogs

It isn't porn. It's . . . umm . . . a novel voyage of self-discovery, interaction with like-minded people across the globe and a chance to explore transgressive thoughts and feelings in a safely contained way. Oh, and a chance to read about what unbelievably fruity stuff belleGirl69 has been up to this week. If you're having a shandy and looking thoughtful, it's still a shandy.

Shaggy Dog Stories

Jimmy Carr is all very well, but sometimes you just want a good old-fashioned shaggy dog story – one of those interminable jokes that go on forever, and which, by the time you get to the punchline, is always a disappointment. They were made even longer by Ronnie Corbett, who would lengthen the already long joke by ad libbing about this, that and the other. But what are we doing, you don't want us rambling on about shaggy dog stories – we've whetted your appetite for a real one, haven't we? Do you know the one about the parrot on the cruise ship? Well, once upon a time, there was this cruise ship . . . See **Cruise Ship**.

Share-Sized Packets of Crisps

Share? Says who? If we want a serving suggestion for a packet of crisps, we'll ask for one, thank you very much. Obviously, the fact that the bag of kettle chips contains about the same wodge of potato as a Walker's Variety Six Pack means that to eat the whole thing yourself makes you a right greedy bastard. But, sometimes, they just slip down so easy. The fact that you're ignoring the 'share' suggestion and selfishly wolfing the lot only makes the experience even more pleasurable.

Sheds

Every man needs a shed. Sometimes an attic will suffice, but it's normally a shed you're after. Ostensibly a place to keep man things, such as tools and, er, more tools, a shed's primary purpose, of course, is as a space for a man to hang out, to 'potter' and generally just get a bit of peace and quiet. There's always a bit of shed assumption amongst womenfolk that all the time her bloke is shut away is due to him cracking one off at the bottom of the garden. And while there may be the occasional gentleman who does indeed do just that, the sad fact is that most of us are just in there having a nice quiet cup of tea.

SHEDS

Shop Windows (Checking Yourself Out in)

No matter how many full-length mirrors you have in your house (and everybody should have at least one), you will find it hard to resist checking yourself out in every shop window or shiny car door that you come across. You could rationalize this by explaining that there's always the chance that a stray tail of loo roll has somehow affixed itself to your outfit. The guilty truth is more likely to be that a plate-glass window, or especially a nice shiny black car, will offer you the most forgiving reflection you'll ever see.

She Pees

The festival equivalent of female empowerment is using a she pee – a small paper cone (like icing a cake, but with, well, wee). It's hard not to swagger into a she pee urinal with the same smugness with which men 'pop' into a bush. The wind blowing in your hair, knickers to the side (sorry to sound so technical) getting all macho about the precision of your 'stream'. And if you steal a few spare cones to take home and amuse yourself with in the privacy of your bathroom – who's going to stop you?

Shopping Bulimia

Why can't we just buy something, take it home and be happy with it? Well, if it's not the credit card making sad-eyes at us from our purse, it's the mirror cracking under the strain of an outfit clearly bought by someone blinded by the changing room's fluorescent lights. Much like eating an entire chocolate fudge cake, sometimes you can only feel the awful sense of nausea and regret after the deed is done. The solution? Regurgitating it over the counter you bought it from. Nothing cures the sick feeling in the pit of your stomach after spending £300 in Zara than returning the next day to take it back. OK, so it might be rude to do the shopping equivalent of 'bringing it up'. But it's much better than letting those financial calories add up until your personal debt is the size of an incredibly obese person. Those items still hanging in your wardrobe, you know the ones you planned to take back but never got round to? They're like retching. All the pain and none of the gain.

Shopping in Primark

It used to be the dirty secret of housewives and single mums on a budget, but now it's the fashion destination of choice. God knows, even Anna Wintour probably drops in there to pick up a few 'pieces' (not sure she can land her private jet in Peckham High Street, though.) So why this sudden reversal of fortunes? What could possibly have rescued a store popular with pikeys, where an Iceland carrier bag was the height of accessory chic? It's cheap. Like, *really* cheap. Filthy cheap, in fact. The kind of knock-down prices even street children in Peru would class as a bargain. The brilliance of having this season's Primark smock is bragging that it only cost £8. In the weird world of fashion it's now considered *tacky* to spend thousands in Armani. After all, the real style icons get sent designer clothes for free . . .

Shopping while Drunk

We're going to make some assumptions about you now: assumptions, like their larger relatives, prejudices, are terrible things but also marvellous timesavers. You're a bit tipsy, aren't you? You're buying this book for someone in a panic buy after a couple of cold drinks with your workmates. You don't particularly like the person concerned but you've got to get them *something* and you're in the bookshop now so you might as well. Besides, you've been flicking through it for a while now (you are up the 'S's after all) and the bits you can read without your eyes going all blurry seem all right. Cover's not too bad either. *Looks* like a present. And it's not even that expensive. You could get yourself something as well. There's bound to be something decent in the 3 for 2. Or, if none of the above assumptions are true, then someone's bought it for you. While they're a bit tipsy. They don't like you as much as all that but at least they bothered. That's something, isn't it? What we're saying is this: the unintentional tipsy buy, whether in the dangerously late-opening book and CD emporium or the positively perilous 24-hour Internet is becoming the default response of the cash-rich, time-poor twenty-first-century worker. Still. It's a good result for someone. In this case us. Thanks.

Shoving Stuff under the Sofa

Picture the scene – you have been told in no uncertain terms that unless the sitting room is cleared up before your significant other returns from the shops, WORDS will be exchanged. You go into the room with the best of intentions and start by tidying up the remote controls when accidentally you hit the power button and on comes the TV screen, which just happens to be showing a Bond film you haven't seen for a while. You decide to sit down for just a few minutes to watch the opening sequence but, before you know it, a huge volcano is erupting and people in orange boilersuits are leaping off large steel structures to a certain death. Then suddenly you hear a sound that fills your heart with instant terror – a car is pulling up outside and you survey the scene – newspapers, lager cans, pizza boxes, socks, DVD cases and, inexplicably, loads of dirty pants strewn everywhere as if the sitting room had been transformed into a Tracey Emin installation. Quick as a flash you scoop it all up and shove it in, under and behind the sofa until the room is tidy, the sofa a little bumpy and the key is in the lock. A quick flick of the remote and the room is ready to pass muster. See also **Having a Cleaner**.

Signing Petitions

We're busy people. We're the sort of people who are so busy that anyone with a clipboard thinks we must be slowed down in the street, to take 'thirty seconds' (translation: twenty minutes) to push upon you whatever cause they are championing and asking for your name in support. Your response should be instinctive. You take the pen and, in your best handwriting, add 'Mickey Mouse' to the bottom of their list. They won't be stopping you again. Or rather, if they do, they'll be stopping Genghis Khan.

Simon Cowell

He wears his trousers too high. He is too smug by half. He's phenomenally rich. He's shagged Sinitta. He's responsible for, among other atrocities to the human eardrum, Will Young, Gareth Gates, Michelle McManus and Steve Brookstein. We also feel we should be able to pin Kate Thornton on him too, though haven't quite worked out how. And yet, despite all of this, we kind of like the guy. We think it's because he's the only one on the reality TV panels who actually says what you're thinking – that the boss-eyed wannabe who has massacred 'I Will Always Love You' wouldn't know a tune if it came round and lamped her on the head. For that, respect.

Size Zero

This business is simply the best thing that ever happened. As long as the ideal dress size for young women was something realistic, we felt vaguely obliged to make a bit of an effort, and every January we'd stink out our flats with cabbage soup every day. Now that the fashion elite has dictated that we should all look like concentration camp victims, that eleven o'clock doughnut with our latte isn't an indulgence, it's a sisterly act of defiance.

Sky Plus

First of all there's the social stigma to be overcome: the Sky 'not only have we got loads of telly, but we can record some' solution is, without question, all-conqueringly convenient, enabling adults, for the first time, to record the programme they actually wanted to see without snipping off the last ten minutes. Unfortunately, there's something about it that's just a little bit council – only the lowest social echelons are supposed to care that much about the telly. Broadsheet readers like us are supposed to just catch the odd screening of *La Traviata* on BBC4 more-or-less by accident and spend the rest of their time reading brainy books like, for cxample, this one. Your second problem as a Sky Plus user is trying to avoid judgemental houseguests from flicking through the low-rent tat you've recorded and finding whole seasons of *Star Trek: Enterprise* and nary a snippet of poncy BBC4 opera.

Sleeping at Your Desk (Ways of Disguising that You Are)

If you are prone to post-prandial snoozing at your work-station then you need to prepare your cover stories just in case you get spotted by your line-manager or just a mouthy colleague. 'Power-napping' feels a bit eighties as an excuse and won't cut the mustard in the modern era, 'thinking' just sounds totally lame and 'having a migraine' is rubbish, so why not go for gold with either 'practising a non-invasive form of Buddhist mind-training used by the majority of the Top 100 business moguls in the world', 'repositioning my success valve from my left cranial extremity to my right where it will be more in tune with my chakra' or just 'working out pi to 150 decimal points'. If that works then you will need to think up a way of getting all that dribble out of your keyboard without having to alert IT.

Sleeping in Taxis

It's hard to get a decent kip in a proper black cab: the seats tend to be slightly too slippery and there seems to be a marked surfeit of falling down room. A nice unli-censed minicab, though, is the ideal venue for a pleasant doze after a convivial evening with friends. They're always so deliciously *warm*, for one thing, and the com-forting hum of Magic FM conspires with the hypnotic twinkle of the hologram Koran sticker and the gentle whiff of Magic Tree to evoke a womb-like ambience.

Well, as long as your idea of a womb is a bit stuffy and smelling of air-freshener. The glorious thing about these in-transit power naps is that only real men can have them. While your better half sits bolt upright fretting about being found dismembered in a layby, you can rest on her bosom and sleep the dreamless sleep of the righteous and/or tipsy.

Slimming World

This is much more serious than a slimming club. This is an entire eco-system. This is a 'world' – an entirely different planet for fat people. In a way it's a bit like Scientology, but with fewer celebs and more tea and low-cal biscuits. It's a cult that makes you look at the world in a totally different – and barmy – light. For a start, there aren't days when you fancy a bit of fish and days when you fancy a bit of pasta any more. Oh no. Instead there are 'RED' and 'GREEN' days. Red means you're eating protein and green means you've gone to the carb side (which, quite frankly, is the only time going green is fun). The real stroke of cult-like genius is saved for the initiation ritual – the weigh in. The reinforced scales don't just give your weight, they sing it at the top of their voice and do a silly little dance. And if everyone hasn't got the message loud and clear then the half-starved leader will announce that you're ten pounds heavier than last week – to mutterings of 'she put on'. The goal? To be thinner? Hell no, it's all about getting those gold stars in your Slimming World passport . . .

Slot Machines, Asking Your Partner to Win a Cuddly Toy On

It's cruel, we know. But when visiting the fair with your loved one, it is your duty to ask him to win you a pink fluffy rabbit, however little you want one. He knows he's not going to succeed: you know he's not going to succeed, but he'll feel it an affront to his manhood not to at least give it a go. And when he inevitably fails pathetically, he'll be extra nice to you for the rest of the evening. Job done.

Slot Machines, Winning Cuddly Toys On

Have you ever actually seen anyone *win* on one of those things? Of course you haven't: the missing link between the joystick you're using and the claw it is allegedly meant to control has yet to be discovered. Not that it stops you spunking 50p after 50p in the hope of securing a bright pink fluffy rabbit for your daughter/date. It's important to round up the experience (and shore up your manhood) by explaining how the machine must be 'broken' and 'it's all a fix'.

Slumping (at Your Desk)

Health and safety really want you to sit up straight. In fact they'll even bring down a nasty looking back brace if you persist in slouching like an arsy teenager. But, mysteriously, even though you hear that the human spine was designed to be erect, yours seems to have been made by the corkscrew department. It's as if every muscle in your body has been finely honed to keep your back crunched out of shape. Sitting up straight feels like the equivalent of doing fifty sit-ups. Which is why slumping feels so much better. And really, so much more indicative of your attitude to your job. Less 'I'm ready and alert to tackle anything you throw at me' and more 'piss off I've given up and I'm going home'.

Snakes on a Plane

'Get those motherfucking snakes off my motherfucking plane.' Thus said Samuel L. Jackson in *Snakes on a Plane*, but only because the original film was reshot after Internet movie fans turned the turkey around from straight-to-video inevitability to so-bad-it's-good cult classic. Of course, now everyone else knows it's so bad it's good, it's kind of naff to like it for being kind of naff. But that's just fine by us – it means the secret pleasure of enjoying the film is back there all over again.

Sneezing while Driving

We love that moment when you are going at eighty miles an hour up the M1 on a Friday night and everyone is jostling for position and suddenly the unmistakeable symptoms of an imminent sneeze start welling up: a tickly nose, slightly watery eyes and maybe a muscle spasm below your eyes. There is nothing you can do to stem the inevitable and, as you fend off lorries on the left and 4×4s on the right, you let rip a massive sneeze, spraying the windscreen with snot and, here's the best bit, shutting your eyes for a full second. Let's work that out – travelling at eighty miles an hour means that, for that one second when you have your eyes shut, you have travelled 117 feet. And you know the bad thing about that? The heady cocktail of speed, danger and blindness is actually rather exciting.

Socks with Sandals

Fashion wise, of course, it's a disaster. It's the foot equivalent of going round all day wearing a T-shirt saying 'Look At Me, I'm Old Before My Time'. Yet two points must be made in favour of the socks and sandals combo. Firstly, it's just so *comfy*: so much lighter than wearing heavy shoes, yet still lovely and warm on the old tootsies. And, secondly, have you ever seen our feet? You may think my socks look naff, but would you really want to see my bunions, sores and overgrown toenails instead?

Softcore Porn (as PC Wallpaper)

Well of course you tut when you go down to the post room and they've got that nudie calendar up, it's demeaning to women. They ought to be ashamed of themselves. You generally manage to get all the way back to your desk, maybe even start composing an email to HR, when you notice a little bit of Daniel Radcliffe's tanned arm peeking out from the edge of the screen. Minimize Outlook for a minute and you'll have no idea what you were annoyed about. Pot. Kettle. Ooh . . . David Beckham . . .

Speed Camera Shuffle

How many speed cameras actually contain a working camera inside their yellow box? We're not completely sure, but we do know that it's far less than you think. Nevertheless, whether we're winding down a country road or working our way through roadworks on a motorway, we're not going to risk it and will reluctantly kill our speed accordingly . . . but only for the duration of the camera's white lane range. Once we're past that, it's foot back on the accelerator. Speed up, slow down, speed up, slow down – is there any more glorious sticking-it-to-the-man way to drive? Make it fun for all the family by getting your children to play 'I Spy a Yellow Box'.

Spitting from Tall Buildings

The Tory MP, diarist and roué Alan Clark used to get great satisfaction from pissing on the electorate from the great height of his office window at the Ministry of Defence. We are not advocating quite that degree of misdemeanour, but there is something rather joyous about clearing your throat and launching a 'big greeney' over the parapet to land who knows where. It's a sort of adult version of chucking a water bomb, and there is something both primal and juvenile about it which makes it a joy. If you want to make it even guiltier, you can pick a target and lean right out, having calculated wind velocity and speed of descent through a series of practice shots before picking a target and really hacking up a good one. Oooooh – yuck – did you see the state of that guy's shoulder?!

Spitting in the Urinal

From extensive surveys carried out by this publication's editors hanging around public lavatories, it is clear that upwards of 72 per cent of men will spit into the urinal just before they start micturating (that is micturate as in pass water rather than anything else, you pervert), so we are not alone in this disgusting habit. It is all about marking out one's territory and also about filling that uncomfortable gap between arriving at your chosen urinal, fumbling to get the old fellow out and starting the flow. Heaven forbid you might catch the eye of someone standing next to you!

Splashing in Puddles
It's not a puddle; it's a vortex. A black hole with a force-field so powerful it will suck you and your new Prada wedges in. One minute you were walking along, minding your own business, and the next minute you've jumped in it like a deranged five-year-old. Obviously, this rarely happens on the walk to work, or the journey home from the dentist. No, strangely it mostly occurs when you've been a bit refreshed in a local drinking establishment. Despite the soggy socks and the fear that a passerby might try and have you sectioned, it's comforting to know that you've nudged middle-age just that little bit further away. Well, you don't see OAPs abandoning their zimmer frames and having a good old splash, do you?

Spooks
Government employees, be they spies or social workers, do not tend to dress as well as the cast of *Spooks*. They tend not to have top-of-the-range Apple computers or such elaborate skincare regimes either. In short, espionage is a whole lot less pretty than this Monday night treat might suggest. But when you've just endured the first day back at work, what you need is glamour, not grit. *Spooks* is the editorial staff of *Arena* magazines with guns. And better hygiene. We know. We checked.

Sporting Altercations (Watching on Video)
When it comes right down to it, all sports are just subli-mated boxing. You may not be interested in ice hockey, no sane person is, but when the players throw off their gloves and start a mass brawl on the hard and unforgiving ice, even the most uninterested of us will look up from our knitting to see if anyone loses a tooth. So it is with Formula One. As a sport it's among the dullest on earth, but the incidents of road rage that occur in the pit-lane, with drivers head-

butting each other irrespective of the presence of a crash-helmet, contribute greatly to its position as one of the premier television attractions of our time. Paradoxically, boxing itself has strayed too far from its bare-knuckle roots to stimulate much prurient interest in the general public, but a good old-fashioned dust-up on the football pitch will be broadcast across the world by teatime.

Squeezable Marmite Jars

Some items on our supermarket shelves are design classics and should not, under any circumstances, be meddled with – Kelloggs Cornflakes, Heinz Tomato Ketchup and, love it or hate it, Marmite. Shiny black glass, yellow lid and that comforting olde-worlde label. The sequeezable jar – a great innovation no doubt – an opportunity to get 99 per cent of that love-it hate-it vegetable extract out of a fun squeezable container – but it just feels wrong, wrong, wrong. Eating Marmite should be an experience which revolves around trying to get the end of the knife into some unreachable parts of the upper part of the glass jar and to scrape out every last gloop of the sticky stuff. Much as we appreciate the gesture, we will be sticking to the old-fashioned hard slog which rewarded the dilligent toast-maker.

Stag Nights

In the old days, stag nights were an evening down the pub, followed by the groom being stripped naked and left chained to a lamp-post. Maybe it's to ensure that this humiliation is avoided that the modern stag goes to great lengths to concoct a veritable weekend of entertainment, often far more elaborate than the wedding itself. The further abroad the better (though it's interesting to note that however much we booze and embarrass ourselves, somehow the inhabitants of Prague or Dublin or Amsterdam never have their stags back in Britain). Basically, it's all an excuse for one hell of a piss-up by men reverting to being sixteen-year-olds again. We know we should know better, but we don't.

Stainless Steel Kitchen Utensils

How many kitchen utensils does one really actually need? We reckon you could get away with one sharp knife, a wooden spoon and a corkscrew. But where's the fun in that? Not when you can have one of those metal strips with hooks to hang up every single stainless steel utensil a man could ever need – and quite a few more besides. That ladle, how much use does it actually get? Likewise the pasta tongs – you just stick your fork in like we do, don't you? The metal spoon with holes in, the metal spoon without holes in, that funny flat spatula thing that looks like what the doctor puts in your mouth to say 'aaah' that we've never quite worked out what it's for . . . what do they actually do? Two things, really: firstly, they look great, and make you feel like a proper chef and not a boil-in-the-bag shyster; and, secondly, they make a great noise when you run another stainless steel kitchen utensil along them.

Starbucks

Along with size zero models, Starbucks is the root cause of all evil in modern society (we've checked this out on the web and it's true – evil simply did not exist before 1971, when Starbucks opened its first store). Heck, even Dr Evil in the Austin Powers movies had Starbucks as his base, so it must be true. Expanding at the rate of one new store every 0.02 seconds (we think), statistics show that, by the year 2054, every new building in Britain will have its own branch. We say, why fight it? The coffee's not so bad, and while the atmosphere might be a little plastic, it's a better place to hide from the rain than MacDonald's.

Starship Troopers

Heinlein's influential, prescient, but disappointingly talky sci-fi novel was distilled by *RoboCop* director Paul Verhoeven into a silly, entertaining and apparently satirical futuristic gun porn movie. If you like the idea of giant cockroaches being blown to pieces by Vanilla Ice and that fruity bird from *Wild Things* (and let's be candid, who doesn't?) then *Starship Troopers* is the movie for you.

Steven Seagal

Owners of waxworks across the world pray constantly for a Steven Seagal career revival: 'If only', they say to themselves, 'the salad-dodging sensei would get himself on Big Brother or something.' You can see why, after a hard day of modelling Brad Pitt's craggy moonscape of a face, the Mme Tussaud sculptor longs to just throw a black cloth over an armchair, top it off with a tinned ham and some boot polish hair, and call it Big Steve. They could even make it animatronic, given that he only ever moves his arms anyway. We probably wouldn't go and see it, though. Not if Seagal was on *Celebrity Big Brother*: we'd be glued to the screen in case he McGuyvered a bomb out of the microwave or Erika Elieniak burst out of a cake.

Sticky Fingers

There is a wonderfully perverse pleasure to be had from coating each fingertip laboriously with UHU glue, waiting for it to dry and then peeling the glue off each fingertip with your teeth and then eating it. Truly.

Sting

Firstly, there's the name. What's that all about? It's not that bad being called Gordon, is it? Secondly, there's the worthiness – far flung tribes with plates under their lips? Is that what Sid Vicious died for? Thirdly, there's the tantric sex – sixteen hours to get off? We might like to last a little longer than we actually do, but, really, that's just showing off. Fourthly, there's the music. Jazz? Madrigals? Pato Banton? And yet, despite all of this, we couldn't help ourselves feeling a squeal of delight when we learnt the Police were going to reform, and wondered how on earth we were going to get hold of tickets.

Stirring Hot Chocolate with a Cadbury's Flake

How much more sinful can a thick mug of Green & Black's Hot Chocolate be? The official description sounds like something you wouldn't do in front of your parents, 'When added to hot, fresh milk, the result is a cocoa-rich chocolate drink with a creamy froth, a rounded flavour provided by the chocolate and a balanced sweetness'. Yes, but once you have embraced the creamy chocolatey froth, we always find that we need an extra chocolatey lift to get us into cocoa-bean nirvana – what better than discarding any thought of a normal spoon and using a Cadbury's chocolate Flake instead? As you stir more and more, the 'flake/spoon' combo cleverly starts to melt and add more and more pure chocolate to the sludgy delights. Come to think of it, maybe there is a way of serving it in a chocolate mug that you could eat afterwards? Mmmmm.

Street Portraiture

What do George Clooney, Julia Roberts and someone-who-could-be-Molly-Ringwald-but-we're-not-sure have in common? Of course! They all appear to have, at some point, sat for an unflattering charcoal portrait outside a London tourist attraction! Given his distinguished clientele, it would seem churlish for us not to commission this evidently successful artist ourselves, that we might astound visitors to our home with a charcoal impression of how we would look if our eyes were closer together and our nose that little bit more freakishly large. A fiver well spent. That's Art.

Stubble

Is it just us, or is shaving every day a right royal pain in the backside (we're not talking literally, of course. If it is, then, you need to get a crash course in biology pronto)? Fortunately, many men have discovered that 'the best a man can get' is not the six blade shaving experience, but simply not to bother. Not only do we get an extra fifteen minutes in bed, but we also enjoy the luxury of swanning around at work all day feeling as if we're in *Miami Vice* (though we don't roll our sleeves up: that would be too far). The tipping point when stubble grows into holiday beard, and you go from looking like a rock star to looking like a tramp, is a fine one, so be careful. Whatever you do, don't go down the trimming route. Then it's all getting a bit George Michael.

stuffonmycat.com

What is there NOT to like about this site? Basically thousands of pictures of STUFF on people's CATS (can you see what they've done with the website name there? Clever, isn't it?). The STUFF can range from Pirate Costumes to Fried Eggs and Scrabble Pieces to Cream Cakes. One does wonder whether, in a parallel universe where cats are the dominant species, they are actually getting their own back for all this kind of stuff by building websites called things like stuffonmyhuman.com and doesntmyhumanlookcuteinafurcoat.com, but no one can deny that this is totally cute and laugh-out-loud funny. As long as your cat doesn't catch you laughing.

Sucking Seatbelts

A weird one this, but sucking on seatlbelts can give a sublime pleasure – maybe it is a throwback to being tiny and having a comforter or being a little bit older and sucking on the furry hood of your anorak? Whatever it is, it is certainly primal and urgent. With seatbelts maybe it is the texture of the malleable thick-woven fabric used to construct them and maybe, yuck, it is the salty sweat of all the people who have sat next to me in the passenger seat and secretly prayed to God for a quick release from the terrible driving experience. Were we Tracey Emin, this would be art, 'The Sweat Of All the People In My Car', but we will content ourselves with just sucking it instead.

Sucking the Camembert From Its Deep Fried Coating

Take a full fat cheese and deep fry it in . . . erm . . . full fat and then add some carbohydrate in the form of breadcrumbs and serve with a lovely spoonful of cranberry sauce. The satisfying crunch of the outer coating of crumbs gives way to the oh-so-sinful melting interior – you could just eat it conventionally or, even better, just insert your tongue and suck and coax the gloopy French cheese from inside its breaded cave. Yum, yum, yum.

Sulking

The key to sulking is to never admit you're doing it. It's not that you're sulking, you argue to yourself, it's merely that you're not *engaging* with the person in question. After all, sulking is terribly immature and juvenile, whilst a refusal to engage in conversation is the mature person's method of sticking fingers in one's ears and going 'lalalalalala'. There are many reasons why the need to sulk comes up. Having your DVD choice refused is often a culprit, as is his refusal to take the bins out. The silence during a sulking session is the loudest noise you'll ever hear. And, usually, it's this emotional white noise that breaks one of you down eventually, with the ultimate sulk-breaker 'Fancy a cup of tea?', followed shortly with a tentative 'Are we talking again then?' At this point, friendly relations will be resumed or an icy 'No' will set the sulkathon off again.

Sunday Papers (Not Really Reading)

It's a great British tradition to combine a heart-attack inducing breakfast with a forest-apocalypse array of papers on a Sunday morning. The problem is that, although every paper comes with at least a million sections, you only ever manage to read the shiny, happy magazine, the glossy bit of froth that washes your tenth slice of buttered toast down with fashion barometers, silly celebrity columns and some pretty pictures of the hot new beach destinations. Quite frankly, with the fried breakfast you've just gulped down, reading about rising inflation and Cameron's manifesto on crime might just give you indigestion. Do you feel guilty? Hell, yes. Well, you just personally deforested part of the Amazon and you still couldn't be bothered to read the Al

Gore profile piece. Next weekend, save the world and just buy *Grazia* instead of *The Sunday Times*.

Sunday Times **Rich List**

Like the Millenium Eye, *The Sunday Times* Rich List is a wonderful thing with no evident purpose. Is it a sort of catalogue for gentleman burglars? Or just a whole bunch of wealthy people swanking? Well, of course it could never be the latter, no one could ever be so shallow. We suspect it's much more likely to be a sporting cabal of millionaires just trying to make it interesting for our old pal Raffles. They love a game of chance, the wealthy. You can hardly move in our local betting shop for assorted Rothschilds and Dukes of Westminster giving it large with a fun size biro. And Her Majesty the Queen's a bugger for the scratchcards. It's only a matter of time before *The Times* puts the whole caper online with virtual reality walk-throughs of all the mansions pointing out where the CCTV cameras are. Then we'll see some action.

Sunday Times **'Style'**

And they say it's for women: if you can find a weekly magazine that's *more* full of shapely young ladies in states of undress, we'll give you our tea-chest full of old Razzles.

Sunglasses

There's a time and a place for wearing sunglasses. If you're on holiday on a beach. Or if you're Bono. Pretty much every other occasion for wearing them is posturing and posing, pure and simple. Not that it stops us donning the shades and swanning around like we're a rock star, even though what we're actually doing is sales shopping. In Slough. In January. We know global warming is on its way, but even so, the truth is that getting the shades out before June and after August is still pushing it. As for that trend for not actually wearing your sunglasses, but perching them on your head like a plastic Alice band, well, we know we shouldn't, but we just can't help ourselves. No pictures, please.

Supernanny

The thing to remember about Supernanny is that, with a careful bit of TV editing, we could all be made to look like terrible parents. The other thing to remember is that we are not stupid enough to write in to the programme asking to be on, and thus exposing ourselves to 'ARE THESE THE WORST PARENT IN BRITAIN?' *Daily Mail* exposés. Consequently, we can settle down for an enjoyable hour of top-quality smug TV, as Jo Frost takes someone else's child-care principles apart. Naughty corner, discipline, yadda yadda, yadda; that's great Jo, but watch the sheer joy of what happens when we plonk the child in front of the television instead. We must have missed the episode when someone said, 'Have you got kids of your own, Supernanny? Right then, well pass me the *Fimbles* DVD and shut the fuck up.'

Susannah

With a figure that in any other hands might be considered matronly, and presiding over a series of television shows that consist essentially of sending not-particularly-bright people for an expensive haircut, Susannah Constantine may not, at first blush, seem the most obvious sex symbol. However, her womanly hotness and world-weary, dissolute air gives one the impression that she's done it all before and, given the right provocation, might do it all again. To you.

Swarfega

Man soap. It's composition is unclear – is it reprocessed saliva? Swamp sludge? Reconstituted Kermit? – but its purpose is more apparent: to clean your hands of oil/ grease/ grime/ body parts without going anywhere near that pristine bar of white soap by the sink. Seriously, that's just for show. Woe betide any man who makes the schoolboy error of trying to clean the dirt off his hands with it. A more skilled practitioner reaches for the must-have tub of green slime kept under the sink and gets scrubbing. Lady friends are so impressed – he's done some proper male graft! He's being considerate in cleaning up! – that it's a wonder that

Swarfega hasn't spread its wings into the deodorant/after-shave market. Or maybe they just think it would give its wearers an unfair advantage.

Swearing at Inanimate Objects

As a form of anger release, swearing at inanimate objects is hard to beat. You get it out of your system; you don't get punched back; no one gets hurt at all. That's what we call win-win. Many inanimate objects in life are asking for it, but we'd like to pick out a few of the particular little bastards: screws, especially those ones that go all magnetic on you or fall down between the floorboards; video recorders; cars on cold days; and traffic wardens. Admittedly, the latter are only inanimate once you've knocked them out cold.

Take That

Were you one of those people who were delighted when Take That decided to reform? If you were, you weren't alone. Mark! Gary! Jason! The Other One! Only joking, Harry. Sorry, we mean Harold. A joke again. Of course, it's Howard. We think. Nothing embarrassing so far, except that, because the reunion so takes you back to growing up and fantasizing about, sorry, singing along to the band, it's hard not to revert to your teenage self – screaming and pulling your hair out, and hanging around outside the studio where they are recording. But remember: you are now a thirty-something woman. Keep the fourteen-year-old behaviour for when everyone is out.

Take That (If You're a Heterosexual Male)

There's not many bands who being a fan of can define your sexuality as Take That can. If you're a bloke, and you're making positive noises about any Take That song bar 'Back for Good' (which even the fashion police will agree is a work of genius), be careful. It doesn't matter how heartfelt your defence of Gary Barlow as a songwriter is – no one's going to believe you. *Seriously*, you argue, *he's up there with Elton John.* 'Exactly,' is the response you'll get.

Takeaway Numbers, Storing Them in Your Mobile Phone

The mobile phone address book is a wonderful thing. Rather than having to write down and remember all your friends' phone numbers, there they are ready for you at the push of a button. But face it, whose numbers do you really need on a regular basis? Your mum's, or the one for the local Indian takeaway? It might feel as if you're trying to artificially bump up your number of friends by putting the Taj Mahal in there, but think of it like this – when have they ever let you down? And when was the last time your mate popped round with a freshly cooked chicken tikka masala and a bonus portion of sag aloo? You're right, maybe we should add them to our friends and family as well.

Takeaway, Ordering From a Train

Food available on a train is not always the best, is it? And what about those times when either all the bacon sandwiches are out or the buffet is shut for 'stocktaking'? That's when using your noddle and ordering a takeaway comes in. Urban legend tells the tale of the man who found the restaurant car shut on a GNER train to London. Using his mobile phone and directory enquiries, he got the number of an Indian restaurant in Peterborough and, after convincing them he was serious, persuaded them to meet his arriving train with a curry. As the train pulled in to Peterborough station, there was the delivery man waiting with his food. Imagine a) how great this man must have felt and b) how hungry and jealous the other passengers must have been. If only we had had the nous to think of that.

Taking Photos for Tourists

But always making sure to cut off their heads.

Talcing Your Hair

Once the preserve of scabby students, the soap-dodging way of washing your hair is making a modern comeback. Thanks to the eco movement, wasting water is now a far more sinister crime than sporting a greasy barnet doused in Johnson & Johnson's finest. So why waste half an hour of your life shampooing and conditioning when a shake'n'vac over your head will do? Just don't let anyone ruffle your hair – the mushroom cloud emanating from your head might be a tad embarrassing to explain away. And citing a nuclear fallout of dandruff won't win you any friends.

Talking About Celebs Like They're Friends
'Anyway, and then Ange told him she wasn't having any of it,' you gossip to your friend. 'Really?' she replies. 'After the way she's carried on, that's disgraceful.' Naturally, you're not exactly sure what Angelina Jolie told Brad Pitt, but heresay from *OK!* counts as fact in your book. For God's sake – anyone would think they were your next-door-but-one neighbours. Erm, aren't they? The delusion is too deep-rooted to cure. And anyway, do you know Kate's got a pair of skinny jeans *just* like mine? You know, Kate Moss. *The* Kate Moss. 'And Britney's *really* depressed about her divorce.' In a way, it's fine to talk about them as if they're your very best friend. Well, celebs are the new community, aren't they?

Talking in Elvish
I'narr en gothrim glinuva nuin I'anor

Talking Like a Teenage Girl
The thing about talking like a teenage girl is it's . . . like . . . so much easier? You don't have to think up *adjectives*? You can just, like, make a *face*? Or a little *sound effect*? Yeah? It's totally easier than acting your age. Plus, yeah, people tend to be less suspicious that you're really a twenty-nine-year-old woman out on the pull dressed up like a bloody Bratz doll.

Tatler (*The*)
Once the bible of the morbidly posh, *Tatler* has managed to broaden its appeal to the upwardly mobile parvenu and

gold-digger without shedding its core rugby shirt and pearls demographic. It covers a dizzyingly wide range of subjects from 'Ten City Boys to marry now!' to 'Ten single men with more money then sense'. If marrying money sounds easier than working for a living (and it should do! It is!) then you need to invest some of that money you put aside for caramel highlights in a *Tatler* subscription.

Tea and Coffee Making Facilities

Check into any hotel room and you'll find the same little sculpture in the corner, consisting of a little kettle, some disappointing tea bags and a cupful of mysterious sachets. You have discovered the Tea and Coffee Making Facilities. Given that significantly more tempting beverages are available from the hotel bar, it's difficult to imagine why anyone might consider making themselves a cup of mystery brand hot chocolate instead. Still, after an evening of comically strong holiday cocktails, a mouthful of Ovaltine powder is the ideal remedy for those nasty low blood-sugar headaches.

Teeth Whitening

The whole process feels very surreptitious and rather *verboten*. In exchange for a couple of hundred quid, people in soothing white labcoats will strap you into a chair, tut a lot, clamp your gums apart, suction any stray saliva out of your mouth, paint some hydrogen peroxide potion on your teeth, expose you to some bright and magic light and then pop back to repeat the process (especially the saliva bit) every twenty minutes until your teeth are shiny, clean and as white as they used to be before you started smoking fags, quaffing red wine, drinking double expressos and chewing licorice. You can't stop smiling at every passer-by and in every shiny surface – in the space of one hour you have gone from looking like the lead singer of The Pogues to bearing a striking resemblance to a US TV evangelist.

Telling a Colleague Their Baby Is Beautiful When it Looks Like a Pig

All parents think that their offspring are beautiful, but let's be honest, there's a good sprinkling of ugly Betties and Bills knocking about. Which leaves us with a dilemma – what do we say when presented with a photo of one such moose of a baby, or even worse, the screaming lump itself? *Christ, Sue, let's hope she gets better with age? You wouldn't want a model in your family anyway?* No, the correct response is to praise, and praise good. You know you're lying, she knows you know you're lying, you know she knows you know you're lying . . . but what is she going to do? Is she really going to say, 'Oh stop it, we all know she's an ugly little minger'. Exactly. One-up-womanship at its very best.

Telling Your Colleague Their Partner Is Beautiful When They Look Like a Pig

Can you think of anything more wonderful than being introduced to a mate's girlfriend only to discover that she's a mildly exhibitionistic lingerie model with a single twin sister? Well no, of course, there isn't. But second best is meeting your pal's bird only to find that she's a dumpy gutbucket with a body hair problem. They say love is blind. Let's hope so. Meanwhile, you can meet up for a drink with the happy couple any time you like without ever worrying about accidentally looking down her top. Plus, whoever you decide to ask along, no matter who you're dating at the time, is bound to be at least a shade hotter, and by dint of the secretary effect, will look like a lingerie model. And that's before you start drinking. Who could ask for more?

Temporary Hitler

The natural corollary to the Holiday Beard, the Temporary Hitler is an inch-square moustache that you leave on as a dare on your first morning back at work. Bonus points if you make it to lunchtime without sending the work experience kid out to buy you a packet of disposable razors.

Tennis Instructors

When Chris Tarrant's love-life shenanigans made the headlines in 2006, it brought with it a new sexual stereotype – the bored housewives of Surrey, hanging round in bars and ready for action. We don't fancy Chris Tarrant ourselves, but, can understand what is apparently the Surrey Ladies' most popular male target – the tennis instructor. They're young, they're athletic, stand up close, grabs your wrists and show you the perfect stroke. Mixed doubles? We say, new balls please.

Testing Your Dog's IQ

We have really pushed the boat out for you here and we have even consulted the great psychologist Dr Stanley Coren from the University of British Columbia, author of *How To Speak Dog*. In addition to being a busy man – marking essays, no doubt, attending drinks parties and wearing bow-ties (probably) – he has also tackled one of those great conundrums: how do you test precisely how intelligent your dog is? Big dilemma up until now, but he has added to his canine oeuvre and written a laugh-out-loud guide (*How Smart is Your Dog?*) to doing just that – through twelve easy tests you can find out whether your dog has a higher IQ than your significant other, your boss or even yourself. What is for sure is that he will certainly have a lower IQ than your cat, and that the cat will keep reminding him of this endlessly. They are like that, cats – real wind-up merchants.

Text Message One-Up-Manship

It doesn't matter whether you're one of those new generation texters with overdeveloped thumbs, or an old school phoner who has the predictive messaging turned off as it's all rather 'confusing': for all of us, the joy of text message one-upmanship is there to be had. The key is always to respond in the opposite register to the message that is sent. Responding to an old timer, a quick blast of incomprehensible text speak (txtspk?) leaves you feeling hip and cool.

Writing to a someone who doesn't know what a vowel is a perfectly spelt out, grammatically correct text gives you the warm of glow of feeling well educated. Standard rates apply.

Text Messages (Sending Them While You're on a Date)

Stay safe, we're told. Always let someone know where you're going. Make sure no one puts anything ghastly in your drink (Angostura bitters is one to especially watch out for, it's awful). Get a proper cab home and hang the expense. Most of all, call someone and let them know you're OK. That's all very well, but it doesn't cover hurried text messages saying 'he's a minger!!!' or 'I think he lives with his mum!!!' and especially not 'I love you too, but I have to work late this evening'.

Text Tourettes

Once upon a time it would taketh great scribes a lifetime to craft a sonnet of exquisite grace, rhythm and depth to woo the object of their affection. Now you can just down too many WKDs and text 'OMG U R SO Hot :) :) lol' whilst you're on the loo. Ah, the romance. The only similarity with days of yore is that it took just as long to decipher David Beckham's sex texts in the *Screws Of the World* as it did to work out what the hell Shakespeare was actually going on about.

The Brazilian (in Your Lunch Hour)

Your boss innocently asks 'Where are you going for lunch?' Oh, you know, just off to have hot wax dripped on to my nether regions for the teenage-porn-star-look, you *don't* answer. But wish you could. It's these kind of naughty mid-day secrets that make working worthwhile. Come the afternoon? Yes, you can get those statistics over to head office ASAP – but inside you're lap-dancing the water-cooler.

The Cheeky Girls

It makes you wonder why *The Daily Malicious* is scared of a deluge of Romanian immigrants polluting our green and pleasant lands when the Cheeky Girls and their mafiosa mother are poster-girls for the country. Actually, it doesn't. What it makes you wonder is whether Paul Dacre actually created them, Frankenstein-style, in a back-room of the paper's HQ. The girls, only one boob job removed from looking like Transylvanian transsexuals, are the kind of dead-eyed Internet brides even a modern-day Dracula would say 'no fangs' to. It takes a special kind of 'undead' to take up that challenge. In steps Lib Dem MP, Lembit Opik, and his professed love of one half of the horror-show, Gabriela. He likes her 'for her mind', mind you. This is clearly a woman who has brain cells for cellulite then. Strangely, her intellectual musings sound distinctly like the blurb on the back of a call box calling card. Their new album, *In My Mind (Is a Different World – a Cheeky One)*, may yet reveal the meaning of life. After all, the album includes a cover of Right Said Fred's 'I'm Too Sexy', 'Farmyard Hokey' and a song called 'Cho-co-late', so anything is possible.

The Core

One of the central macguffins of *The Core* is a practically indestructible metal called Unobtanium. It's a shame the scriptwriters didn't have the courage of their convictions and called it Bollockonium. Then the comic potential of this self-confessedly preposterous sci-fi disaster farrago would have been complete. It's basically *Fantastic Voyage*, but underground, instead of up a politician's fundament. It's better than that, though, it's B-Movie perfection: everybody dies at the *exact* moment you expect them to. The IT geek does all the standard IT geek things *and* has fully 50 per cent of the special effects budget spent on his nose. A pouty but frankly slumming Hilary Swank makes climbing into a hundred foot tall Rampant Rabbit look more glamorous and exciting than Doug McClure or a Thunderbird puppet ever could, and at no point does anyone insert *that* apostrophe and space into her name. Wondrous.

The Director's Cut

What's better than settling down on the sofa to watch a nice film? Settling down on the sofa to watch a nice film that's going to last all day, that's what. As it is, the average running time of a cinema release is creeping ever upwards. *Titanic*, which many people believe started this frankly rather silly trend, only clocks in at a blink-and-you'll-miss-it three and a quarter hours. The third *Lord of the Rings* movie offers you a slightly more impressive three hours and twenty-one minutes in the cinema or well over four hours on your sofa. Now that's a sit *down*. Admittedly, there are longer movies, *The Cure for Insomnia* (really) is more like a video installation than a proper movie, but it promises something like eighty-seven hours of sitting on the sofa eating biscuits. Unfortunately it's only been shown once and they don't seem to have it in our local Blockbuster.

The Dutch Oven

All land animals suffer, at least to some extent, from flatulence. Some say that termites are the worst offenders. Some prefer to pin the blame on cows. We would humbly suggest that, until these species master the art of the Boxing Day sandwich – loaded with turkey, stuffing and lovely little silverskin onions – they can only contend for the silver medal in the wide world of fart. Launching one's own signature fragrance is normally a solitary pleasure, though, and we all know that the most *special* moments in our lives are only truly complete when we share them with our loved ones. That's why popping fresh in the comfort of the marital bed, and then inviting the light of your life to spend a few precious moments with her head beneath the duvet is perhaps the greatest and most illicit pleasure of all. If the little woman needs a small amount of gentle encouragement to sample your output then that's entirely normal. After all, women are shy and retiring creatures and quite frequently deprive themselves of life's little joys. Sometimes you need to share your happiness. Sometimes you need to give her the gift that keeps on giving, the

Dutch Oven. If you can pull off the same trick in a car, it's called HotBoxing, and you might need a couple more Magic Trees. If you can stink out a city, it's called a Dirty Bomb and there's a Mr Bin Laden here with a job offer for you.

The Economist

'No one ever got famous by staring out of the window', ran a famous *Economist* billboard ad. You might have seen it, as we did, by staring out of a train window. At the time, we cursed their cleverness, but then we thought, what if we actually read *The Economist* ourselves, and then the next time we saw one of those 'staring out of the window' ads, rather than feeling small and worthless, we'd feel all smug and superior instead? There's some side reward of getting up to date with geo-politics and economic trends, but we needn't bother you with that here.

The Game by Neil Straus

The thought that a respected Rolling Stone journalist would decide to hang out with a group of Pick-Up Artists, learn their craft and then sell it to millions worldwide through a despicable book entitled *The Game*, which reduces the whole nature of Boy Meets Girl into a premeditated series of well-rehearsed pseudo-psychological misogynist moves, is bad enough, but the fact that he makes the book so goddamm compelling and unputdownable is even worse! So the next time you go out 'peacocking' or 'sarging' a PUA and you need a 'wing man' to help you 'throwing a square', let me know, and if you are a girl and one of us walks up to you and uses the oldest trick in this book, by saying, 'Excuse me, can you help settle an argument I have been having with my girlfriend', then you know what is on my bookshelf.

The Hits

MTV is great. However, we don't have MTV because we're too tight to fork out for the satellite package it comes with – so we've got *The Hits* instead in which to fill those brain-numbing hours. Full marks for the Ronseal channel title, *The Hits* shows you, yes, the hits in several different orders. Sometimes they sprinkle the videos with one of those wacky phone-ins to fleece money from teenagers. These are called something like Love Doctor, and once you have spent £1.50 texting your name and that of your boyfriend, it spits it back on screen as '*Carrie + John = 17%. Oh dear, guys, it looks like someone is getting their TLC elsewhere . . .*' Whereupon your boyfriend has to spend the next twenty minutes defending himself from what can only be described as randomly generated televisual accusations, while getting clobbered with a cushion as he tries to catch an eyeful of Britney Spears. Maybe you should have got MTV after all?

The Man Booker Prize (Watching People Lose)

The best bit of the TV coverage of the literary love-in that is the Man Booker Prize has nothing to do with who has won or what they have written but is, of course, the face of defeat – of those short-listed authors whose role at the event changes instantly from CONTENDER to LOSER when the winner's name is announced. Watching their faces at the precise moment they realize that the last four years of writing have all been in vain is a guilty pleasure par excellence. A typical loser's face goes from serious contemplation (as the Chairman of the Judges winds up to the money-shot) to practised nonchalance as the name is announced, to too-fast over-exuberant camaraderie with the winner (who is now striding up the podium) and then gritted-teeth vitriol as they listen to the acceptance speech. A joy to behold.

The Sicilian (Bikini Wax)

It's basically a Brazilian that 'let itself go' and went to the fur side. Known in professional circles as a 'fulsome bush', its only nod to male enjoyment is that it refrains from growing down the leg. That would be too uncouth. Think

The Good's Life's Felicity Kendall, not Pamela Anderson on the porn channel. Best worn with hairy legs, pyjamas and a place booked at spinster bootcamp.

The Vicar of Dibley

Yes, it's got Dawn French in it. Yes, it's written by Richard Curtis. Yes, it's got that telling-a-bad-joke-badly skit at the end of each episode. Yes, it's a BBC sitcom set in the cosiest of settings that a killer from *Midsomer Murders* could do wonders with, given twenty minutes and a chainsaw. Yet somehow, as with half the nation, we end up watching it every Christmas. And laughing.

'The World of Cheese' Webcam

Those helpful fellows at www.cheddarvision.tv in Somerset have set up a webcam to allow you to watch their 44lb (20kg) truckle of Cheddar spend twelve months maturing. In the first three months a mere 400,000 people have watched the cheese mature. It is simply hypnotic and, if you are really lucky, you might even (as we did once) see expert cheesemaker Tom Calver put his cheesy hand into shot to shave a bit off for testing. Until someone invents the 'Watching Paint Dry' webcam, we are hooked. What? They have? Where? www.watching-paint-dry.com. Oh well – the domination of cheddarvision was nice while it lasted.

Therapy

Years ago people told their deepest darkest secrets to their family. Actually, scrub that. People *committed* their deepest, darkest secrets with their families. And then spent a lifetime politely not mentioning it. Now it's good to talk. But not with your family, that would be weird. And not with your friends. Mainly because most of your bitchy whinges are about them. Which is why therapy is now God. In a world where everything has a price tag, paying for someone to endure your egotistical rantings and agree that it's probably all someone else's fault is priceless. In a way, visiting a counsellor is rather like gazing into a mirror for an hour. Except with the mirror occasionally asking: 'How do you *feel* about that?' Well, don't get me started, you reply, happy to be in the land of MeMeMe. The problems set in when you start to get issue-envy over other patients. You start to worry that your spat with the boss might seem a trifle inconsequential when the next patient probably survived satanic abuse after their family was wiped out in a freak plane crash. Thank Christ for false memory syndrome . . .

Thierry Henry

Why aren't more footballers attractive? Wayne Rooney may get your bloke all excited with meaningless gibberish about being 'naturally gifted' and 'the best player of his generation', but let's face it, he looks like a sack of spuds, and that's on a good day. Thank the football lords, then, for Thierry Henry, a cool sliver of Gallic gorgeousness among the usual meat and two veg. Put simply, the guy's got va-va-voom. He's got style, he's got class, and the way he moves is almost balletic. If your boyfriend's making you watch the football *again*, it's all but compulsory to compare his favourite sport to his least favourite dance. It's just a shame that Thierry doesn't wear the same sort of tight garments as the Nureyevs of this world.

Thinking Up New Words for Breasts

Yes, we all know that in the twenty-first century men can have them too, but nevertheless we still retain a fascination bordering on obsession for those delectably bouncy orbs of flesh. Just as the Inuit have about a million words for snow, so we normal blokes – for whom the world exists principally as a showcase for jiggling melons – have devised approximately twelve billion terms for boobies. The best part is, you only have to invent a word for norks and every other man on earth knows what you mean. You mean bristols.

Thinking Up the Perfect Crime

We all like to think we are cleverer than the last murderer we saw on a Poirot episode who stupidly left his glove at the scene of the crime, or the criminal mentioned on *Crimewatch* who removed his stocking mask in full view of the cameras, so the notion of thinking up the perfect crime is a wonderful way to while away a bathtime. You are swiftly transported from your Catford bubble bath to Las Vegas, where you are fixing the roulette wheel, scooping the jackpot and then flying off to a mega-yacht with Julia Roberts by your side. As she leans in to kiss you, you wake up all of a sudden and discover the water is cold and your toe is stuck in the tap.

Threshers

It happens every time: you need a bottle of wine to take to a dinner party. But you can get three if you pay for two. That five minute dash home to stash the two spare bottles will mean you miss the train and get non-stop sniping all night from your punctuality-obsessed partner. There are still two bottles of Banrock Station in the fridge, though. Worth every minute.

Tim-Tams

At last! An excuse for having an Australian friend! Chocolate AND biscuit AND mysterious tea sucking abilities all in one magical package. Just don't think about the food miles. This is a biscuit with a serious carbon footprint.

Toast Binges

By day a normal kind of snack. Butter me up two slices for breakfast, you say. At dinner add a tin of baked beans and bingo. But by night it's a different matter. Under the cover of darkness, the ingredients in a loaf of Warburton's ferment into the crack cocaine of the carbohydrate world. Two slices is *never* enough. In a sweating, butter-drenched frenzy you cannot be sated until the whole loaf is gone. Demolished. Just a few charred crumbs left that you recklessly snort up. When anyone asks the next day, you casually say, 'Yeah, I had a couple of slices.' Then feign total wonderment at why there's no bread left.

Toboganning Down the Stairs in a Duvet
Wrapping yourself in a big fat double duvet and then tobogganing down the staircase is a great way to start the day or to end it if you are very drunk.

TomKat
We never really had the Spice Girls down as cultural commentators, but with their number one hit '2 Become 1', they neatly encapsulated that modern celebrity phenomenon – the couple who are so close, their individual identities just melt away. Hello there, TomKat! How are you doing, Brangelina? What's new, Pebbie? That's Paul Daniels and Debbie McGee, by the way. We made that one up ourselves: you should try it too, it's great fun. Jorandre, Coyne, RussellBranythinginaskirt, we could go on.

Topshop
It's hard to imagine the time when Topshop was just a cheap high street shop. Now it's beyond a brand, it's the entire collective consciousness of every girl between the age of eighteen and twenty-five. It has its own radio channel, flagship stores, vintage sections, boutique labels, catwalk shows – it has Kate Moss as a designer for God's sake. It's what Neverland was to Jacko, for shoppers. If you can't see the object of your desire on the racks, you need only look into the eyes of the 24/7 plasma screens pumping out pop for inspiration. Which is why getting back from planet Topshop and bumping back down to earth in the privacy of your bedroom can be such a shock. Yes, you really did just buy a size zero mini bubble-skirt in gold foil. And, yes, your full-length mirror did just spontaneously combust at the sight of you wearing it. And, yes, you did lose the receipt on the bus home, thanks to your shopping coma.

Torrential Rain (Using as an Excuse to Stay In and Watch the Telly All Day)

Blame George Bush. Due to some weird weather thing, it's absolutely bloody pouring. Again. And it always picks the weekend to really crap down, doesn't it? There's probably some black and white thingy about World War Two on FilmFour, and all Blockbuster will have left is *The Prince and Me*. True enough, there's one of those gastropubs up the road and you could go and spend the afternoon on their sofas pretending to be the cast of *Friends*, but there's a whole load of *outside* between your house and there, and you've got a perfectly good sofa in your front room. All of a sudden sending the manly Hunter Gatherer out for some Ben & Jerry's and a comforting Julia Stiles fairytale sounds like the best idea in the world. Compared to the notion of looking like a drowned rat in public, putting up with the odd over-informed comment about Spitfires sounds like a price worth paying. Global warming? We love it.

Touche Eclat

Every wax-faced celeb in the land claims to owe their shimmering good looks to Yves St Laurent's wonder-product. And even though you suspect that a trip to Mr Nip/Tuck in Harley Street might have had more to do with it, it's more fun to believe the dream. Especially a dream that exterminates eye-bags *and* comes in a fetching gold ingot package that even a pirate would hyperventilate over.

Tourist Menus

You are in foreign climes and have barely worked out the essential words and phrases (Yes, No, Two Beers, Please) before tackling that first all-important visit to a local restaurant. After lots of non-verbal communication (smiling is always good), you are seated at a prime table and are faced with a huge totally unintelligible menu with an enticing single-sheet of paper headed MENU TOURISTICO paper-clipped to the front. You are now faced with a dilemma – do you make the effort to respect local cultures and sample indigenous cuisine or plump for the easy option? So that will be MENU TOURISTICO for two (hold two fingers up at this point) with chips and could you bring some ketchup, please. Now.

Tracey Emin
She's a stranger to soap, she likes a laugh, she's always got some fags and she doesn't care whether you make the bed or not. Every man's dream woman.

Tramps (Putting Them Down in Front of Your Girlfriend Like it Makes You Cool or Something)
In these commercially-fixated times, everybody seems to have some sort of mission statement or charter. None more so than the homeless. The tramps of yesteryear have been rebranded, and have developed a clear mission statement that is memorable and gives them visibility in the market-place. No longer content with traditional commercial activities, like having fights with themselves in shopping precincts and sleeping in parks, they have developed a clear mission statement (to get some spare change) and identified a revenue source (us) which will enable them to complete key objectives. Street beggars are very concerned with brand identity. They have a certain image to maintain and cultivate in order for them to be successful at what they do. The modern homeless person is all about obtaining spare change, so the modern homeless person brand reflects that. He has a grimy undernourished appearance that communicates 'I require spare change'. The modern homeless person reinforces his brand by a) asking for spare change, and b) having a skinny dog. If nobody gives a street beggar some spare change, he's doing something horribly wrong. As long as the modern homeless person stays focused and maintains his brand behaviour consistently, the modern homeless person brand is effective. So, when you come out with venerable cracks like 'how do I know if this change is spare? I haven't died yet!' or 'Why would I want a bigger shoe?', you're not only repeating

gags that were old when Jasper Carrott was young, you're obstructing a modern urban professional in the course of his self-determined objectives. Still, it's a bit of a bloody chuckle after a couple of shandies.

Trashy Magazines

What you actually went to the newsagent for was an upmarket broadsheet that could give you insightful information and opinions on the political situation in the Middle East. What you left with was a cheap tat mag aimed at Sheila in Swindon. Why? Obviously your curiosity about world politics had to take a backseat to your absolute, desperate desire to find out Sid's message from the grave, or how Eileen had possibly managed to mistakenly pull her ovary out of her left nostril. Which is why we are a nation of no-brains who know more about hermaphrodites than the Hezbollah. Trouble is, these magazines are like crack – one hit of that headline and you're hooked. Just make sure you hide your stash.

Trinny

About forty feet tall and possessed of an austere beauty that is near irresistible to the less assertive man, Trinny Woodall is – as I'm sure we've said before – popular television's most alluring principal boy.

True Crime

Just in case you felt too safe in your own home, along comes true crime to remind you that behind every next-door neighbour lies a sex-crazed serial killer. Luckily, thanks to Fred West and the Yorkshire Ripper having a monopoly on murder in the UK, most of the horrific events seem to happen in America, where it takes at least fifty-two women to go missing before the local police get a 'strange hunch' that something might be amiss. The problem with true crime on telly is that, unlike horror films, there isn't actually any grisly footage to show. Just Edna from three doors up commenting that she saw him moving the dustbin in a suspicious manner in 1972. And you know, as much gravitas as poor Edna tries to give the whole proceedings, it's hardly pure horror. Which is where the nifty camera work comes in. Shaky, black and white shots of the killer's house are dangled before your eyes, with a portentous voice over announcing it as the scene of 'at least ten truly horrific murders'. Yeah, but it still looks like a CCTV version of *Property Ladder*. When you can look out of the window and see a real-life stabbing for yourself, you have to wonder how long the genre can last.

Trying New Hairdressers
The rule of hairdressers is that, no matter how expensive and celebrity-endorsed your previous stylist was, they made an absolute *butchery* of your hair. Your new hairdresser will hold clumps of your hair up with the distaste people normally reserve for cow dung, and tut loudly to imply you were lucky not to have been arrested for crimes against hair. The irony is, they'll then go on to absolutely destroy what you thought was a perfectly nice hairstyle, leaving you sobbing in the toilets afterwards, facing the prospect of having to go back to your original stylist and endure the same 'Who *butchered* you hair?' speech from them.

Tucking Your Willy in Between Your Legs and Pretending to Be a Girl
We have all done this – stood there for a moment and thought 'I wonder what I would look like as a girl'. You have two options – firstly, to wait for your partner to go out, lock the door, try on a (not so) Little Black Dress, stuff a brassiere with a pair of socks, try on some rouge and a smidge of lipstick and then parade around the bedroom looking like Danny La Rue and then getting caught out badly when your soon-to-be-ex-lover comes back unexpectedly; or, secondly, just tucking your meat and two veg between your legs, covering your hairy chest and imagining just for a moment the liberating feel of not having a

trouser snake dictating your almost every mood. But, before you get too carried away, you think about the nightmare side-effects of being a woman (shopping, not being able to decide what to wear, having to be able to convincingly say you have got a headache) and you relax your grip and shout '*Ecce Homo*' in a very butch way at the mirror.

Turning Your Eyelids Inside Out
There was a kid one of us was at school with who taught us all how to do this – it hurts a bit and takes a bit of clever manipulation, but you do end up looking like an alien, so it is well worth the effort.

Twin Shower Head
Excuse the pun, but two heads are indeed better than one – this natty accessory for your power shower from those nice people at www.crazygadgets.com allows you to replace your boring solitary shower head and get up close and personal with your back-scrubbing mate of choice.

Twinned Towns
Who was it who first thought to transfer the concept of identical children to places of co-habitation? We don't know, but if they hadn't, then 'Welcome to the City' signs would be a lot duller. We think that's all town twinning is – does anything else actually happen? Essentially, it adds a vestige of cosmopolitan glamour to an otherwise rundown industrial wasteland – a vestige that dissolves pretty much the instant you pass the sign. Do the twinned towns in France and Italy make a song and dance of being 'twinned with Grimetown?' No, we suspect they might have forgotten to put that on their signs as well.

Ugly Betty

It's the new *Sex and The City* – but with braces and a poncho. It has to say something about the state of modern womanhood that we've swapped Carrie Bradshaw as our icon de jour for the geek-chic of Betty. Whilst Carrie wrote a smart column, drank cocktails out of her Manolos and had filthy sex with men called Mr Big, Betty dreams of writing as she picks up her boss's dry cleaning, has really bad hair and a boyfriend who appears to have had his chin amputated. The message being? Collectively, we've let ourselves go. Who's got the energy to identify with someone who sees shopping as an Olympic sport, and summarizes her life in pithy witticisms every night before she goes to bed. Give us a real woman like Betty, who looks like shit and grunts her way through life in a totally uncomprehending way, staggering from misfortune to mishap, a true heroine with a loser boss, bitchy colleagues and a backside that will never see the inside of Balenciaga tight-fit jeans. Stick your glossy magazines, how much more fun to hang out with Betty and her Bronx buddies eating nachos and knitting ponchos. So from now on, braces, not Botox, are the facial accessories to sport.

Ultimate Force

Series one contained moderate Professionals-style hokum. Series two was more of the same, with a slightly tubbier Grant Mitchell in it. Series three saw the departure of Chris Ryan as technical adviser, the advent of the first female SAS officer in fact or fiction and the transformation of the show into a weekly Steven Seagal movie with slow-motion shoot outs and ever-more implausible plotlines. The strange thing is, the better it got, the lower the ratings dipped, until *UF* was eventually dropped after series four. If you like guns, macho posturing and fat squaddies then *Ultimate Force* is the show for you.

Undetectable Maladies

Reader, do you ever feel that you don't get quite enough time off from work as you should? That's why you need an undetectable malady to bump up your holiday quota. The problem with making up colds or twenty-four-hour flu bugs is that people expect to see some sort of residual symptom, and it can be quite difficult to remember to sniff every fifteen minutes. But select, say, a 'bad back', 'migraine' or 'sinus problems' and, when you return to the office, no one is going to be any the wiser. It's wonderfully self-perpetuating: the more time you take off for the symptom, the more real it seems. And the fact that it can come on at . . . ooh, ow, sorry, bit of a twinge there. Going to have to lie down now.

Universal Remotes

Inspired by those adverts for some kind of shampoo or another in which some bird or another struggled to take both shampoo *and* conditioner into the shower and was relieved to hear that some product or another combines both functions into one gloopy unguent, those canny boffins at Boffin HQ have developed a remote which controls tv/video/DVD/satellite/surround sound/garage doors/ volume of partner's nagging and intensity of orgasm. Marvellous little gadget were it not for the small print that says 'Operates basic remote control functions and may not operate every function found on your original remote' – in which case, it's probably best just to keep all the others to hand just in case. Fun idea, though.

University Challenge, **Actually Getting a Question Right On**

Quiz shows on television are there for you to shout the answers at – it's not latent autism, it's joining in. But while your strike rate on *Who Wants to Be A Millionaire* or *The Weakest Link* might leave you looking at least moderately intelligent, attempting the same with *University Challenge* leaves one feeling really, really dense. Did we actually learn anything during our two decades of education? *Oh come on, viewer,* you can almost hear Paxman snap, *do at least try to make an effort.* Imagine, then, the sheer joy of, after having shouted out twenty wrong answers in a row, actually getting one right. Admittedly, it's normally the pop culture one rather than a question of real substance, but that doesn't detract from your belated feeling of smugness as Paxo and the geeks struggle with the concept of 'Scissor Sisters'.

Using the Post at Work

It's a hassle enough to get to the Post Office in your lunch hour without working out all those new fangled rules about what size the letter should be. We say, take the difficulty out of your day by slipping it into the mail sack at work. Quite how you go about it is down to how confident you're feeling. If it's to a member of your own family, will you change their name so no one will twig? If it's to a home address, will you add in an artificial line or two ('Personnel Department, Friends Group PLC') to make it sound more plausible? And have you really got the nerve to send your brother's present to Australia ('Contents: Clothes, sorry, important documents')? Of course you have: just don't write 'Happy Birthday, bro!' in big letters down the side.

Valet Parking

Like grated cheese in a bag, and many other inventions targeted at the morbidly lazy, valet parking is an American innovation. Still, like every other kind of parking uncommon in the UK, it works like this: you pull up within 'fat guy rolling distance' of whatever all-you-can-eat buffet you are attending that evening and a young Mexican gentleman takes on the onerous task of re-enacting *The Fast and the Furious 3: Tokyo Drift* while you are inside. You are engaged in a dramatic recreation of *La Grande Bouffe*. Basically, everybody wins. Especially the garage that has to repair your car's suspension after it's been taken over a few sweet jumps and then had a great canapé-filled whale climb back into it. It's a shame we aren't offered valet parking more often over here. It's due, we suppose, to the shortage of parking spaces. And Mexicans.

Vampire Lust Issues

Watching shlock horror re-runs is the perfect way to revisit any childhood psychological damage of an evening. The 1970s obsession with mashing up horror and sex into vampire lesbo slut films sent out some pretty mixed messages to your young impressionable self. The story was always quite simple. Count Dracula is a bad man. You know, the type that you shouldn't accept sweets or a sugared fang off when you're playing out. But here's where the moral logic gets, well, skewered. Because, although the bad Mr Dracula does like sticking his bits into good girls in Daz white nighties, what he *really* likes is a naughty lady who's gagging for a go on his incisor. She's the kind of girl who finds herself floating around Transylvanian castles of an evening, Bacardi Breezer in one hand and heaving bosom in the other. So inflatable are her assets that, when she gets pierced by his teeth, you almost expect to hear the hissing sound of balloons being deflated. Of course, going over to the dark side turns her into more of a raving nympho than she already is, and she goes out hunting for more sex with a bit of neck-produced tomato ketchup on the side.

Overall, it feels like one big tourist board ad for the dark lord and his bunch of merry vampires. So blame *Daughters of Dracula*, not drugs and drinking, for the loose knicker elastic of modern women.

Vi(codin) Habit
It's amazing the amount of Hollywood celebrities who go into rehab for painkiller addiction. And just as most of us are mouthing into our sleeves, 'coke addiction', it turns out that in the US pain relievers are the equivalent of shooting up ten grams of heroin. Vicodin. Even saying it out loud makes you feel slightly glamorous and dangerous, without the need to, say, hang out in crack dens with Pete Doherty. Obviously it's not available here in the UK, meaning that poor celebrities are forced to actually go into rehab for class A drugs. But what's that on the shelf next to those Boots paracetomol? Disguised in a humble Ibuprofen packet? Step forward Ibuprofen Plus. Our very own painkiller, cut with pure codeine – some kind of lovely opiate. And you can take it at work. God, you can even 'do one' in front of the boss. So develop a back injury, bosh a packet a day and say hello to the Priory and goodbye to any form of gainful employment for a few months. With sick pay, naturally.

Vibrating Duck
Fancy a duck anyone? At first sight, this is a cute bright yellow little floaty duck for the bath, but inside its little beak their lies a sensuous little secret – um . . . it can be used as a 'hand held massager' thanks to its built-in motor. Yes, fitted inside its tummy is a small motor which gently vibrates when you press its back. So next time you need something that is good at relieving dynamic tension reach for your duck . . .

Vitamin Pills (Not Taking)
In the same way that taking super-strength codeine pills with a hangover is a true pleasure, taking ten zillion

vitamin pills before bed is an act of pure horror. Which is why avoidance is such exquisite bliss. The thrill of living dangerously far outweighs the risk of overnight liver failure by leaving the Solgar Milk Thistle untouched. The only downside is that this kind of vicarious living can cost at least £80 a month at Fresh & Wild.

Vogue

In a world where magazines are getting thinner and less glossy, and are printed on such flimsy paper that you can read the numbers of the chatlines on the back cover while you're looking at the contents page, it's nice to pick up something as substantial, meaty and unapologetically expensive as a copy of *Vogue*. Pricier than many books, or DVDs even, and with a perfume sample insert that smells like the same really upmarket glue every month, *Vogue* is an unchanging touchstone of quality that we can cling to when everyone else in the waiting room is reading *Hot Stars*.

WAGlomania

Coleen is self-appointed chief WAG – Wives and Girlfriends, do keep up (apparently she blanks the under-graduate wannabees). But, in fairness, you would have delusions of grandeur too if you were the face of George at Asda. This Queen Bee syndrome can be contracted from the simplest of successes. But the key to feeling superior is to *act* with great benevolence. So, if you're the proud parent of a new upwardly mobile postcode, don't gloat *too* much. And make a big deal of the *up-and-coming* nature of your friends' humble abodes. After all, there's a fine line between your current dizzy heights and the depths of your inner Ugg boot wearer.

WAGS Boutique

How can the worst hour on British television also be the most compelling? The concept: give two teams of footballer's WAGs their own shops and let, er, battle commence. Great, you might think: so that'll be Posh and Coleen versus Louise Rednapp and Cheryl Tweedy. Er, no. One presumes they must have been busy doing whatever it is real WAGs actually do. Hello, ex-girlfriend of Michael Essien (and technically, therefore, not a WAG). Hello, lady friend of Marc Bircham, whoever the hell he is (Captain of QPR. But we only know that because we Googled him).

Hell, why not add some groupie who is hanging around the Chelsea training ground – at least she's *seen* a Premiership footballer. No drama, no stars, it's the show that has nothing. The only reason you're still watching is because you can't quite believe it's on.

Waiting Outside the Changing Room (in Womens' Clothes Shops)

It's all upside: you've obviously got a girlfriend, so you're safe. So women will smile at you. Some of the more maladjusted will actively flirt with you. It's a chance for a nice sit down and every now and then a wayward curtain will give you a glimpse of something you shouldn't see. Double points if it's in a bra shop. Triple points for Agent Provocateur.

Walkers Sensations Thai Sweet Chilli Crisps

It starts with the ridiculous packaging showing twelve seductive gleaming red chillis dodging two cascading crisps arranged in a tasteful 'just got out of bed' look on a white ceramic square dish (of the type probably owned by the Noel Edmond's lookalike on the cover of the retro Mastermind board game) and it ends with you picking bits of disodium 5'-ribonucleotide and hydrolysed soya protein out of your teeth. But it is impossible to resist a food product that tells you (almost audibly, in a Fenella Fielding meets Marilyn Monroe voicetrack) that 'in this bag, real chilli creates a gentle heat, while a dash of soy sauce, onion, tomato and garlic add a delicate sweetness for a sublime taste contrast'. A wicked shopkeeper also told us that Walkers have added Vintage Cheddar and Red Onion Chutney, Slow Roasted Lamb with Moroccan Spices, Gently Infused Lime and Thai Spices, and Oven Roasted Chicken with Lemon and Thyme. Enough already – we give in.

Walking on Cracks in the Pavement

One of the authors of this book was told by his granny that, if he walked on the cracks in the pavement, a large teddy bear would run out from around the next corner and eat him. Not suprisingly this put him off almost for life until he had a long hard think about it and began to doubt his granny's veracity – if this genuinely happened then why wasn't it ever reported on the news? He has happily walked on the cracks ever since, until now, when he has filled his son's mind with thoughts of teddy bears policing pavement crack-walking infringements and they both now dutifully walk with their feet slap bang in the middle of slab after slab.

Walking Round the House Naked when No One Else Is in

This is tremendously liberating and, as long as you keep the curtains shut and remember not to open the door to any postmen or plumbers (unless you are actually an 'actress' in an adult movie), capturing the whole naturist experience in a safe and controlled environment is a rather joyous experience – although do be careful if the cat jumps on your lap.

Walking Under Ladders

When you are a little chap this deliberate flaunting of this seemingly ridciulous superstition was something you under-took with great trepidation, but now you are a grown-up you take this in your stride and get a tiny little thrill from doing it. The fact that, in medieval times, a leaning ladder was thought to ressemble the gallows and so by walking under it you were in some way prefiguring your own death isn't scary at all, is it? Neither is that fact that the triangular shape a ladder makes leaning up against a wall supposedly represents the Holy Trinity and that by walking through it you are diss-ing God and embracing Satan. Hang on a sec – gallows, Satan, death? We thought it was just about buckets of paint, so maybe just for a little while longer we will walk on by.

Watching Comedy DVDs on Your Laptop Whilst Ironing

Maybe it is the appeal of combining something innately un-manly with something innately blokeish that gives ironing while watching watching DVDs on your laptop such appeal. The added bonus is, of course, that no one is going to challenge your choice of programming unless, of course, they want to take over the ironing as well. In which case you can leave them to it and go and watch your film of choice on a bigger screen in the sitting-room. Bingo.

Watching People Being Sick

We were recently travelling from London Charing Cross to London Bridge at 8.00 p.m., a short journey and one that we do every day. It was, as ever, a packed commuter train. As we entered our chosen compartment, a scruffy-looking bloke was standing (well, swaying, actually) in the middle of the aisle next to a concerned looking friend of his who was saying things like, 'Are you sure you don't want some fresh air?' and 'Let's try to find you a seat'. His swaying friend ignored him and started to make burpy, throat-clearing noises. The six commuters sitting to his left looked up from their *Metros*, their laptops and their books and looked down again. The train lurched forward, as did, in a gloriously syncopated fashion, our scruffy friend, projectile vomiting what looked and smelt like six pints of lager and a couple of kebabs high into the air. It hung there in true cartoon style and then rained down over the aforementioned commuters coating their hair, their clothes, their laptops and the windows and seats around them with the contents of his stomach. We have never seen such chaos and, to be honest, never laughed so much either on the way home. Good work, scruffy lager-kebab fellow. We salute you. Maybe he was a dry-cleaner seeking to drum up business?

Watching the Match in the Pub (When You Don't Like Football)

It's easy to get the idea that every other bloke in Britain likes football, and knows all about it. Not so. There are these three old chaps in a pub in Shaw that used to be mates with Jimmy Frizzell and they've managed to convince every other man in Britain that if you don't like football you're somehow not all man. The only reason that we allow this ridiculous charade to continue is that it presents the finest excuse yet conceived for men to disappear off to the pub for arbitrary 'important' fixtures, like the Charity Shield, the first game of the season, a mid-season derby or a vital six-pointer against Melchester Rovers. Women, being almost universally immune to the mesmeric influence of the Mackeson-sipping Oldham triumvirate, assume that our devotion to these groups of millionaire illiterates is genuine and allow us to slope off for a splendid piss-up. The only price we pay is having to wear a rather uncomfortable, distinctly non-fairtrade T-shirt which is probably a fire hazard. Worth every sweaty minute.

Watching Your Fat Cat Trying to Get Through the Catflap

One of the editors of this esteemed tome has a tabby called Leo who is so fine and plumptious that the whole process of him getting through the catflap has become a complex and balletic manoeuvre that is a combination of momentum and pure science. First Leo gets his front paws and head as far through the flap as possible by running at it (well – as fast as a cat weighing 20lbs can) before easing his huge fur-covered carcass halfway through. He then kicks off with his hind legs and, for a few seconds, hangs there in a see-saw of feline construction – neither in nor out, neither here nor there. To the uninitiated this looks like stasis, but then an almost imperceptible ripple starts from his tail and moves up, up, up until his body starts to slip silently out of sight through the flap like a great ocean-going liner leaving the shipyard for the Tyne. Almost before you know it his left leg waves goodbye as finally the task is accomplished and he is gone. Marvellous.

Wayne Rooney

Well, yes, obviously he does look a bit like a potato. Or actually, now you mention it, a little more like a radish. But he's a very, very rich potato. With evidently very low standards.

After all, between us, Coleen's not exactly Angelina Jolie now, is she? In fact, we could probably outshine her given ten minutes in front of the mirror and a Primark trolley dash. So whereas he's neither as chiselled as Beckham nor quite as dizzyingly minted, Wayne Rooney scores by being that little bit more *attainable*. After all, the chocolates you can reach from your sofa are twice as sweet as the ones in the shop.

WD40

What does the WD stand for? No idea. What about the 40? Nope, you've got us there too. But what we do know is that this aerosol can is one of life's most precious substances, ceremoniously passed down from father to son at the birth of their first child. 'What's this for?' asks the new dad. 'Everything,' the father replies, with a knowing nod. And he's right – there is literally nothing that cannot be sorted by a spray of WD40. Knackered bike? Squirt. Squeaky door? Squirt, squirt. The Middle East Peace Process? Excuse me, Kofi, you might be needing this. Just don't let your girlfriend get hold of a can: the day that happens will be the day she realizes that she doesn't actually need to put up with a man about the house after all.

Wearing Shades Indoors

Sometimes, thanks to being blinded by your own coolness, it becomes necessary to wear shades indoors. Preferably the oversized Marc Jacobs variety. Naturally, other people imagine you are either a) celebrity, or b) a total idiot. The moment when you put your HSBC solo card, not a Black Amex, behind the bar usually clears up the confusion. Luckily, it's too damn dark to see everyone's withering stares through your shades – so you can focus on the most important person in the room: yourself.

Wearing the Ultimate Rubbish Souvenir T-shirt

If you've ever walked down Oxford Street in London or the Golden Mile in Blackpool or, frankly, through any tourist trap anywhere in the world, you will know what we are talking about – those T-shirts which say 'My INSERT RELATIVE etc went to INSERT NAME OF CITY/ COUNTRY/TOURIST ATTRACTION and all they brought me back was this lousy T-shirt'. Wearing this T-shirt signals a number of things – firstly, that your relatives have no taste whatsoever for buying it and that, secondly, neither do you for choosing to actually wear it. The bad thing is that we secretly want one and will try our best to wear it in bed with a suitable veneer of irony.

Weasel Coffee

If you find the myriad choice of coffees in your local Starbucks have begun to bore you then may we suggest you accompany us to Vietnam to sample the delights of Weasel Coffee? It has a piquancy that will titillate your palate and should appeal to the tastes of high-end drinkers the world over. It attracted our attention not because of the taste so much but because it is made from coffee beans that had been eaten and excreted by weasels, which apparently enhances the taste of the beans. There is even a chain of coffee shops in Vietnam specializing in weasel coffee, so if you fancy ingesting something that has been transported through a weasel's digestive tract then please join us!

Weekend First

Upgrading at the weekends to the untold luxuries of British Rail first class travel (i.e. your own hand-tooled leather Parker Knoll reclining armchair, your personal Thai foot masseur, Michelin-starred cuisine, fine wines, shag-pile carpets, a Victorian roll-top bath and a home cinema) all for the princely sum of a tenner. Firstly, it makes you wince as you throw your deeply-held beliefs about a class-less society to one side as you leave the standing-room-only world of screaming children, drunken fans and broken air-conditioning for your private wing of the 11.37 from Wolverhampton and first-class fare. Secondly, it makes you laugh out loud when you think how much some of the people around you have paid for the full standard fare.

Weighing Your Poo

Banish, please, all thoughts of a freshly laid turd gracing your mother's old-fashioned kitchen scales. Our method is a simple 'weigh yourself before you have taken a dump and then weigh yourself afterwards'. A quick bit of subtraction and, hey presto, you can work out the weight of your poo. For the advanced poo weighers amongst you, we suggest you then search the house for an object that weighs the same as your faecal matter – there is something weirdly pleasing about holding a large peppercorn grinder in front of you and thinking 'gosh my poo is heavy'. You never know when this sort of information may come in handy, and it is a great ice-breaker at cocktail parties. On Sky One's *Braniac*, Richard Hammond introduced an entire item featuring this method (although he declined to participate himself) and the winner produced a poo the weight of a small kitten. Bless!

Westlife

It's very easy to slag off Westlife, the band to whom Boyzone passed the boy band baton, and who then couldn't be arsed to pass it on to anyone else. And, yes, their songs might not exactly push the boundaries of contemporary music back a bit. But, at the same time, credit where credit's due. They're the boy band whose USP is that they don't actually dance! No difficult routines to learn, no visits to the gym to keep fit and trim. All they have to do is sit on stools and grin at each other as if to say, we can't believe we're still getting away with this. And then two thirds of the way through the song, when the chorus goes up a gear, they stand up and everyone cheers. Imagine that – being paid shedloads of cash and everyone thinks you're great because you can stand up! If only we'd thought of it ourselves.

What Happens on Tour Stays on Tour

There are various slices of philosophical wisdom around which one can live your life: 'do unto others what you want others to do unto you' is one; 'love thy neighbour' is another. But, really, is there any maxim more delicious than the rock star staple, 'what happens on tour stays on tour'? For those of us who aren't rock stars, of course, then 'tour' is replaced by such alternatives as 'holiday' or 'spring sales conference', but even in these more grimy Travelodge settings, the maxim still holds its charm, just about. All we say is, don't think too hard about the logic of the saying, or, indeed, where its authority comes from: trust us, you don't want to see how well it holds up in an argument. And if you're foolish enough to use it as justification with your girlfriend, the only tour you're going to be going on is one of the casualty ward.

Where the Heart Is

Sunday night? Worried that everyone else you know is out have a good time while you cower like a frightened little mouse on your sofa too scared to have any fun because you've got to be up for work in the morning? Still, if you really can't have any fun, there's always *Where the Heart Is*. Comforting Northern stereotypes sleepwalk through simple but strangely incomprehensible plots surrounded by scenery that makes the wobbly walls of *Crossroads* look like the bloody Pyramids. It's like a hot water bottle for your mind. Lovely.

White Van (Hiring a)

A white van is the working man's 4×4: it's all about the raised elevation giving you that sense of superiority on the road, both metaphorically and literally. But while the 4×4 driver has to cope with sneers from environmental types, there are no such objections to white van drivers for one simple reason: we're not scared of a Chelsea mother taking Fifi and Trixibelle to school, but we're petrified that Shane from Essex might step out and kneecap us. Imagine, then, the sheer joy when moving house or some such thing which requires you to hire a transit for the day, and included in the rental price is a one day pass to Club White Van Man. That's right, for twenty-four hours you too can appreciate the sheer thrill of driving badly and getting away with it, sing along out of tune to classic rock on Virgin and honk your horn at anyone in the vicinity wearing a dress. Just make sure it's the *Star* and not the *Guardian* folded up on the dashboard – otherwise they'll know you're a fraud.

Wikipedia

Do you remember how you used to get those guys who came round trying to sell you thirty-six volumes of the *Encyclopedia Brittanica*? Well, if you wondered whatever happened to them, just log on to Wikipedia and you'll find out. By which we mean, of course, that Wikipedia has superseded the *Encyclopedia Brittanica* as the fount of all knowledge, rather than Wikipedia containing a page about what happened to ex-*Encyclopedia Brittanica* door-to-door salesmen. Though, if it did, we wouldn't be surprised, such is its range of entries. How accurate is Wikipedia? Let's be frank – we all know it's not 100 per cent reliable. But what price truth when you've got a ready-made answer in 0.5 seconds flat? If it wasn't for combining this wonderful site with the joys of cut and paste, we'd still be researching this book now. (Note to lawyer: that last bit is a joke)

Wikipedia Random Article Generator

The mission of the Wikipedia Foundation is to 'empower and engage people around the world to collect and develop educational content under a free license or in the public domain, and to disseminate it effectively and globally'. It is rather like Rome these days on the Internet – basically all roads lead there. If you want to know about stuff then someone will have written a hugely detailed article about it, had it fact-checked by the Wikipedia community and posted it up there, and anyone can suggest editorial changes. Totally awesome, amazingly up-to-the-minute and no doubt partly responsible for the increase in grades for course work in many countries around the world. The bit we like best is the Random Generator on the left of the screen – one click and you can summon up a random article from its 1.6 million pieces. Today we were taught about the Armenia politician Artashes Geghamyan, the Italian philosopher Francesco Bianchini and the 2001 New Zealand film *Crooked Earth*. What a great way to start the day.

Wine-in-a-Box

It's hard to know where to begin thanking the 1980s. But wine-in-a-box is a good place to start. OK, so the 'bouquet' is the equivalent of Chernobyl happening up your nose – but who can argue with an alcoholic beverage that you can mainline straight into your mouth? That's right. Perch it on the arm of the sofa after a hard day at work. Flick to *Location, Location, Location* on the TV. Assume the horizontal position and imbibe.

Winning the Father's Race on Sports Day

This isn't about sport. It's about proving a point and finally wiping the smile off that total arse-wipe of a father of that bullying little brat in your son's class. This is payback time and, as far as tactics are concerned – anything goes. And if as a bonus your son is able to say 'my dad's faster than yours' and a few yummy mummies take a little more notice of you at the school gates, then every little bit helps.

Wireless Networks (Hacking into Somebody Else's)

One of the laptops this book was written on has a nifty device called a Wireless Catcher which keeps its electronic eyes and ears open. If the laptop gets into range of someone else's unsecured network, it lets you know in no uncertain terms and at the click of a mouse you are using it free of charge. Marvellous stuff.

Women Drinking Pints

Why is it attractive when the fairer sex do this? It's not as if it works the other way round – women don't get all hot under the collar at the sight of a bloke sipping gently on a cocktail. I guess it's the same thing as seeing a female in a suit, or in your jumper – donning the masculine mantle is just, well, sexy. Well, just as long as they don't pick up the other male drinking traits of belching, fighting and taking a piss in a street doorway on the way home.

Woolworth's Pick'n'Mix

What M&S is to the middle classes, Woolworth's is to the chavs. Which is why the toffs get simply organic honey-poached salmon on a bed of wilted spinach, and the riff-raff get to shoot up a sugar-fix at the pick'n'mix counter (as if they didn't already have enough e-number ASBOs). Really, Woolies' (as it's affectionately known) makeshift sweet shop is confectionery's answer to Jordan's wedding pictures in *OK!* You're compelled to buy them, then feel sick a few minutes later. First you start off with the trusty old favourites – Liquorice Allsorts. A bit like your nan, but in sweet form. Then, feeling a bit daring, you move on to Cadbury's Celebrations and a few Rose's Orange Creams, with a bit of said effluent oozing on the wrapper. Finally, high on inhaling Sherbet Scraps from your paper bag, you dish up some Percy Pigs and Coconut Mushrooms. At the checkout, the real shock will be the price. Yes, you just spend £10.12 on fizzy sweets you didn't want, when there's a DVD player on discount for £9.99.

Working at Home

One of the joys of modern working life is the concept of working at home. Of course, when we say working at home, what we really mean is 'working' at home, for why get stuck into that report when there's Jeremy Kyle and *This Morning* to watch? For real connoisseurs, there is the advanced model, working 'at home', where so confident (or so don't give a monkeys) is the 'worker' that they don't even bother staying at home but head straight for the pub/shops instead. Don't feel bad about your bonus holiday – think of it instead as clawing back all those hours of overtime you've put in over the years.

Working-Class Tories

It sounds like a contradiction in terms, but across the nation's working men's clubs, a select few trade pictures of Margaret Thatcher in her pussy-bow blouse heyday like they're Catholic saintly icons. The Iron Lady holds a place dear in their real-bitter drenched hearts. It is the shadow of her towering reputation that casts a warming shadow over modern Conservative ponces like David Cameron. Ravey Dave's tree-hugging, wind-turbine powered ascent to the throne of the Tories is only tolerated in Northern, industrial cities because he's a direct descendent of her Ladyship. See, Thatch, as she's fondly called, had a proper work ethic, rising from her humble green-grocering roots by pure graft and a nifty perm'n'set at the local high-street hairdressers. Her vision of a classless society, owning their own council houses, was like crack to the older generation working class. Who cared if they didn't have jobs? At least they had the right to fit satellite dishes on the roofs of their privately owned estate homes.

Wristwatches (Insanely Expensive)

Ever wondered what the time was in Rio de Janeiro? Ever wondered what the time was in Rio de Janeiro *while you were at the bottom of the sea*? If you need to tell the time, you can get a £20 Swatch. Or ask a policeman. You do not need a hand-milled stainless steel military-spec chronometer crafted to the finest tolerances by Swiss horologists. Not if you're still going to be late to everything anyway.

www.abebooks.com

Imagine the biggest antiquarian bookshop in the world with a fully searchable database and every book a click away and you have just imagined www.abebooks.com. For anyone trying to clear a bit of shelf-space, this site is a total no-no – before you know it you will be ordering up copies of childhood favourites that got given away when you left home, replacement copies of books people borrowed and never returned, and maybe even books by people with the same name as you to impress the neighbours with. But leaving that to one side, just imagine you urgently need a first edition of the King James Bible and you have a cool $11.9 million to spend, or if you are operating on a more modest budget then one of 200 copies of Beatrix Potter's privately printed 1902 edition of *The Tale of Peter Rabbit* can be yours for a mere £27,500.00. We love the fact that Jonkers Rare Books in Henley-on-Thames include a note that postage within the UK will cost an additional £5 – as if someone will have spent almost £30K on a book and then trust it to the vicissitudes of the British postal service to deliver it.

www.dailycandy.com

Reading the sublime Daily Candy's daily email is like having a very loyal posh friend who keeps you in the loop on everything from sample sales, fashion tips and shopping to useful and acceptable gifts. It can be delightfully off-the-wall, beautifully illustrated and pleasingly dotty and random – a typical entry on the London edition (edited by the lovely Kinvara Balfour) is headed *Rare Sights Of London – Free Parking Spaces, Bus Conductors, East African Bongos and Real Tits.* Indeed. What a dinner party that would be.

www.dontdatehim.com

Officially, www.dontdatehim.com is a powerful online community of women from around the world which provides an informative wealth of articles about dating and relationships; advice to help you make 'better decisions in finding a man you love'; and, of course, the 'postings of hundreds of thousands of women who are creating a global sisterhood on the Internet!' The real reason we use it is that it has a hilarious database of terrible dates and men that you just shouldn't touch with a large bargepole. We like the sound of Philip from Idaho, about whom we are told, 'I advise any woman to keep her wallet closed around this man, he does like his gifts but when the relationship ends he will expect any tiny thing that he might have given you back, while he will keep all your gifts to him'. Don't fancy him? Then try Dr Dick from Manhattan, who sounds like a serial naughty man – about whom one girlfriend said, 'If you lost your Elizabeth Arden lipstick 'Maple Sugar' under the seat of Phil's car in about late November, I still have it'. See you in the Live Forum!

www.dullmen.com

On one level, www.dullmen.com is a cyber-world where quiet men wearing slippers, cardigans and drip-dry shirts can fall asleep over back issues of *Saga* magazine in button-back chairs listening to Classic FM. On another more interesting level, this is a place where people are debating important issues like whether there are more clockwise or anti-clockwise luggage carousels in international ariports and whether the rain in Spain does, in fact, fall mainly on the plain and is as such unmissable.

www.wreckedexotics.com

What's more interesting than pictures of a beautiful car that you'll never own? It's pictures of a beautiful car that you'll never own, but the muppet who *can* afford it has wrapped it around a tree. It just never stops being funny. If we were brainy enough, we'd be bandying words like *Schadenfreude* and *hubris* around at this point, but quite honestly we're so busy laughing at that Aston Martin that some Arabian prince has written off that we can barely breathe.

X-Rated Harry Potter

Strictly speaking, loving kids' films is for either, well, kids, or men (big kids, as we like to call them). But we made an exception for Harry Potter. Why? Well, it's like inhaling the nostalgic scent of childhood. Wizards, people with cute names like Dumbledore, golly gosh antics of what basically amounts to middle-class kids at boarding school – but on a broomstick. You knew you were with Harry. You could watch the one you missed at the cinema on Christmas Day with your mum and dad and not be troubled by the modern world of sex, sleaze and scandal. Until Daniel Radcliffe grew up. And grew some mighty fine pectorals along the way. Suddenly sitting through a Harry Potter film feels like a tour through the rotten underbelly of child porn. One minute you were salivating over topless pictures of him in stage show *Equus*, telepathically firestarting your vibrator by mistake. The next minute this little boy in round specs is staring out of the screen as the wholesome Harry Potter. Wrong. Wrong. Wrong. Basically, you can never watch the films in the same way again.

Yogarexia

It's hard to be an oasis of Zen, floating on a lotus leaf to a state of perpetual enlightenment, when the person on the mat next to you has her leg wrapped round her neck. And you can't even touch your toes. Actually, you can't even scratch your bum without pulling a hamstring. 'Whatever place you're at is perfect, honour it,' coos the yoga teacher beatifically. As if. Yoga is all about getting a better body and being more bendy than the person next to you. It's a hard-core, competitive sport which is highly addictive. Even though you know it should be all about achieving inner calm, you can't help but hope it'll get you a super-toned bum along the way. Which is why you spend every day doing the downward dog, dreaming of washboard abs. Sorry, Buddha.

Yorkshire Pudding from a Packet
Who's got time for a great British tradition when Sainsbury's do a pre-mix for 99p and *X-Factor*'s on in half an hour?

YouTube
If idly gazing out of the window at work isn't as much fun as it used to be, you need some YouTube in your life. We guarantee you'll see more car crashes, skateboard mishaps and wardrobe malfunctions than you'll see in . . . ooh . . . an *hour* of staring out of the window. You can easily lose a whole afternoon grazing the links, starting with a straight-forward bit of old Led Zeppelin concert footage and ending up with a tubby German lip-syncing showtunes. Best of all, because it's on your computer, it looks a bit like work, until you realize that the whole office is standing behind you watching in silent horror as Dean Martin duets with Orson Welles in an ill-advised stab at bonhomie. Yes, since the Google buyout, more of the content is just advertising, but in a world where *Big Brother* can be the most-watched television show in Britain, the adverts are frequently the best bits.

Your Blog (Obsessively Checking the Hits On)
Every man, woman and child in the Western World has now got a blog. Most of them are awful. Ours all are.

Nevertheless, the temptation to log into Google's AdSense site every hour to check how many people have read your incisive critique of the local bus service will punctuate many a working day or romantic evening.

Yummy Mummies

Years ago, the sign of a good mum was a pair of sensible shoes and set hair. The act of motherhood was, by its nature, a negation of everything that defines you as a woman. Instead you morphed into a post-baby blob of wet wipes, rendering you an unidentified species when it came to sexuality. Not any more. Holding up celebrities like Kate Moss as a beacon of inspiration, the modern-day mother cares more about her boob job than breast feeding. The school run is sponsored by Prada and she's more likely to nip out for a chemical peel than to change nappies. No doubt the next step will be botox for babies – well, who wants to see unsightly frown lines during a screaming fit? Ironically, the fact that the yummy mummy's bum isn't the size of a small country after the birth means she's more likely to get up the duff again.

Zero Bids on eBay

If you're hitting the Prozac at the lack of interest on the counter, the bids will have you in a full-on personal melt-down. It can be a cruel world out there, and even a million on the counter and a good few watchers don't guarantee any bidders. Nothing in the world is as personally humbling as seeing a big fat zero bid for your cerise pink winter coat. OK, so you might not want it *now*, but at some point you *loved* it. You even parted with a lot of hard-earned cash for it. Subliminally, what eBay is saying is that you are a person of no personal taste, that on a hugely successful auction site literally heaving under the weight of exchanges, no one deemed your bit of tat as worthy. On some level, it almost as personally crushing as unsuccessful Internet dating. But not *quite*.

Zoo / Nuts / FHM (Interviews as Excuses for Pictures of Young Actresses in)

Yeah, we're really interested in Lindsay Lohan's opinions on the situation in Darfur. We're slightly more interested in what she finds attractive in a man. Given that she's unlikely to join the UN Security Council or pop into our local for a Breezer, we'd rather dispense with the fig-leaf of an interview to justify those fruity pictures. In fact, we'd prefer it if she'd dispense with that fig-leaf too.

Zoo Magazine (Apocalyptic News Stories Regarding Al-Qaeda in)

You could, of course, always get your news and current affairs fix from some lightweight journal like *The Times* or *The Spectator*. The only problem with this approach is the comparative paucity of punchy, attention-grabbing and easily-understood headlines, like 'Holy Mother of Christ, we're all going to die', the rarity of double entendres involving the phrase 'Dirty Bomb' and the poor availability of pictures of semi-clad young dental hygienists from Staines when the news gets too terrifying and you just need to look at something that reminds you that you were breastfed. Indeed, given how a certain degree of embonpoint can offer comfort to a worried man, it's curious that only one major news journal offers these features. The journal is, of course, *Zoo* magazine. Every issue can be relied upon for detailed pictures of ex-Soviet RPGs or AK-47s being demonstrated by bearded, tanned and evidently very cross young men who have evidently decided that blowing things up is the best way to get on in life. Every yin has its yang, though, and you can also depend on *Zoo* for poor-quality photographs of impressionable young women who have decided that their best opportunity for advancement lies more in the area of slipping their blouse off. The balance thereby achieved makes *Zoo* the only organ in which you can safely read about ricin plots without engendering unnecessary, debilitating anxiety. Beat that, Boris Johnson!

Now that you have spent the last few hours/days/months reading our book/looking over someone else's shoulder/ standing in a bookshop and generally tutting/blushing/ yawning, we thought it was time that you, gentle reader, looked deep inside your soul and 'fessed up to just how many of our confessions you share. Here follows a handy list of all the *Shopping While Drunk* confessions – please tick as appropriate.

IMPORTANT NOTE: Fill the answers in using a pencil and erase immediately afterwards unless you want colleagues/friends/lovers/children to discover your darkest secrets.

Honest answers only. Have you indulged in these secret desires/obsessions/habits/thoughts?

Name	Never A	Occasionally B	Quite a Lot C	Every Day D
Abu Hamza	☐	☐	☐	☐

Mostly As – So Square

Or more likely you're a pathological liar. Really, in the modern world harbouring secret obsessions with Peter Andre and sniffing your toenails is just a fact of life. Don't delude yourself otherwise. It's futile. Please, for our sake, come out of the wrongness closet and get sinning.

Mostly Bs – Nicely Naughty

Perfect: you bite your toenails – but like Bill Clinton, you never inhale. You love Richard Madeley in a kitsch way – but you never considered having a naked screensaver of him on your computer. Not once. Well maybe that *once*, but you were very drunk. What a balanced individual.

Mostly Cs – Get Help

Actually, don't. It's much more fun this way. So what, you bought the entire collection of novelty *Baywatch* dolls when you had bid-goggles on eBay. And, yes, you did play naked air guitar at your neighbours BBQ. Is it a crime? Not according to your police statement it isn't.

Mostly Ds – Freak Alert

You're scaring us. Step away from the Scooch CD. Look, we're all for this modern sin lark – especially if it gives us carte blanche to drink strong beer through a straw and wear flip flops with socks. But we may have to call your therapist if you don't sort yourself out.

	A	B	C	D
Abu Hamza	☐	☐	☐	☐
AC/DC	☐	☐	☐	☐
Accessorize	☐	☐	☐	☐
Accommodation Allocated on Arrival	☐	☐	☐	☐
Adding Cheese	☐	☐	☐	☐
Adopting Little Brown Babies (to Enhance Your Celebrity)	☐	☐	☐	☐
Agent Provocateur	☐	☐	☐	☐
Airfix Models	☐	☐	☐	☐
Airline Seats (Reclining)	☐	☐	☐	☐
Alpha Women	☐	☐	☐	☐
Alternative Fireplace DVD	☐	☐	☐	☐
Amateur Footage on the News	☐	☐	☐	☐
American Idol	☐	☐	☐	☐
Ankle Bracelets	☐	☐	☐	☐
Anne of Green Gables	☐	☐	☐	☐
Anne Summers (Nurse's Uniform)	☐	☐	☐	☐
Announcers Saying 'We Interrupt this Programme'	☐	☐	☐	☐
Annual Bonus	☐	☐	☐	☐
Anti-Wrinkle Creams	☐	☐	☐	☐
Apple Product Announcements	☐	☐	☐	☐
Aquadrops	☐	☐	☐	☐
Arctic Monkeys	☐	☐	☐	☐
Aromatherapy	☐	☐	☐	☐
Artful Combing	☐	☐	☐	☐
Arthouse Cinema	☐	☐	☐	☐
Asking Leading Questions	☐	☐	☐	☐

	A	B	C	D
Asking the Waiter Questions	☐	☐	☐	☐
Australian Princess	☐	☐	☐	☐
Baby-Talking to Men	☐	☐	☐	☐
Back, Crack and Sack Waxing	☐	☐	☐	☐
Backhanded Compliments	☐	☐	☐	☐
Backstage Riders	☐	☐	☐	☐
Banana Caramel Frappuccino Blended Coffee	☐	☐	☐	☐
Bananarama	☐	☐	☐	☐
Band on the Run	☐	☐	☐	☐
Bandslash	☐	☐	☐	☐
Bandwagon Jumping	☐	☐	☐	☐
Banksy	☐	☐	☐	☐
Banoffee Pie	☐	☐	☐	☐
Bar Snacks	☐	☐	☐	☐
Be Here Now	☐	☐	☐	☐
Beating Your Child (at Tennis)	☐	☐	☐	☐
Beauty and the Geek	☐	☐	☐	☐
Beaver Shaver	☐	☐	☐	☐
Bedroom Posedown	☐	☐	☐	☐
Being a Homezilla	☐	☐	☐	☐
Being a Snob	☐	☐	☐	☐
Being a Strict Parent	☐	☐	☐	☐
Being a WAGabee	☐	☐	☐	☐
Being Asked to Move Down the Train (Watching Passengers Ignoring)	☐	☐	☐	☐
Being Duped by Newspaper Headlines	☐	☐	☐	☐
Being Late	☐	☐	☐	☐

	A	B	C	D
Being Nicer to Temps than You Are to Your Secretary	☐	☐	☐	☐
Being 'On a Break'	☐	☐	☐	☐
Being the Office Fire Marshal	☐	☐	☐	☐
Being Welcomed by Name at a Restaurant	☐	☐	☐	☐
Betting Shops	☐	☐	☐	☐
Big Boy Condoms	☐	☐	☐	☐
Big Brother *Contestants (of Limited Intelligence)*	☐	☐	☐	☐
Big Brother*'s Little Brother's First Cousin's Aunt*	☐	☐	☐	☐
Big Lunch, a	☐	☐	☐	☐
Bingo Wings	☐	☐	☐	☐
Biting Your Toenails	☐	☐	☐	☐
Black Opaque Tights	☐	☐	☐	☐
Blackpool	☐	☐	☐	☐
Bloating (Blaming Everything on It)	☐	☐	☐	☐
Body Type (Lying About on Internet Sites)	☐	☐	☐	☐
Bog Books	☐	☐	☐	☐
Boob Jobs	☐	☐	☐	☐
Book Groups	☐	☐	☐	☐
Book Signings	☐	☐	☐	☐
Borat (Fancying)	☐	☐	☐	☐
Bought It in the States. Coupla Bucks	☐	☐	☐	☐
Bourbon Biscuit Sucking	☐	☐	☐	☐
Boyfriend's Baseball Cap	☐	☐	☐	☐

	A	**B**	**C**	**D**
Boyfriend's Jumpers	☐	☐	☐	☐
Brangelina	☐	☐	☐	☐
Bread-Free Sandwich	☐	☐	☐	☐
Brides of Botox	☐	☐	☐	☐
Brighton on a Bank Holiday	☐	☐	☐	☐
Broken Digestives	☐	☐	☐	☐
Burning the Dinner	☐	☐	☐	☐
Bushisms	☐	☐	☐	☐
Butter	☐	☐	☐	☐
Buying 'It' Bags	☐	☐	☐	☐
Buying a Box of Chocolates (For Yourself)	☐	☐	☐	☐
Buying New Tools (When You Know You Have What You Need Somewhere in the Cellar But You Can't Be Arsed to Look For It)	☐	☐	☐	☐
Buying the Outfit in the Window	☐	☐	☐	☐
Call Centre Rage	☐	☐	☐	☐
Cancelling Dental Appointments	☐	☐	☐	☐
Cancelling Lunch	☐	☐	☐	☐
Carrier Bag Fraud	☐	☐	☐	☐
Carveries	☐	☐	☐	☐
Cashmere	☐	☐	☐	☐
Cassettes	☐	☐	☐	☐
Casualty	☐	☐	☐	☐
CDs with Sexy Covers	☐	☐	☐	☐
Celebrities (Too Fat)	☐	☐	☐	☐
Celebrities (Too Thin)	☐	☐	☐	☐

	A	B	C	D
Celebrity Autobiographies, Failing to Sell	☐	☐	☐	☐
Celebrity Golf	☐	☐	☐	☐
Celebrity Sex Tapes	☐	☐	☐	☐
Chakra Crystal Bracelets	☐	☐	☐	☐
Changing Rooms (the Gym)	☐	☐	☐	☐
Changing Song Titles in a Puerile and Stupid Way	☐	☐	☐	☐
Charity Shop Clothes	☐	☐	☐	☐
Charity Shops (Looking to See How Much Your Donations Are Being Sold For in)	☐	☐	☐	☐
Chavumentaries	☐	☐	☐	☐
Checking the History Bar of a Friend's Internet Explorer	☐	☐	☐	☐
Cheese on Toast	☐	☐	☐	☐
Cherie Blair	☐	☐	☐	☐
Chicken Fillets	☐	☐	☐	☐
Chip and PIN	☐	☐	☐	☐
Chocolate Nutella	☐	☐	☐	☐
Chopsticks	☐	☐	☐	☐
Chorizo	☐	☐	☐	☐
Chris Moyles	☐	☐	☐	☐
Christina Aguilera	☐	☐	☐	☐
Christmas Cards (with Cuddly Animals)	☐	☐	☐	☐
Christmas Decorations (the Naff Kind)	☐	☐	☐	☐
Christmas Tree Chocolate	☐	☐	☐	☐
Chucking a Sickie	☐	☐	☐	☐
Chuggers	☐	☐	☐	☐

	A	B	C	D
Cirque du Soleil	☐	☐	☐	☐
City Shorts	☐	☐	☐	☐
Cod	☐	☐	☐	☐
Cola and Mentos	☐	☐	☐	☐
Coldplay	☐	☐	☐	☐
Collecting After Dark Postcards	☐	☐	☐	☐
Comment Whore (Being a)	☐	☐	☐	☐
Competitive Bingeing	☐	☐	☐	☐
Competitive Dieting	☐	☐	☐	☐
Competitive Shopping (Food)	☐	☐	☐	☐
Computer Top Trumps	☐	☐	☐	☐
Concocting Elaborate Excuses for Being Late (When You've Overslept)	☐	☐	☐	☐
Conferences	☐	☐	☐	☐
Control Top Tights	☐	☐	☐	☐
Conversations About the Weather	☐	☐	☐	☐
Cop Groupie (Being a)	☐	☐	☐	☐
Corner Shops	☐	☐	☐	☐
Crashing Over	☐	☐	☐	☐
Crisp Linen Sheets and Plumped-up Pillows	☐	☐	☐	☐
Cruise Ship	☐	☐	☐	☐
Crying at Work	☐	☐	☐	☐
Cushioned Loo Roll	☐	☐	☐	☐
Cut and Paste	☐	☐	☐	☐
Cutting People Down to Size	☐	☐	☐	☐
Daily Express Headlines about Diana Death	☐	☐	☐	☐
Death Metal Bands (Publicity Photos of)	☐	☐	☐	☐

	A	B	C	D
Debt	☐	☐	☐	☐
Decaf, Skinny, Soya Latte to Go	☐	☐	☐	☐
Deepak Chopra	☐	☐	☐	☐
Deluxe Rabbit	☐	☐	☐	☐
Dennis, Les (in Extras)	☐	☐	☐	☐
Dismantling Sweeties	☐	☐	☐	☐
Disney Toothpaste	☐	☐	☐	☐
Disposable Nappies	☐	☐	☐	☐
Disrupting Meetings	☐	☐	☐	☐
Doing Absolutely Anything Apart From the One Thing You're Actually Meant to Be Doing	☐	☐	☐	☐
Doing DIY with a Hammer	☐	☐	☐	☐
Donny Tourette	☐	☐	☐	☐
DVD Recorders	☐	☐	☐	☐
Drinking Tonic Water Neat	☐	☐	☐	☐
Driving a Better Car than Your Dad	☐	☐	☐	☐
Drunk Texting	☐	☐	☐	☐
Eating a Secret Extra Portion while Preparing Food	☐	☐	☐	☐
Eating at Supermarkets	☐	☐	☐	☐
Eating Breakfast at Your Desk	☐	☐	☐	☐
Eating Food in Front of the TV	☐	☐	☐	☐
Eating Ice Cream as a Late-Night Treat	☐	☐	☐	☐
Eating Ice Cubes	☐	☐	☐	☐
Eating Paper	☐	☐	☐	☐

	A	B	C	D
Eating Sandpaper	☐	☐	☐	☐
Eavesdropping in Restaurants	☐	☐	☐	☐
eBay Counters	☐	☐	☐	☐
Eddie Irvine	☐	☐	☐	☐
Egg and Bacon Croissant	☐	☐	☐	☐
Elderflower Cordial	☐	☐	☐	☐
Electric Toothbrushes	☐	☐	☐	☐
Email Kisses	☐	☐	☐	☐
Emmerdale	☐	☐	☐	☐
Empty Calories	☐	☐	☐	☐
Equilibrium	☐	☐	☐	☐
Estate Agents, Time-Wasting	☐	☐	☐	☐
Eyebrow Eating	☐	☐	☐	☐
Failure (Other People's)	☐	☐	☐	☐
Fake Tan	☐	☐	☐	☐
Family Picture Screensavers	☐	☐	☐	☐
Fathers for Justice	☐	☐	☐	☐
Fearne Cotton	☐	☐	☐	☐
Fellating Hotdogs	☐	☐	☐	☐
Fez, a Tiny One with a Plastic Strap	☐	☐	☐	☐
FIFA 07	☐	☐	☐	☐
Filling Water Bottles Up with Tap Water	☐	☐	☐	☐
Flirting (Cynical)	☐	☐	☐	☐
Football Celebrations	☐	☐	☐	☐
Football Phone-Ins	☐	☐	☐	☐
Footballers' Cribs	☐	☐	☐	☐
Foreign Trains' Sanitary Arrangements	☐	☐	☐	☐
Foreigner	☐	☐	☐	☐
Free Newspapers	☐	☐	☐	☐
French Maid TV	☐	☐	☐	☐

	A	B	C	D
French Toast	☐	☐	☐	☐
Friends Re-Runs or the One that We're Watching Even Though We've Seen it Sixteen Times Already	☐	☐	☐	☐
Friends' Sisters (Fancying)	☐	☐	☐	☐
Gap, US Size 8	☐	☐	☐	☐
Garage Calendars	☐	☐	☐	☐
Gay Men Fancy You	☐	☐	☐	☐
Genesis	☐	☐	☐	☐
George Bush's Command of Eng. Lang.	☐	☐	☐	☐
Getting Ready to Go Out	☐	☐	☐	☐
Gillette Fusion	☐	☐	☐	☐
Girlfriend's Inability to Set the Video (Laughing at)	☐	☐	☐	☐
Giving Her Lingerie	☐	☐	☐	☐
Glass of Wine (with a Midweek Meal)	☐	☐	☐	☐
Global Warming	☐	☐	☐	☐
Glossy Fashion Mags (for Women)	☐	☐	☐	☐
GMI	☐	☐	☐	☐
God Bothering (in Emergencies)	☐	☐	☐	☐
Grand Theft Auto	☐	☐	☐	☐
Green & Black	☐	☐	☐	☐
Gruesome Birth Stories	☐	☐	☐	☐
Green-Shifting	☐	☐	☐	☐
Gun Porn	☐	☐	☐	☐
Gym Playlists	☐	☐	☐	☐
Haddock in Beer Batter	☐	☐	☐	☐
Hag Fag (Madonna)	☐	☐	☐	☐

	A	B	C	D
Hairbrush (Using as a Microphone)	☐	☐	☐	☐
Hairy Legs	☐	☐	☐	☐
Handsome But Dimwitted Barmen	☐	☐	☐	☐
Harry Potter, Reading with an Adult Cover	☐	☐	☐	☐
Hat Wearing	☐	☐	☐	☐
Having 100 Per Cent Feedback on eBay	☐	☐	☐	☐
Having a Bath in the Afternoon, with a Cup of Tea, Listening to the Radio	☐	☐	☐	☐
Having a Breakover	☐	☐	☐	☐
Having a Celebotomy	☐	☐	☐	☐
Having a Cleaner	☐	☐	☐	☐
Having a Good Side (in Photos)	☐	☐	☐	☐
Having a 'Long Lunch'	☐	☐	☐	☐
Having Stupid Computer Passwords	☐	☐	☐	☐
Hayseed Dixie	☐	☐	☐	☐
Headphones (Not Plugged in)	☐	☐	☐	☐
Helping Self to Things from Neighbour's Skip	☐	☐	☐	☐
Hen Nights	☐	☐	☐	☐
Hiding CDs	☐	☐	☐	☐
High Definition	☐	☐	☐	☐
Highlighter Pens (Over-Using)	☐	☐	☐	☐
Holiday Beard	☐	☐	☐	☐
Holly Willoughby	☐	☐	☐	☐
Holy Toast	☐	☐	☐	☐

	A	B	C	D
Home and Away	☐	☐	☐	☐
Homemade Soups	☐	☐	☐	☐
Home Office (Getting a)	☐	☐	☐	☐
Hoovering Up Things That You Shouldn't	☐	☐	☐	☐
Hotel Rooms, Adding Drinks on to Other People's	☐	☐	☐	☐
Hotpants	☐	☐	☐	☐
Hughmima	☐	☐	☐	☐
Humumga	☐	☐	☐	☐
I'm Fine (Said Moodily)	☐	☐	☐	☐
Iceberg	☐	☐	☐	☐
Ignoring All Traffic Signals (If You Are a Cyclist)	☐	☐	☐	☐
Ikea Hating	☐	☐	☐	☐
Imagining What Your Colleagues Look Like Naked	☐	☐	☐	☐
Inevitability of Britain's Inability to Deliver Large-Scale Projects on Budget and on Time	☐	☐	☐	☐
Insectilix Lollies	☐	☐	☐	☐
Intensive Conditioning (Hair)	☐	☐	☐	☐
Internet Questionnaires	☐	☐	☐	☐
iPod Nano	☐	☐	☐	☐
Jack Nicholson, Doing Impressions of	☐	☐	☐	☐
James Hewitt	☐	☐	☐	☐
Jamie Oliver	☐	☐	☐	☐
Jamie Oliver Recipes	☐	☐	☐	☐
Jazz Hands Dancing	☐	☐	☐	☐

	A	B	C	D
Jazz, Pretending to Like	☐	☐	☐	☐
Jeremy Kyle	☐	☐	☐	☐
Jingles	☐	☐	☐	☐
Joey Barton	☐	☐	☐	☐
Jokes About Samantha on Sorry I Haven't A Clue	☐	☐	☐	☐
Jonathan Ross	☐	☐	☐	☐
Jordan and Peter	☐	☐	☐	☐
Kaballah	☐	☐	☐	☐
Kate Beckinsale	☐	☐	☐	☐
Kate Moss	☐	☐	☐	☐
Keeley Hazell	☐	☐	☐	☐
Keeping Things in the Loft	☐	☐	☐	☐
Keira Knightley	☐	☐	☐	☐
Ken Bruce	☐	☐	☐	☐
Kendal Mint Cake	☐	☐	☐	☐
Kerry Katona	☐	☐	☐	☐
Keyboard Fastidiousness	☐	☐	☐	☐
K-Fed	☐	☐	☐	☐
Kicking Your Legs in Joy	☐	☐	☐	☐
Kissing Girls (to Wind Boys Up in Clubs)	☐	☐	☐	☐
Knocking Off Early	☐	☐	☐	☐
Larry David	☐	☐	☐	☐
Lawn-Mowing	☐	☐	☐	☐
Leaving Your Wife/ Girlfriend/Female Flatmate to Deal with Workmen	☐	☐	☐	☐
Leggings	☐	☐	☐	☐
Let Me Entertain You	☐	☐	☐	☐
Licking Things	☐	☐	☐	☐
Lighting Your Farts	☐	☐	☐	☐
Lindsay Lohan	☐	☐	☐	☐

	A	B	C	D
Listening to Music When You're Meant to be Working	☐	☐	☐	☐
Lists	☐	☐	☐	☐
Live Television, Being Able to Pause	☐	☐	☐	☐
Living the Playboy Lifestyle (While Your Wife is at Her Parents)	☐	☐	☐	☐
Local Radio Adverts	☐	☐	☐	☐
Local Weather Forecasts	☐	☐	☐	☐
Loch Ness Monster (Retaining an Open Mind About)	☐	☐	☐	☐
Lock-Ins	☐	☐	☐	☐
Looking for CDs whilst Driving	☐	☐	☐	☐
Losing on eBay	☐	☐	☐	☐
Lost (Putting Up Fake Theories on Messageboards)	☐	☐	☐	☐
Lost (Watching on Video to Skip Past the Endless Adverts)	☐	☐	☐	☐
Lurking	☐	☐	☐	☐
Lush Soap	☐	☐	☐	☐
Lying About the Number of Boyfriends You Have Had	☐	☐	☐	☐
M&S Pyjamas	☐	☐	☐	☐
Make-Up (Practice Runs)	☐	☐	☐	☐
Making Tea Upwards	☐	☐	☐	☐
Making Up Stories about How Your Train Was Late	☐	☐	☐	☐

	A	B	C	D
Making Yourself Sneeze	☐	☐	☐	☐
Male Mascara	☐	☐	☐	☐
Marie Antoinette				
(the DVD)	☐	☐	☐	☐
Meet The Fockers	☐	☐	☐	☐
Memory Sticks	☐	☐	☐	☐
Messageboards	☐	☐	☐	☐
Michael Winner	☐	☐	☐	☐
Michel Houellebecq				
(Re-reading the				
Porny Bits in)	☐	☐	☐	☐
MILF	☐	☐	☐	☐
Mineral Water	☐	☐	☐	☐
Minty	☐	☐	☐	☐
Mobile Phone Games	☐	☐	☐	☐
Monkey Picked Tea	☐	☐	☐	☐
Moobs	☐	☐	☐	☐
More to Love	☐	☐	☐	☐
More to Share				
(Dairy Milk)	☐	☐	☐	☐
Motorcycles (Buying Them				
when You're Forty)	☐	☐	☐	☐
Moustache Waxing	☐	☐	☐	☐
Mutton Dressed				
as Lamb	☐	☐	☐	☐
My Monopoly	☐	☐	☐	☐
MySpace Shoot				
(Doing One)	☐	☐	☐	☐
Nasal Hair (Trimming)	☐	☐	☐	☐
Nathan Barley	☐	☐	☐	☐
National Enquirer	☐	☐	☐	☐
Navy SEALs	☐	☐	☐	☐
News Junkie (Being a)	☐	☐	☐	☐
News of the World	☐	☐	☐	☐
Newspaper Diaries	☐	☐	☐	☐
Nibbling Warts	☐	☐	☐	☐

	A	B	C	D
Nicholas Hoult (Illegally Hot)	☐	☐	☐	☐
Nicknames	☐	☐	☐	☐
Nigella Lawson	☐	☐	☐	☐
1980s Brat Pack Films	☐	☐	☐	☐
Nintendo Wii	☐	☐	☐	☐
Nipple Tassels	☐	☐	☐	☐
Noel Edmonds (Self-Help)	☐	☐	☐	☐
Non-Egg Eggs	☐	☐	☐	☐
Non-Iron Shirts	☐	☐	☐	☐
Not Getting Up Till after Lunch	☐	☐	☐	☐
Not Keeping New Year's Resolutions	☐	☐	☐	☐
Not Reacting in the Way People Expect	☐	☐	☐	☐
Not Remaining Seated Till the Plane Has Stopped Taxiing	☐	☐	☐	☐
Not Waiting for the Train to Leave the Station	☐	☐	☐	☐
Novelty Pens	☐	☐	☐	☐
Nu Rave	☐	☐	☐	☐
Ogling	☐	☐	☐	☐
Old School Reports	☐	☐	☐	☐
Organic Food Stores	☐	☐	☐	☐
Original Features	☐	☐	☐	☐
Owning a Guitar	☐	☐	☐	☐
Parking in the Toddler Zone at the Super-market when Your Toddler is Thirteen	☐	☐	☐	☐
Parking	☐	☐	☐	☐
Parrot	☐	☐	☐	☐

	A	B	C	D
Partworks	☐	☐	☐	☐
Paying Bills Late	☐	☐	☐	☐
PDAs	☐	☐	☐	☐
Peeing in the Back Garden	☐	☐	☐	☐
Peeing in the Sink	☐	☐	☐	☐
Peeling Sunburnt Skin Off	☐	☐	☐	☐
Period Pants	☐	☐	☐	☐
Personal Ads in the Guardian Guide	☐	☐	☐	☐
Personalized Number Plates	☐	☐	☐	☐
Pet Blogs	☐	☐	☐	☐
Pete Doherty	☐	☐	☐	☐
Photoshop	☐	☐	☐	☐
Pigs	☐	☐	☐	☐
Pink iPods	☐	☐	☐	☐
Planning which Relatives to Ignore when You Win the Lottery	☐	☐	☐	☐
Playing Buzzword Bingo During Important Meetings	☐	☐	☐	☐
Playing Spot-the-Tranny	☐	☐	☐	☐
+1 Channels	☐	☐	☐	☐
Poker Night	☐	☐	☐	☐
Porn Movies, Watching the Free Five Minutes when Staying at a Hotel	☐	☐	☐	☐
Porn Names	☐	☐	☐	☐
Porn Stars, Exposing More of a Knowledge of in Public Than is Advisable	☐	☐	☐	☐

	A	B	C	D
Power Girl	☐	☐	☐	☐
Practising Your Signature	☐	☐	☐	☐
Pretending Something Was in the Sale (When it Wasn't)	☐	☐	☐	☐
Pretending to Be Blind	☐	☐	☐	☐
Pretending to Be Out when You Are in	☐	☐	☐	☐
Pretending to Like Your Colleague's New Haircut	☐	☐	☐	☐
Pretending to Listen	☐	☐	☐	☐
Pretending You Can't Work the Washing Machine	☐	☐	☐	☐
Pretending You Haven't Eaten (When You Have)	☐	☐	☐	☐
Pretending You Never Got the Email	☐	☐	☐	☐
Pretending You've Eaten (When you Haven't)	☐	☐	☐	☐
Prince Harry	☐	☐	☐	☐
Princess Diana (Implausible Conspiracy Theories About)	☐	☐	☐	☐
Problem Pages	☐	☐	☐	☐
Property Sites, Virtual Tours	☐	☐	☐	☐
Provincial Nightclubs	☐	☐	☐	☐
Pubic Art	☐	☐	☐	☐
Public Schoolboys	☐	☐	☐	☐
Public Schoolgirls	☐	☐	☐	☐

	A	B	C	D
Punchline	☐	☐	☐	☐
Punning	☐	☐	☐	☐
Putting Tomato Ketchup on Everything	☐	☐	☐	☐
Putting Weird Stuff in the Toilet	☐	☐	☐	☐
Putting Your Cat into Different Positions	☐	☐	☐	☐
Quote . . . Unquote	☐	☐	☐	☐
R&B Grinding	☐	☐	☐	☐
Radio Quizzes (Cheating Using Google)	☐	☐	☐	☐
Rag Mags	☐	☐	☐	☐
Rave Anthems (Old)	☐	☐	☐	☐
Ray Lamontagne	☐	☐	☐	☐
Reading on the Toilet	☐	☐	☐	☐
Reading XRRF & Passing the Jokes Off as Your Own	☐	☐	☐	☐
Recordable DVDs	☐	☐	☐	☐
Rehearsing Your Exit Interview (Again and Again)	☐	☐	☐	☐
Relationship Advice U-Turns	☐	☐	☐	☐
Remote Control (Putting on the Television)	☐	☐	☐	☐
Rewriting History	☐	☐	☐	☐
Riding a Motorbike (Just So You Can Turn Up to Work In the Clothes)	☐	☐	☐	☐
Rockumentaries	☐	☐	☐	☐
Rotherham Shower	☐	☐	☐	☐

	A	B	C	D
Roy Chubby Brown	☐	☐	☐	☐
Running For a Bus (Kind of)	☐	☐	☐	☐
Rural Daydreams	☐	☐	☐	☐
Russell Brand	☐	☐	☐	☐
Ruth Badger	☐	☐	☐	☐
Saddam Hussein, Watching Being Hung on the Internet	☐	☐	☐	☐
Sandals, Wearing to Work	☐	☐	☐	☐
'Satisfaction' (the Benny Benassi video for)	☐	☐	☐	☐
Saying the Word 'Hot!'	☐	☐	☐	☐
Saying You Are in a Meeting	☐	☐	☐	☐
Scarlett Johansson's Smile	☐	☐	☐	☐
Scented Candles	☐	☐	☐	☐
Scientology	☐	☐	☐	☐
Scissor Sisters	☐	☐	☐	☐
Screen Wipes	☐	☐	☐	☐
Second Breakfasts	☐	☐	☐	☐
Second Life	☐	☐	☐	☐
Secret Messages	☐	☐	☐	☐
Self-Help Books	☐	☐	☐	☐
Sex (With Knickers on)	☐	☐	☐	☐
Sex Blogs	☐	☐	☐	☐
Shaggy Dog Stories	☐	☐	☐	☐
Share-Sized Packets of Crisps	☐	☐	☐	☐
Sheds	☐	☐	☐	☐
Shop Windows (Checking Yourself Out in)	☐	☐	☐	☐
She Pees	☐	☐	☐	☐

	A	B	C	D
Shopping Bulimia	☐	☐	☐	☐
Shopping in Primark	☐	☐	☐	☐
Shopping while Drunk	☐	☐	☐	☐
Shoving Stuff under the Sofa	☐	☐	☐	☐
Signing Petitions	☐	☐	☐	☐
Simon Cowell	☐	☐	☐	☐
Size Zero	☐	☐	☐	☐
Sky Plus	☐	☐	☐	☐
Sleeping at Your Desk (Ways of Disguising that You Are)	☐	☐	☐	☐
Sleeping in Taxis	☐	☐	☐	☐
Slimming World	☐	☐	☐	☐
Slot Machines, Asking Your Partner to Win a Cuddly Toy On	☐	☐	☐	☐
Slot Machines, Winning Cuddly Toys On	☐	☐	☐	☐
Slumping (at Your Desk)	☐	☐	☐	☐
Snakes on a Plane	☐	☐	☐	☐
Sneezing while Driving	☐	☐	☐	☐
Socks with Sandals	☐	☐	☐	☐
Softcore Porn (as PC Wallpaper)	☐	☐	☐	☐
Speed Camera Shuffle	☐	☐	☐	☐
Spitting from Tall Buildings	☐	☐	☐	☐
Spitting in the Urinal	☐	☐	☐	☐
Splashing in Puddles	☐	☐	☐	☐
Spooks	☐	☐	☐	☐
Sporting Altercations (Watching on Video)	☐	☐	☐	☐
Squeezable Marmite Jars	☐	☐	☐	☐
Stag Nights	☐	☐	☐	☐

	A	B	C	D
Stainless Steel Kitchen Utensils	☐	☐	☐	☐
Starbucks	☐	☐	☐	☐
Starship Troopers	☐	☐	☐	☐
Steven Seagal	☐	☐	☐	☐
Sticky Fingers	☐	☐	☐	☐
Sting	☐	☐	☐	☐
Stirring Hot Chocolate with a Cadbury's Flake	☐	☐	☐	☐
Street Portraiture	☐	☐	☐	☐
Stubble	☐	☐	☐	☐
stuffonmycat.com	☐	☐	☐	☐
Sucking Seatbelts	☐	☐	☐	☐
Sucking the Camembert From Its Deep Fried Coating	☐	☐	☐	☐
Sulking	☐	☐	☐	☐
Sunday Papers (Not Really Reading)	☐	☐	☐	☐
Sunday Times Rich List	☐	☐	☐	☐
Sunday Times 'Style'	☐	☐	☐	☐
Sunglasses	☐	☐	☐	☐
Supernanny	☐	☐	☐	☐
Susannah	☐	☐	☐	☐
Swarfega	☐	☐	☐	☐
Swearing at Inanimate Objects	☐	☐	☐	☐
Take That	☐	☐	☐	☐
Take That (If You're a Heterosexual Male)	☐	☐	☐	☐
Takeaway Numbers, Storing Them in Your Mobile Phone	☐	☐	☐	☐
Takeaway, Ordering From a Train	☐	☐	☐	☐

	A	B	C	D
Taking Photos for Tourists	☐	☐	☐	☐
Talcing Your Hair	☐	☐	☐	☐
Talking About Celebs Like They're Friends	☐	☐	☐	☐
Talking in Elvish	☐	☐	☐	☐
Talking Like a Teenage Girl	☐	☐	☐	☐
Tatler *(The)*	☐	☐	☐	☐
Tea and Coffee Making Facilities	☐	☐	☐	☐
Teeth Whitening	☐	☐	☐	☐
Telling a Colleague Their Baby Is Beautiful When it Looks Like a Pig	☐	☐	☐	☐
Telling Your Colleague Their Partner Is Beautiful When They Look Like a Pig	☐	☐	☐	☐
Temporary Hitler	☐	☐	☐	☐
Tennis Instructors	☐	☐	☐	☐
Testing Your Dog's IQ	☐	☐	☐	☐
Text Message One-Up-Manship	☐	☐	☐	☐
Text Messages (Sending Them While You're on a Date)	☐	☐	☐	☐
Text Tourettes	☐	☐	☐	☐
The Brazilian (in Your Lunch Hour)	☐	☐	☐	☐
The Cheeky Girls	☐	☐	☐	☐
The Core	☐	☐	☐	☐
The Director's Cut	☐	☐	☐	☐
The Dutch Oven	☐	☐	☐	☐
The Economist	☐	☐	☐	☐
The Game *by Neil Straus*	☐	☐	☐	☐

	A	B	C	D
The Hits	☐	☐	☐	☐
The Man Booker Prize (Watching People Lose)	☐	☐	☐	☐
The Sicilian (Bikini Wax)	☐	☐	☐	☐
The Vicar of Dibley	☐	☐	☐	☐
'The World of Cheese' Webcam	☐	☐	☐	☐
Therapy	☐	☐	☐	☐
Thierry Henry	☐	☐	☐	☐
Thinking up New Words for Breasts	☐	☐	☐	☐
Thinking up the Perfect Crime	☐	☐	☐	☐
Threshers	☐	☐	☐	☐
Tim-Tams	☐	☐	☐	☐
Toast Binges	☐	☐	☐	☐
Toboganning Down the Stairs in a Duvet	☐	☐	☐	☐
TomKat	☐	☐	☐	☐
Topshop	☐	☐	☐	☐
Torrential Rain (Using as an Excuse to Stay In and Watch the Telly All Day)	☐	☐	☐	☐
Touche Eclat	☐	☐	☐	☐
Tourist Menus	☐	☐	☐	☐
Tracey Emin	☐	☐	☐	☐
Tramps (Putting Them Down in Front of Your Girlfriend Like it Makes You Cool or Something)	☐	☐	☐	☐
Trashy Magazines	☐	☐	☐	☐
Trinny	☐	☐	☐	☐
True Crime	☐	☐	☐	☐

	A	B	C	D
Trying New Hairdressers	☐	☐	☐	☐
Tucking Your Willy in Between Your Legs and Pretending to Be a Girl	☐	☐	☐	☐
Turning Your Eyelids Inside Out	☐	☐	☐	☐
Twin Shower Head	☐	☐	☐	☐
Twinned Towns	☐	☐	☐	☐
Ugly Betty	☐	☐	☐	☐
Ultimate Force	☐	☐	☐	☐
Undetectable Maladies	☐	☐	☐	☐
Universal Remotes	☐	☐	☐	☐
University Challenge, Actually Getting a Question Right On	☐	☐	☐	☐
Using the Post at Work	☐	☐	☐	☐
Valet Parking	☐	☐	☐	☐
Vampire Lust Issues	☐	☐	☐	☐
Vi(codin) Habit	☐	☐	☐	☐
Vibrating Duck	☐	☐	☐	☐
Vitamin Pills (Not Taking)	☐	☐	☐	☐
Vogue	☐	☐	☐	☐
WAGlomania	☐	☐	☐	☐
WAGS Boutique	☐	☐	☐	☐
Waiting Outside the Changing Room (in Womens' Clothes Shops)	☐	☐	☐	☐
Walkers Sensations Thai Sweet Chilli Crisps	☐	☐	☐	☐
Walking on Cracks in the Pavement	☐	☐	☐	☐
Walking Round the House Naked when No One Else Is in	☐	☐	☐	☐

	A	B	C	D
Walking Under Ladders	☐	☐	☐	☐
Watching Comedy DVDs on Your Laptop Whilst Ironing	☐	☐	☐	☐
Watching People Being Sick	☐	☐	☐	☐
Watching the Match in the Pub (When You Don't Like Football)	☐	☐	☐	☐
Watching Your Fat Cat Trying to Get Through the Catflap	☐	☐	☐	☐
Wayne Rooney	☐	☐	☐	☐
WD40	☐	☐	☐	☐
Wearing Shades Indoors	☐	☐	☐	☐
Wearing the Ultimate Rubbish Souvenir T-shirt	☐	☐	☐	☐
Weasel Coffee	☐	☐	☐	☐
Weekend First	☐	☐	☐	☐
Weighing Your Poo	☐	☐	☐	☐
Westlife	☐	☐	☐	☐
What Happens on Tour Stays on Tour	☐	☐	☐	☐
Where the Heart Is	☐	☐	☐	☐
White Van (Hiring a)	☐	☐	☐	☐
Wikipedia	☐	☐	☐	☐
Wikipedia Random Article Generator	☐	☐	☐	☐
Wine-in-a-Box	☐	☐	☐	☐
Winning the Father's Race on Sports Day	☐	☐	☐	☐
Wireless Networks (Hacking into Somebody Elses)	☐	☐	☐	☐

	A	B	C	D
Women Drinking Pints	☐	☐	☐	☐
Woolworth's Pick'n'Mix	☐	☐	☐	☐
Working at Home	☐	☐	☐	☐
Working-Class Tories	☐	☐	☐	☐
Wristwatches (Insanely Expensive)	☐	☐	☐	☐
www.abebooks.com	☐	☐	☐	☐
www.dailycandy.com	☐	☐	☐	☐
www.dontdatehim.com	☐	☐	☐	☐
www.dullmen.com	☐	☐	☐	☐
www.wreckedexotics.com	☐	☐	☐	☐
X-Rated Harry Potter	☐	☐	☐	☐
Yogarexia	☐	☐	☐	☐
Yorkshire Pudding from a Packet	☐	☐	☐	☐
YouTube	☐	☐	☐	☐
Your Blog (Obsessively Checking the Hits On)	☐	☐	☐	☐
Yummy Mummies	☐	☐	☐	☐
Zero Bids on eBay	☐	☐	☐	☐
Zoo / Nuts / FHM (Interviews as Excuses for Pictures of Young Actresses in)	☐	☐	☐	☐
Zoo Magazine (Apocalyptic News Stories Regarding Al-Qaeda in)	☐	☐	☐	☐

Now add up your scores in time-honoured magazine-style fashion and see what our patented Shopping-While-Drunk-Ometer (patents pending) reveals about your personality.

Acknowledgements

The authors would like to thank their dear friend and researcher Mr G O'gle, Sean Rowley, über-agent James Gill at PFD (always a useful man to have in your corner) and, at John Murray (Publishers), their firm-but-fair editors Ellie Birne and Helen Hawksfield, marketing supremo James Spackman and publicity guru Nikki Barrow.

Amanda would like to thank Mum and Dad, Ali, Ange, Joy, Helen and Milo, the fat, ginger, psychotic cat.

Tom would like to thank Jo, Josephine and Scooch (his cat, not the Eurovision flops. He'd only be thanking them if they offered to fall on their swords for their weak attempt at representing the nation).

Michael sobered up briefly to express his gratitude to his lovely wife Cassie, his increasingly entertaining daughter Leah, his 'other' agent, Susan Smith, and all the patient shop assistants who have at some time pressed unwisely chosen DVDs into his unsteady hands.

Simon would like to thank Sarah Ballard, Claire Gill and Ariella Feiner at the office and at home, his nice wife Helen, his son Jack T (for his withering 'not another list book' looks) and Leo and Ted (the brothers – aah!).